Mao Tse-tung:
A Guide to His Thought

DATE			

MAO
TSE-TUNG:
A Guide to
His Thought

Alain Bouc

translated by
Paul Auster and Lydia Davis

St. Martin's Press   New York

Copyright © 1977 by Alain Bouc
All rights reserved.
For information, write:
St. Martin's Press
175 Fifth Avenue
New York, N.Y. 10010
Manufactured in the United States of America
Library of Congress Catalog Card Number: 76-62749
ISBN: 312-00000-0

Library of Congress Cataloging in Publication Data

Bouc, Alain.
Mao Tse-tung: a guide to his thought.

Includes texts by Mao Tse-tung.
Bibliography: p.
1. Mao, Tse-tung, 1893-1976. 2. Heads of state— China—Biography. I. Mao, Tse-tung, 1893-1976.
DS778.M3B6813   951.05'092'4   76-62749

ISBN 0-312-51397-6

Contents

INTRODUCTION

**No one since Lenin has had such
a powerful effect on history.**

—André Malraux

There are many ways of portraying a political figure, from academic dissertations to simple slogans, from historical research to eyewitness accounts, from journalistic reports to supposedly definitive analyses. Professor, militant, journalist, researcher— each has his own style and his own methods. My primary intention here is not to write a scholarly work but to call attention to a political presence; in analyzing such a complex figure, I have tried to go beyond slogans and clichés, and my principal aim has been to emphasize what might possibly form an answer to the questions asked by people in the West.

Mao Tse-tung died in Peking in the early morning of September 9, 1976. No one can deny that this founder of a civilization and pioneer of Marxism in the Third World has had a profound effect on the 20th century. Yet his influence in the West is still negligible. Mao Tse-tung's strategies have overwhelmed China, aroused its cities and its countrysides; to some extent, they have also shaken up the rest of Asia. But in our countries, they have had little resonance and are hardly more than the subject of casual conversation—or at most the focus of controversy among a small number of extreme Leftists.

The reason for this, one might say, is the difference in national objectives. China has been fighting feudalism, poverty, and humiliation since the beginning of the century, and it has opted for socialism; in the West, people are no longer faced with these problems. Take France, for example. For a long time now—during the Third, Fourth, and Fifth Republics—it has been trying to break away from a traditional form of democracy which has not succeeded in becoming truly democratic. Therefore, people say, the specific problems of the Chinese are very different from those of the French, or of the West in general.

So at least think the people who look at the world and see only the differences between nations, the separation of countries or even continents one from another, who conceive of the universe as broken into autonomous units in which each individual in his own home thinks only of himself.

It takes a lot of stubbornness or blindness to hang on to such misguided and anachronistic attitudes, to ignore the larger trends that are shaping the second half of the 20th century. At least in France we should expect to find less of this kind of short-sightedness: Didn't the victory of Vietnamese nationalism at Dien Bien Phu topple a government? Didn't the Algerian rebellion overthrow several governments and destroy a Republic? Have we forgotten that, as recently as 1960, the French Republic included several African peoples? And in all the new regimes that have replaced French colonial government, hasn't a recovered sense of dignity always been accompanied by some reference, even if only token, to socialism? France, more than any other Western country should be aware of the importance of the Third World, and of socialism in the Third World.

This political short-sightedness cannot be explained away either by the dissimilarities in our situations or the fact that China is so far away. To understand this indifference to China, which is disguised by a pretense of curiosity, we must also take into account the inadequacy of our information. China is always presented to the Western public as foreign, strange; as long as Mao Tse-tung is regarded merely as "emperor of the blue ants," he will seem intriguing but remain unimportant. What is more, the people who carry on arguments about China within revolutionary or supposedly revolutionary movements—groups both overly politicized and too little informed—have seldom made a serious study of the subject of their disputes. Too often, they claim to know who Mao is but are ignorant of the most important things he has done, and judge his thoughts without ever having glanced at his books.

Yet the historic dimensions of the man demand our study, our serious attention. Because, when one-fifth of the human race is caught up in a single passion, the dynamics of the entire world change. Because, as our troubled societies seek their own path, they owe it to themselves to become familiar with the different social experiments in the world. And because Mao Tse-tung's China—the country that he called a "poor blank page" at the time the People's Republic was founded—today shows more originality and contains more energy than any other nation in the Third World.

Many books have been devoted to Mao Tse-tung. Primarily what I want to do here is to emphasize, through a description of the man himself, the depth and influence of his political thought. The study of Mao Tse-tung's ideas can contribute to, or help to formulate, a richer conception of politics; at the very least, it can provoke reflection. Not in the realm of intangible abstractions, but here in the West today, for Westerners who question their society and the world in which Asia plays an ever-growing and already crucial role.

Of course my approach is very different from that of a Chinese. In this book, I have not examined everything Mao Tse-tung has said or done, but everything he has said or done that might interest people in the West.

The reader should not be surprised therefore if I give only limited attention to Mao Tse-tung's theories of people's war. Armed struggle is clearly not the order of the day in the West; moreover, the idea of the "urban guerilla," which was defended in the past by certain groups of the extreme Left, hardly corresponds to Maoist strategy. Also, I have ignored Mao Tse-tung the calligrapher and have studied Mao Tse-tung the poet only insofar as he is the poet of the revolution.

What I have stressed are the larger political problems, the problems of socialism and democracy, violence and dictatorship. I have devoted several pages to outlining some answers to the broader issues raised both in the East and in the West, most notably the search for a balanced society and the definition of social and individual morality—issues to which Mao Tse-tung, in the great Chinese tradition, has devoted many passages of his writings.

For centuries the effort to learn from the experiences of other nations, to draw lessons from them, has proved useful. But it is a risky practice. One must remain critical and not be carried away by the idea of a system conceived with a different place in mind. This is a problem particularly in the case of Mao Tse-tung. First of all because in his writings the leader of the Chinese Communist Party has not shown much interest in anything outside his own country, with the exception of the Soviet Union and more recently, the countries of the Third World. Mao Tse-tung lived *in* China and *for* China. He devoted all his energy to raising out of poverty the hundreds of millions of his fellow countrymen; he hardly ever left his national territory.

This is partly because during the long civil war and the resistance against Japan, there was no need for an elaborate foreign policy; a few simple principles were enough to establish the militants' attitude. Only on very rare occasions did Mao Tse-tung express his views about the politics of other countries and the struggles which he believed Communists should be engaged in abroad. And so I must start by discussing Mao Tse-tung's reflections about his own country, and not the sort of global, multinational analyses which Marx, Lenin, or even Stalin—to name only the leaders and theoreticians of the socialist movement—ventured to make.

Mao Tse-tung was not given to writing long essays in the Germanic style on history, economics, or philosophy, as Marx did. In fact he was interested only in socialism or, more precisely, in the practical struggle to achieve socialism. To him the situation was clear: the socialist cause is the only just and good cause, the only cause worth dying for. Yet omelettes cannot be made without breaking eggs, and he saw no need to cavil about the obvious. Nor was he given to philosophizing about the loneliness of the man of action, about the need to "dirty one's hands," to "be engaged;" there is none of the rhetoric of Camus, Malraux, Sartre, or De Gaulle. In all that sort of talk, he sees nothing but absurd uneasiness about the main problem: the need to liberate the people through the establishment of socialism.

The essence of socialism, he says, is to "take as one's criterion the collective interests and the interests of the individual and to judge every word and every action by this criterion." All his work attempts to answer these questions: how to establish socialism, how to maintain it, how to teach it, how to discover what kind of art it can have. Consequently people who think the idea of socialism is misguided, who believe that an individual contains all of human nature, that the satisfaction of private desires is enough to explain the course of the world will find nothing in Mao Tse-tung to interest them and will refuse to admit that there is any depth to his thinking. Everything we know about Mao Tse-tung relates to a struggle, to campaigns both military and ideological. Unlike Marx, he rarely leaves the fight in order to wander into the realm of concepts, of notions of liberty, the dignity of work, or creative leisure.

What basically concerns Mao is the essence of the Chinese Revolution, its soul and its origins; he himself commands attention because of the extraordinary power of his personality. For decades he embodied China's dignity and its recovered unity. Behind him and with him until the day of his death the country, the Party, and the people readied their weapons, forged their tools, fought poverty, accepted collectivism, and continued in search of a remote prosperity. In Mao Tse-tung China found a leader who could keep this enormous effort from falling apart in the face of unexpected obstacles, from being frightened off by failure. He was one of those great figures whom Hegel called "cosmo-historic," whose role "was to become aware of the Universal, to understand that their world is necessarily on its way to a new stage, and to make this new stage their goal and devote all their energy to reaching it."

Mao Tse-tung took on this role as catalyst of the popular forces long before the People's Republic came into being. He acquired his experience of battle and formed the essential part of his doctrine during the period of underground activity, in the tragic times when several thousand poorly armed men fled from the over-equipped troops of the central government, in the glorious times when the "liberated districts," already comprising more than one hundred million men, began to build the new society. Mao Tse-tung's experiences during this long period of combat were without doubt more diverse than those of either Marx or Lenin.

The essential fact is that this revolution is taking place in a Third World country. It has left behind the blast furnaces, docksides, and suburbs to build its victory at the edge of rice fields, on mountainsides, and in the heart of the forests. Mao Tse-tung and his comrades fought their battle alone, and they alone are responsible for their victories and their defeats; they owe nothing or almost nothing to Moscow, which makes their achievement all the more noteworthy. The Paris Commune and the October Revolution raised hopes (and awoke fears) throughout Europe, but hardly anywhere else. What Mao Tse-tung proposed—that the most numerous and most impoverished peoples of the world rally behind socialism—upset the political balance of the world once and for all.

The originality of the Chinese Revolution has become apparent only as the years have gone by, particularly during the last years of Mao Tse-tung's life. The break with Russia, turned bourgeois, allowed China to assert itself as a Third World country, to associate itself with areas of extreme poverty and hunger, and in this way to recover the original impetus of socialism—the great coalition of the poor against the rich, the struggle against the masters of the machines.

It is hard to talk about a man who arouses such strong feelings. The biographies written by his enemies try to disparage him; the ones that come out of China portray an unblemished hero, one who has never been defeated, who won victory after victory through the sole force of his genius, his fervor for work, and his love of the people. Yet it should be obvious that one does not fight for thirty or forty years without suffering defeats, without making mistakes of judgment, without at the least bending the law, without resorting to violence for reasons of Party or state.

It is also evident that Mao Tse-tung was able to clarify his ideas only over the course of the years. The ideas of specific eras influenced him—those of Sun Yat-sen at the outset, those of the International during a later period, those of Stalin's entourage during yet another. He did not define his own ideas right away; later, he hesitated before condemning Krushchev's line. He needed time before he could assert his point of view, and more time before he could impose it. Though he won numerous political victories, his path was by no means an unbroken series of triumphs. The Party he founded has undergone too many trials, both before and after it took power, for it to be portrayed in a simple manner.

This is all the more true since the important decisions of the Chinese Communist Party were usually made collectively. Sometimes Mao Tse-tung's hand was forced by his associates and he unwillingly ratified a policy which seemed wrong to him.

Nevertheless Mao Tse-tung's career presents a picture of remarkable, even exceptional unity. Despite the decades gone by, no one can deny the essential consistency of the man who asked the Party in 1927 for wholehearted support of unorthodox peasant rebellions and who likewise in 1966 asked the Politburo to approve the student rebellion and to brave the storm of the Cultural Revolution. The man who unwaveringly supported the Vietnamese and Cambodian resistance against America, and who in 1927 tried to resist the Kuomintang in spite of its crushing superiority in arms.

What is astonishing when we compare Mao Tse-tung to other great figures in history is that his life came to a peaceful end. It is rare that great heads of state or leaders in war, especially revolutionaries, experience such serenity near the end of their days.

The deaths of Alexander, Caesar, Robespierre, and Napoleon were tragic. True, they were swept along by the larger currents of history, but it is equally true that they were too passionate or ambitious, that they crushed too many innocent flowers along the way not to tempt fate themselves in the end. "The man of action," wrote De Gaulle, "almost always has a strong dose of egotism, pride, cruelty, craftiness." And further: the leader "is distant, because authority is always accompanied by prestige, and prestige by remoteness." But if these notes of De Gaulle's still apply to many contemporary leaders, they do not ring true for leaders of the socialist movement—not for Marx, Engels, Lenin, Ho Chi Minh, or Mao Tse-tung. The leader of the Chinese Communist Party does not resemble those morose and solitary men, those melancholy conquerors out of the past, any more than did the leaders who came before him in the proletarian revolution. He more than once brushed with tragedy and death, but he was able to build his life out of the battle he fought alongside the masses. They saw in him the force of their own unconscious aspirations and their hope for a better life. They acknowledged his prestige and put their faith in him. His life therefore ended without upheaval, without disenchantment.

Mao Tse-tung:
A Guide to His Thought

one/
Mao Tse-tung: His Life

1/A Life of Struggle

There are men associated with every
phase of a revolution; some follow
it through to the end, and others
begin it but do not finish it.   —Chateaubriand

Mao Tse-tung's life spanned the whole history of China's humiliation and China's awakening. He was born at the end of 1893,
when the country had just gone through what was perhaps its
most difficult period. Two years later, Japan was to humiliate the
Empire; six years after that, an international expeditionary force
would pillage Peking. By the turn of the century, China had lost
its sovereignty over the adjacent territories: France was occupying
Indochina, the Portuguese were in Macao, Britain had seized
Hong Kong, Burma, and Nepal. Japan had demanded Okinawa
and Taiwan, and was preparing to annex Korea. The Czars controlled the southeastern regions of Siberia. And in China itself
foreigners were taking over more and more divisions of the
Chinese administration.

But in South China, where Mao was born, and particularly in
Hunan with its history of heroism, everyone still remembered the
glorious struggle of the Taipings—the fighters of the "Supreme
Peace"—whose insurrection had mobilized people of all classes
throughout the country and had nearly overthrown the Empire.
This was a peasant uprising in some ways reminiscent of the
great French *jacqueries* in the Middle Ages, but already modern
in its anti-imperialist orientation and its desire for reform.

In the 1840s there were no less than one hundred peasant upris-

3

ings in China. It was the great famine of Hunan, in 1849, that sparked off the rebellion, which was organized farther to the south. Moving up from Kiangsi toward the north, the insurgents fought a great battle at Changsha, a city sixty-five miles from Mao's birthplace, where he would later embark on his clandestine activities. Everywhere they went the Taipings burned title deeds to land and confiscated the goods of the rich. Their newly founded government proclaimed agrarian reform on the principle that land belonged to those who tilled it. It gave equal rights to women and did away with the ancient system of land taxes. The venture ended tragically in 1864 with a military disaster, but it had already dealt a death blow to the Empire. Millions of peasants had been willing to sacrifice their lives to fight feudalism and drive out the foreign invader. And, when a new peasant resistance arose many years later, with Mao Tse-tung's encouragement, the rebels from Hunan seemed to be the direct heirs of the great insurrection of 1851. Moreover, the uprising had incited other peasants to follow suit, and the struggle continued until the mid-1880s in various parts of Eastern China and in regions inhabited by national minorities.

From the Pine Forests of Shaoshan to the University of Peking

It was into this rural world—a world beaten down but not completely resigned—that Mao Tse-tung was born on December 26, 1893. Against a background of steep mountains sparsely covered with scrub, of wooded hillsides, red earth, and pine trees where thousands of birds sang, of small rice fields which descended stepwise to the bottom of a valley, of pools covered with water lilies: this was the Shaoshan countryside where he spent his childhood. The family home was a large frame building with an inner courtyard, stable, and sheepfold typical of the region. His father had gradually become rich; shortly before his death he owned eighteen *mou* of land. Eighteen *mou* is not much more than two and a half acres, but in Hunan, which was so very poor, that was enough to place the family above the average. Two laborers came to help work the earth.

Mao Tse-tung remained in the village with his family for sixteen years. Starting in adolescence, relations with his father became strained. Mao Tse-tung preferred his uneducated but kind-hearted mother to this man whom he saw as conservative, authoritarian, and greedy. Mao was raised and educated in the old style; in primary school he studied the great Chinese classics under the eye of a stern old teacher. Except for his fits of anger and his defiance of his father, there was nothing extraordinary about Mao's life—the life of a typical peasant boy.

Like his fellow peasants, Mao Tse-tung was aware of China's destitution. In 1909, there was famine: some ate and some went hungry. The employees on his father's farm worked hard, ate little and badly, and were abused. Mao disapproved of his father. He wished that his mother, a devout Buddhist, would not submit so readily to his father's authority. In Shaoshan, he saw public executions and rebels' heads grimacing at the end of pikes. It was in his birthplace that he learned the basics—poverty, oppression, the generosity of a mother, and the gentleness of his native land, which he never forgot.

In 1910 Mao Tse-tung cut off his pigtail and set out barefooted for Changsha, his little bundle on his shoulder. It was autumn. For three days he walked through the green landscape. He had just spent several months in a higher primary school not far from Shaoshan. He had read the theoreticians of the contemporary reformist movement and had formed some political convictions. Life in the city of Changsha inspired him to assert himself. Then came the fall of the Manchurian Empire. He joined the Republican revolutionary army and spent six months in it. Then he resumed his studies. One month of commercial school was enough to discourage him. He tried other institutions in Changsha without success; during the whole of 1912 he chose to work alone in the library. The following spring he entered Normal School. This was the great turning point, the moment that marked the later emergence of Mao Tse-tung the master, the teacher that he prided himself on remaining all his life, at least in spirit. In those dark classrooms and cramped dormitories Mao Tse-tung discovered the world of ideas—British and German ideas, as it happened, since this was about all that the translators of that time were interested in (Darwin, Stuart Mill, Adam Smith, Kant, Feuerbach, Paulsen, and Hegel). He also studied Chinese philosophy.

In 1913 he turned twenty. All the young men talked about saving China from decadence, but none of them knew how to go about it. Should they copy the West, should they reform existing structures, should they return to traditional ways? Mao Tse-tung was not sure. He devoured books in order to find a solution. He wrote copious notes, adopted positions, rejected some ideas and accepted others. His scribblings, (now on display at Changsha) show how serious his reading was and how characteristically anxious he was always to extract a practical lesson from the text.

At this time he was won over by the idea of revolution. He was not sure what to do, but he was aware that what people around him were suggesting was not enough. He noted in the margin of a book: "I believe reform is necessary; as when you burn an object, utterly destroy it, then entirely recreate it." This was true for China and for all of society. Or: "Like a mother who becomes pregnant and gives birth to a new child." Mao was speaking of reform but thinking of revolution—without perhaps realizing it clearly, as yet.

The Announcement of the October Revolution

Mao returned home for the winter vacation. One night he said to his fourth sister-in-law Wang Shu-nan, who was coming downstairs to look for him: "Good news! Good news!" And his face radiated joy as it never had before. Wang asked him: "What good news? What treasure have you found?"

Mao lifted his hands and said, stressing his words: "Oh, this news is even better than finding a treasure. Listen! Russia has become Communist, we are certainly going to follow its example and bring about a revolution, establish Communism . . . ."

"It's all very well to say establish Communism, but lots of heads are going to fall . . . ."

"Heads will fall, heads will be chopped off, of course, of course. But just think how good Communism is! The state won't bother us any more, you women will be free, marriage problems won't plague you any more!"

Wen-hui Pao of Hong Kong, November 20, 1957

Little by little he established his style, constructed his personality. He left the classrooms and went to investigate the small factories of Changsha with a group of sympathizers. Several months before receiving his degree he set off into the countryside of Hunan. He covered four districts in one month, walking almost three hundred miles. He knew nothing about Marxism, but already several future leaders of the Communist Party were among his friends. In *New Youth* he discovered the writings of Ch'en Tu-) hsiu—the future secretary-general of the Chinese Communist Party—attacking Li Li-san, who would assume similar duties one day.

He set up a virtually free night school for illiterate workers just a few yards away from the Normal School. He devoted very little time to the latter. Most of his efforts were spent on evening work. In the evenings he did his best to lead the "New People's Study Society," which could already be considered a revolutionary organization. It urged its students to become politically engaged; it also organized trips to France, where the young Chinese expected to be initiated into the world of European industry and to have their first contact with the Western proletariat and with ideas about worldwide revolution.

In the autumn of 1918 Mao Tse-tung received his degree and left for Peking. For several months he had a small job in the university library. There he met the most prominent intellectuals of the extreme Left of the time, including his superior Li Ta-chao, the head librarian and a translator of Marxist works into Chinese. Little by little Mao gave up his anarchist tendencies in favor of Marxism. In this same year, at the age of twenty-five, he fell in love with the charming Yang K'ai-hui, the daughter of one of his former professors in Changsha. He married her three years later.

Mao returned to his province in 1919 and threw himself more directly into politics by publishing the *Hsiang River Review*. This journal appeared in July and was banned one month later by the governor of Hunan. In three of the four issues that appeared, Mao Tse-tung expressed his beliefs of the moment—the ideas of a lively young man who retained several general themes from Marxism and combined them with his own reflections. His first important article was "The Great Union of the Popular Masses." In this article he rejected all individual measures as being powerless to save China. He declared that general mobilization was necessary:

"One glance at history shows us that all historic developments, whatever their significance, started with the uniting of a group of people . . . . What determines victory or failure is the strength or the weakness of this union, and whether its fundamental ideology is new or outmoded, correct or false." Mao Tse-tung noted in passing that in Russia, "last year, the great union of the popular masses faced the great union of the aristocrats and the capitalists, and it won a victory on the issue of social reform."[1]

During the period immediately after World War I, Chinese youth were looking beyond China to foreign countries. They studied the Bolshevik revolution; they rebelled against the dealing at Versailles and the gifts offered to Japan by the West. In the large "May 4th Movement" of 1919, workers joined the angry students in demanding respect for territorial sovereignty and for the dignity of China. The towns were seething with excitement. At the end of the year Mao Tse-tung organized a student strike at Changsha directed against the governor of Hunan. Mao had to leave the province immediately and went to Peking and Shanghai. Previously he had declared himself an idealist, but as he later confided to Edgar Snow, by 1920 he had become "in theory and to some extent in action, a Marxist."

In the autumn, having returned to Changsha, he established a Communist cell and a branch of the Youth League. He had just discovered the *Communist Manifesto* and Kautsky's *Class Struggle*. Now the principal of an elementary school, he expanded his political activities, started a bookstore, and became involved in the workers' movement of Hunan.

A Double Career

In July 1921 Mao's ardent radicalism qualified him to be included in the founding of the Chinese Communist Party, which met for five days in a small school for girls in a district of Shanghai. He took control of the Party organization of Hunan, whose influence extended as far as the large coal mines of Anyuan in the neighboring province of Kiangsi. At that time the Communists in the region numbered only in the dozens, and Mao devoted much of his time to union-organizing activities. In September 1922 the miners of Anyuan, organized by Mao Tse-tung, Liu Shao-ch'i—future Chief of State—and Li Li-san—future leader of the "hard" line—achieved very successful results with a strike which has remained famous. During the Cultural Revolution it was said that Mao and Liu had opposing ideas about union organization. Certain anti-Communist historians give all the credit for organizing that early strike to Li Li-san. The matter is not

---

[1]The text of the article can be seen at the Shaoshan museum. *China Quarterly* has published a translation of it.

clear. But several facts are beyond dispute: (1) Mao Tse-tung and his brother Mao Tse-min participated actively in the movement; (2) Mao Tse-tung had been in contact with the miners as early as autumn of the previous year; (3) the September 1922 strike involved 17,000 workers, including the railwaymen of the P'ing-hsiang line; and (4) the miners of Anyuan later formed the nucleus of the 2nd Regiment of the First Army based in the mountain range known as the Chingkongshan (1928).

Mao Tse-tung entered the central committee of the Party at the time of the Third Congress (June 1923). He was given organizational duties. In order to carry them out he went to Shanghai and established himself there. That same year the Communists came to an agreement with Sun Yat-sen's Kuomintang about conditions for cooperation. They agreed to dual-party membership, and Mao Tse-tung began his career in the Kuomintang.

The Communists' objective was clear: an alliance with a large progressive party against the feudal forces would assure them a national dimension and allow them to consolidate their position in the country while awaiting the moment—which would come much later, once feudalism had been done away with—for criticizing the bourgeois positions of the Kuomintang and fighting to seize power themselves. This is the classic "united front" policy. So there is nothing dishonorable about Mao Tse-tung's short but brilliant career in the Kuomintang, and the apparently obligatory silence on this subject in the People's Republic is surprising.

In January 1924 Mao Tse-tung became an alternate member of the Central Executive Committee of the Kuomintang. He was a member of the Shanghai Bureau of the Kuomintang and in February became chief of its organization bureau in that city. As far as he was concerned, this meant the Communists had control of one of the key political posts in the nation. But many radicals within the Chinese Communist Party criticized this policy of cooperation with the Kuomintang. Perhaps that explains why Mao left this post in 1924. In November 1926, however, Mao Tse-tung rose in the hierarchy again: he became the *de facto* head of the Kuomintang's propaganda department.

Meanwhile he and other Communists had turned their attention to developing ties with the rural areas. The Chinese Communist Party had "infiltrated" the Peasant Movement Training Institute in Canton, which was under *de jure* Kuomintang control. In a report made to the 2nd Congress of the Kuomintang in 1926 Mao Tse-tung insisted on the need to intensify work in the rural areas.

The following month he joined the Committee for the Peasant Movement, most of whose members were Communists who hoped to impose their politics on the whole of the Nationalist organization. In May, he became the secretary of a committee by the same name formed within the Communist Party in Shanghai.

But the hopes which the Communists had placed in the Kuomintang soon evaporated. The two organizations fought for control of the United Front. Sun Yat-sen's successor, Chiang Kai-shek, whom the Communists were supporting in his struggle for national unity, tried to get rid of them. In March 1926 he imprisoned the Communist instructors at the Whampoa Military Academy, one of whom was Chou En-lai. In May, he forbade members of the Chinese Communist Party to occupy management positions in the commissions of the Kuomintang's Central Committee. Mao Tse-tung left the department of propaganda but kept his post at the Canton Peasant Institute. The Party was divided: the radicals wanted to break away, while the "right," including Ch'en Tu-hsiu, gave in. Later, Mao Tse-tung would say that the 1927 massacres had opened his eyes to the nature of the Kuomintang, which might imply that in 1926 he still cherished some illusions about it.

"The Communists had always profited a great deal from the teaching of the generalissimo (Chiang Kai-shek). If he had not been the man he was, people like Mao himself would not have been able to rid themselves of their Rightist opportunism in order to take up arms against his regime. In fact, it was Chiang who taught them how to fight, the United States being only a secondary school teacher."

Reported by Edgar Snow in *le Nouveau Candide,*
December 11, 1965.

By the summer of 1926 Mao felt that the Chinese revolution had to have the support of the countryside. P'eng P'ai (who had pioneered this effort), Jen Pi-shih, Lin Po-ch'u, and others were taking their work into the rural areas. The countrysides of Hunan, Kiangsi, and Hupei were stirred up by agitators. At the end of 1926, full of uncertainty, Mao Tse-tung decided on a brilliant move. He returned to Hunan for more than a month, in order to study five districts and his native town of Shaoshan. He brought back a document that aroused worldwide interest, the "Report on an Investigation of the Peasant Movement in Hunan," one of the most brilliant articles he had ever written and one in which his whole personality was already asserting itself.

The March 1927 report is one of the great documents of the socialist movement. For the first time, the peasants acquired the dignity of revolutionaries—on an equal standing, or almost so, with the urban proletariat. They were the principal strength of the revolution. Moscow published the document. Bukharin praised it in front of the Soviet Party's Central Committee when it met in May. Around the same time the Soviet Union printed several of P'eng P'ai's equally "heretical" reports. But the majority of the Chinese Communist Party was not in the least prepared to follow the movement, nor, of course, was the Kuomintang, whose rural support lay among the conservatives. In April, Chiang Kai-shek massacred the Shanghai Communists: the break had come, belated and bloody.

From Party Rebel to Party Leader

Mao Tse-tung quarreled with his party. He left the Fifth Congress, in May 1927, discouraged at having his ideas about the peasant movement rejected. He was not reelected to the Politburo. The Leftist faction of the Kuomintang had dropped out of the Chinese Communist Party, which went underground and began to organize a series of revolts. Shortly after the Nanchang insurrection, a plan for revolt by units of the Nationalist army, which occurred in early August and marked the birth of the Red Army, the Chinese Communist Party changed leadership and Mao Tse-tung once again became a member of the Politburo. After the failure of the so-called "Autumn Harvest Uprising in Hunan," (September 1927) he led what remained of his troops—about one thousand men—up into the Chingkang Mountains. The saga of the underground began. It was to continue until the taking of power.

The Party was in upheaval. Mao was accused of Leftist adventurism. He was condemned by the Party in Hunan as well as by the Politburo and the International. Nevertheless, other troops made their way to the mountains of Kiangsi, notably those of Chu Tehand P'eng Teh-huai. In June 1928 the wind changed direction: these few thousand ill-equipped soldiers won their first victory. Mao Tse-tung, in charge of the political leadership of the troops, stressed the importance of ideology. He and Chu Teh defined the principles of people's war ("Why Is It That Red Political Power Exists in China?" etc.). A series of defeats while carrying out the orders of the Politburo to attack towns induced them to break with the "putschist" line once and for all. The base of Communist power in 1931 lay far from the towns. The Red Army drove back the troops of the Kuomintang, which tried three times to wipe it out. In 1931 the first All-China Soviet Congress proclaimed the establishment of the Chinese Soviet Republic, and Mao Tse-tung was elected Chairman. He became "Chairman Mao."

Most of the leaders of the Chinese Communist Party joined this little Republic, but not without challenging the authority of its head. At that time even Chou En-lai often sided with the group of students who had returned from Moscow, and for a time he replaced Mao in the army's political commissariat. For several years Mao Tse-tung did not write—or at least did not publish— anything of primary importance. In some sense he was pushed to the side. This was undoubtedly the darkest period of his career, even though he was still officially Chairman of the Republic.

Those in command of the Party rejected the main principle of a people's war: to withdraw, in order to weaken the enemy and prepare for a counterattack. They wanted to fight on equal terms with an army that was far superior to theirs. In 1934 the situation at Kiangsi became untenable. The advancing enemy was wiping out unit after unit. The disaster did not however bring on a rout: the troops remained behind their commanders and headed north, pursued by Nationalist forces. This was the famous Long March, which lasted from the fall of 1934 to the fall of 1935. It involved a series of defeats, ambushes, and flights during which the Red Army lost almost all of its manpower but the Party gained a leader.

In January 1935, a top-level conference held in the newly captured town of Tsunyi, in the province of Kweichow, led to a small *coup d'état*. The leaders of the largest detachment of the Red Army appointed Mao Tse-tung to lead them. It is unlikely that any regular meeting of the Politburo took place. Not all the historians are certain that Mao was even a member of the Politburo at that time. However that may be, he emerged from Tsunyi in full control of the Party. Once again, Mao Tse-tung had violated strict legality, broken the rules, in order to impose the right policy. Since then the Party has often taken pains to justify *a posteriori* his assumption of power in 1935.

In the hills of Shensi, the Red Army recovered gradually from its defeat. Mao Tse-tung managed the affairs of the liberated districts, and without encountering any real opposition he planned China's democratic and socialist future. He formulated his philosophical theses and worked out the strategy of partisan warfare. He also prepared for the formation of an anti-Japanese United Front with the Kuomintang—the same Kuomintang which had just killed most of the soldiers of the Red Army.

No doubt it required a great deal of self-restraint on the part of the Communists not to execute Chiang Kai-shek when he was taken by surprise and captured at Sian in December 1936 and even greater self-restraint to form an alliance with him against the invader. There still remain many obscure points about the Sian incident; what is certain is that Chou En-lai was in the forefront at that time, and not Mao Tse-tung. According to Rotschild, former Belgian ambassador to China, the Soviets intervened to save Chiang's life, and Molotov supposedly confided this to an American leader in 1944. This hypothesis needs to be confirmed. In any case, for several years the Communists had been insistently urging the Kuomintang to put an end to the civil war and join in a united resistance. The outcome of the Sian incident gave them what they wanted. All the wisdom, cunning, and rigorous thinking of the Communist leaders is evident in the reprieve they granted Chiang Kai-shek—the better to destroy his reactionary forces ten years later. But at that point a United Front was absolutely essential. The Japanese, who had controlled Manchuria since 1931 and Jehol since 1933, were preparing to invade the whole of China. Several months after the Sian negotiations, Tokyo sent in troops with orders to conquer Eastern China.

The Japanese army advanced and then halted. While the two Chinese camps—Communist and Nationalist—consolidated their positions, the Communists set up an almost independent economy in the regions they controlled. This was the experimental model for the future People's Republic. Mao Tse-tung outlined revolutionary principles for organizing the "liberated" regions. They would be self-sufficient, depending only on the meager resources of the underdeveloped countryside: a crafts industry would be developed for weaving and making clothes; small factories would provide a full complement of arms; soldiers returned from the front would plant crops and work in the fields; as for the peasants, they would cooperate with the troops and be provided with guns. The soldiers would behave with discipline and self-restraint; they would not rape or steal, they would pay a fair price for what they bought, and they would speak politely to the civilians. This typically Maoist ethic called the "Nanniwan spirit"—after a small model district in Shansi—later became part of the golden legend of the Red Army, and eventually became an essential element of the People's Republic even in peacetime.

Mao Tse-tung, whom journalists had begun to discover in his Yenan retreat, was not yet all-powerful. According to his biographer Jerome Ch'en, the first praise did not appear until 1938—written by Lin Piao—for his "general leadership." A number of Mao's former enemies in fact still held key positions in the Party, and still objected to the political and military ideas of the leader of the Chinese Communist Party as unorthodox. In 1942 Mao Tse-tung vigorously attacked dogmatism, stereotyped jargon, and sectarianism, ridding himself of the hair-splitting quibblers of Leftist ideology: this was the great rectification movement which would continue until 1944, definitively establishing his authority.

In 1943, the Party ratified the decisions of the Tsunyi conference and officially placed Mao Tse-tung at the head of the Central Committee. At the end of the war against Japan, in 1945, the Communists held their 7th Congress. The thought of Mao Tse-tung became the dominant ideology of the Chinese Communist Party, along with Marxism. The Party had become Maoist. China would not be long in following suit.

In August 1945, several days after the bombing of Hiroshima, Mao Tse-tung flew to Chungking, the Nationalist headquarters. For six weeks, acting on the advice of American diplomats, he was involved in discussions with Chiang Kai-shek. The negotiations, continued by Chou En-lai after Mao's return to Yenan, ended in a cease-fire agreement signed by the two adversaries on January 10, 1946. No one had any illusions of success. The truce suspended for only a few weeks the hostilities begun in the fall. Mao Tse-tung, who was settled in the Yenan region, conducted the civil war from then on. After the Nationalists took Yenan in March 1947 he led his troops on a zigzagging trail through the whole of Northern Shensi. In the north of China the situation changed in favor of the Communists, and here they instituted agrarian reform during the summer of 1947.

The following year the People's Liberation Army launched its general offensive and carried off victory after victory against an enemy which outnumbered it, but which incarnated oppression and corruption in the eyes of the people. In March 1949 Mao

Tse-tung set up the Central Committee and army headquarters in Peking, which Lin Piao's army had just conquered. Communist troops crossed the Yangtze, seized Nanking and Shanghai, and then conquered South China. The Nationalists either surrendered in whole divisions or else left China, where they were no longer welcome. To crown this series of victories, on October 1, 1949 Mao Tse-tung proclaimed the founding of the Chinese People's Republic to a delirious crowd gathered in Peking's T'ien An Men Square, declaring, "China can now stand on its own feet!"

Revolution without Civil War

The man who had once been an underground fighter and a clandestine agitator held official posts from now on. At the age of 56, he became Chairman of the Chinese People's Government, in other words, head of the regime. But the time of honors was not a time of rest. The machinery of the state had to be set up, the "people's democratic dictatorship" had to be organized, and in addition to the enormous burden of domestic duties, diplomatic relations had to be established with the outside world. South China was not yet completely liberated in December 1949 when Mao Tse-tung left for Moscow to negotiate a treaty of friendship, alliance, and mutual assistance. He had bitter discussions with Stalin, who believed that Mao was another potential Tito. Stalin tried to take advantage of the divisions within the Chinese delegation, particularly in order to win over Ch'en Po-ta, who had already had talks with Moscow several weeks before. After two months of difficult negotiations, Stalin agreed to sign the treaty. Its terms were hardly generous, but the People's Republic would essentially be able to count on the support of the Soviet Union.

As soon as he returned to Peking, Mao Tse-tung tackled the first large-scale domestic reforms. National finances had to be reorganized. In April, he explained his views to the governmental commission of the Central Committee: if a radical transformation of the country's economy were to take place, three conditions would have to be fulfilled: agrarian reform would have to be achieved, industry and commerce would have to be rationalized, and military and administrative spending would have to be cut drastically. Late in the same month, the marriage law gave women legal equality and ended their enslavement of thousands of years. The agrarian reform in June represented a rationale and justification of the regime to a majority of peasants. In this same month China lost hope of unifying its territory in the near future by recovering Taiwan. On June 27—two days after the beginning of the Korean War—Harry Truman ordered the 7th Fleet to take up position in the Straits of Taiwan to prevent a landing by the Communists. At the end of October, as they were driving back American troops which had reached the Yalu border, Chinese soldiers left national territory for the first time, causing the United Nations to condemn the People's Republic soon afterward. China's diplomatic isolation would last for more than twenty years.

Where the peasant question was concerned, Mao Tse-tung had no intention of imitating the USSR. He wanted permanent revolution, but in stages. After dividing up the lands of the landlords and rich peasants, which transformed agricultural workers into a mass of small farmers, the regime asked the peasants to form mutual aid teams, and then cooperatives, along lines that were more and more collectivist. But it was not enough to organize, it was still necessary to destroy the remains of the society of the Kuomintang, which were present everywhere. Mao Tse-tung distrusted not only the bourgeoisie, but also the Party which he had founded. Too many cadres had looked beyond China for their ideas, when they weren't happy just to dig them up from the Moscow handbooks. If steps were not taken to prevent it, some of these cadres might form a new ruling class and govern the country from inside their offices, ignoring the people.

This was why, after eliminating notorious counter-revolutionaries, Mao Tse-tung asked his fellow countrymen— whether or not they were Communists—to denounce the errors of the cadres, the faults of the bureaucracy, and borgeois acts of sabotage. These movements were called the "Three Antis," aimed at the Party and the state, and the "Five Antis," aimed at the bourgeoisie.

These two nationwide campaigns consolidated the new regime, strengthened the people's dictatorship and curbed the tendency to slacken off after the victory. They foreshadowed other typically Maoist rectification campaigns, such as the movement of the Hundred Flowers in 1956–57, the Movement for Socialist Education in 1963, which would become the Cultural Revolution, and finally the Lin Piao Criticism Movement and the Movement for the Rectification of Work Methods in 1973–74.

Long after the days of its underground activity, the regime tried to organize itself along more traditional lines. With the end of the Korean War there came a general reordering. In 1953 the first five-year plan, modeled on the Soviet plans, went into operation, laying the foundations for the first modern industry. The country drew up a constitution. In 1954 the First National People's Congress was held. Mao Tse-tung took part as representative from Peking and was elected Chairman of the People's Republic. But then the first crisis broke out within the Politburo: Kao Kang, Vice–Prime Minister and Party leader in the northeast, tried to take over as head of the government, backed by a fraction of the Party and by his industrialized "independent kingdom" of Manchuria; he also advocated closer ties with Moscow—with the support of the Soviets, naturally.

As for the army, its memory of the bloody Korean ordeals was still fresh: it gave up on guerilla warfare, put the emphasis on armament, and asked for funds. It established requirements for advancement, gave out ranks to its soldiers, and appointed field marshals.

Mao Tse-tung was not very pleased with what was going on in China at this point, as hierarchies were being formed and laws laid down everywhere. He kept his distance. What interested him was the progress of socialism, primarily in the countrysides. On the strength of investigations carried out by the new cooperatives, he announced in 1955 that the peasants were ready for collectivism. Within a few months the plans for cooperatives were perfected. From here, Mao Tse-tung went on to socialize the entire industrial sector and all of wholesale trading. The operation was successful and did not cause any serious trauma.

At this point differences arose with Moscow. Krushchev had visited Peking in 1954 and the following year had restored to China the privileges that Mao Tse-tung had been forced to concede to Stalin at Port Arthur and in Sinkiang. But, from the podium of the 20th Soviet Party Congress early in 1956, Krushchev brutally denounced the errors of the former Soviet dictator, and he did this in terms which Mao Tse-tung found extreme, uncalled-for, and ill-timed. Subsequently, China supported the changes in the Polish regime and showed a discreet sympathy for the Hungarian uprising in its first days—though the Chinese attitude changed when Nagy's government asked to withdraw from the Warsaw Pact. The Chinese Communist Party, with Mao Tse-tung and Chou En-lai at its head, ventured to give some quiet advice to the socialist camp: It pointed out the dangers of "great power chauvinism" and insinuated that the tragedy at Budapest would not have taken place if the Communists had always respected the rules of internal democracy. As for the personality cult, it was unhealthy, and, practising what it preached, the 8th Congress withdrew from the Party statutes all reference to Mao's thought.

The great campaign of the Hundred Flowers ("Let a hundred flowers bloom, let a hundred schools of thought contend"), which occurred in 1956 and 1957, meant to show that the Party was not afraid of popular criticism, that it even sought it. The press devoted columns to citizens' complaints about the high-handedness of party cadres or authoritarianism in the factories; the universities were shaken by intellectual debates. But after several months, the movement began to go astray. The letters published no longer simply called attention to faults, they questioned the very principle of socialism; some felt that the point was no longer to correct mistakes but to fight Communism itself.

The campaign had to be stopped; it had become dangerous to the regime. At this point, the experiment which had begun in a liberal spirit turned into a struggle against right-wing and conservative elements, among whom were several important figures in the non-Communist parties. The following year, a few of them lost their positions. But the criticisms voiced against officials and Party members during the first period of the Hundred Flowers had not remained a dead issue: they had resulted in the ouster of some three hundred thousand offenders.

That same year, 1957, China began to wonder about developments in the Soviet Union. Did the first Sputnik show the "superiority of the Socialist regime" or did it simply indicate that Moscow was more preoccupied with technological progress than with revolution? In November Mao Tse-tung went to Moscow at the head of a large delegation. There he criticized Krushchev's ideas about peaceful coexistence and pointed out that it was necessary to persist in the struggle against imperialism, since the latter was losing ground. His remarks have become famous:

"The direction of the wind has changed in the world. In the struggle between the socialist camp and the capitalist camp, either the West wind will prevail over the East wind, or the East wind will prevail over the West wind . . . . The imperialist camp does not include more than about four hundred million people and it is divided within itself. There will be an 'earthquake' there. At the moment, the East wind prevails over the West wind."

The Soviets subsequently claimed that there were racist ideas in this speech, and that the East wind represented Asia threatening Europe. Yet there is no question that at the time Mao placed the Soviet Union in the Eastern camp.

Infighting and Controversy

The time had come, Mao believed, for China to assert its own course of action. The domestic situation seemed satisfactory. Production was increasing within an economy that was now entirely socialized; the campaign of the Hundred Flowers had strengthened the authority of the Party. Mao was also thinking about who his successors would be. In January 1958 he asked the leaders of the Party to think of a replacement for him as Chairman of the Republic. He would hand over the everyday duties to other people so that he could withdraw to the "second front"— that of ideological reflection and control. The decision was to be announced in December of the same year, when China was several months into the experimental Great Leap Forward.

Since the spring of 1957 the country had more or less abandoned the Soviet model: it was now attempting to achieve advanced collectivism in a backward and preindustrial economy.

In May Mao Tse-tung and Liu Shao-chi'i presented to the Party Congress the guiding principles behind the Great Leap Forward. China, liberated as it was from the shackles of bureaucracy, should give free rein to the people's creativity. Material incentives should give way to collective motivation, as part of a massive mobilization of human resources. In the months that followed, rural cooperatives regrouped themselves into people's communes; peasants became part-time workers in the village factories; intellectuals participated in manual work. In August, at the time of the meeting at Peitaiho, there was talk of a changeover to Communism "in the near future." In the euphoria caused by the excellent harvest, people accepted uncritically the announcement of a 60 to 90 percent increase in grain production.

Even Mao Tse-tung allowed himself to be carried away by the enthusiasm. In September, during an inspection tour in Wuhan, he asserted that the harvest had incresed by "several hundred billion pounds," in other words by over 150 million tons (production in 1957 officially rose to 185 million tons). Even though these figures were impossible, it should be pointed out that they were more modest than those quoted by the *People's Daily,* which on November 28 bravely reported a harvest of 375 million tons—a 100 percent increase in one year. The harvests of 1958 were certainly very good, but they were believed to be absolutely miraculous. During the autumn local cadres in various places became excited and spread "rumors of Communism," withdrawing a portion of goods and livestock from production teams and brigades in order to contribute it to the communes, requisitioning market-garden produce without compensation, organizing free soup kitchens, and so on. The peasants rebelled against this at the beginning of 1959 and a rectification movement, set in motion at the Central Committee's Chengchow meeting in November, restored the situation early the following spring.

The Party was divided. Some of its members felt that the fever which had seized the entire country was unhealthy; it was superseding the national plan and causing the neglect of land and machines in its concern for an immediate record production. For Mao Tse-tung on the other hand, this unprecedented mobilization of the people was a great victory and the mistakes that had been made did not in any way affect its positive aspects, since the people learned from them. "Where else could we have found an accelerated training school capable of educating hundreds of millions of men and millions of cadres?," he said several months later at Lushan, in answer to people who disparaged the movement.

He vigorously called to account those who were upset by the "blunders" a mass movement can make: "Just look at the way Marx and Engels spoke of the Paris Commune and how Lenin spoke of the Russian Revolution! Have you noticed the way Lenin criticized the renegade Plekhanov and 'the bourgeois gentlemen and their flunkeys,' 'the dogs and the pigs of the dying bourgeoisie and of the petit bourgeois democracy that drags itself along after it'? If you haven't, please take a look at it!" (annotations to the article entitled "On the Correct Attitude for Marxists to Have towards the Revolutionary Mass Movement," August 15, 1959).

But there were many people in the Party, both in the top echelons and at the lower levels, who practiced a policy of obstruction. In 1957 the *People's Daily* had refused to publish news about the National Conference on Propaganda Work. Now again, in 1959, Mao Tse-tung could not persuade the Party newspaper to publish a report by Ch'ang Ch'un-ch'iao on the fight against bourgeois habits. Several leaders, who are in fact still in office today, were opposed to publication because, they declared, one could not get rid of capitalism that easily.

Resistance, hesitation, and obstruction would not have mattered if the economy had continued to make progress. But the very bad harvests of 1959, largely caused by drought, showed that China was still very far from being able to ensure a steady output of food, that it did not have a stable agricultural base, and that there was no question of an imminent conversion to Communism. The most conservative leaders came to the fore again, and, with the discreet backing of the Kremlin, regrouped behind the Minister of Defense, P'eng Teh-huai, who had led the attack on the failures of the Great Leap Forward at the famous meeting of the Central Committee at Lushan (July–August 1959).

Confrontation with P'eng Teh-huai

Using a familiar tactic, Mao Tse-tung's enemies took advantage of the mistakes made (everybody had agreed to put an end to the strange fantasies of the year before) in order to criticize the movement as a whole. They prolonged the debate and spoke of democracy and liberty. They took advantage of the fact that since the summer of 1958, the Soviet Union, which was still theoretically "the leader of the Socialist camp," had expressed disapproval, through Krushchev, of the experimental people's communes. In short, it was not just a matter of reexamining production objectives, but of questioning the fundamental policy.

P'eng Teh-huai circulated an "opinion letter," sending one copy to Moscow, in which he denounced the exaggerations that had been made, the petit bourgeois fanaticism, and the prominent place given to politics: "Certain comrades believe that giving primary consideration to politics makes up for everything else." And he added: "It is harder to correct manifestations of Leftism than to free oneself from conservative ideas."

Mao Tse-tung launched a violent counterattack: "At Lushan, I made three remarks: we accomplished great things; quite a few problems remain; the future is bright. But after that, a number of new problems arose, with Rightist opportunism frenetically attacking the Party. There are no longer any more 'rumors of Communism' . . . or unrealistic overstatements. At present *the problem is not to oppose the 'Left,' but to oppose the Right* . . . . After fighting Leftist tendencies for several months, it is natural that a leaning toward the Right should appear. There have been real mistakes and inadequacies; but we have corrected them. And yet these people continue to demand correction. They cling to that and attack our general line in order to try to make us deviate from it.''

P'eng Teh-huai was repudiated by the Central Committee; Lin Piao replaced him in the Ministry of Defense. But Mao Tse-tung had not won a complete victory. Many other leaders continued to criticize the Great Leap Forward, or at least the manner in which it was carried out. Liu Shao-ch'i was able to make use of this dispute to pose as a sort of arbitrator and extend his influence. Even Lin Piao—on whom the head of the Party would rely so much in the course of the following years to change the direction of events—did not hesitate to express serious reservations about the 1958–59 experiment as being "excessive," "extreme," "going beyond the limits" of what was reasonable. T'eng Hsiao-p'ing, the Party Secretary, suggested that "a donkey is certainly slow, but at least it rarely has an accident." Mao Tse-tung's prestige undeniably suffered from the difficulties encountered by the Great Leap Forward. Some years later, at the beginning of the Cultural Revolution, he would reproach T'eng Hsiao-p'ing for having more or less kept him out of government affairs since 1959. In April 1959 Liu Shao-ch'i replaced Mao Tse-tung as President of the Republic. Mao Tse-tung was giving up control of daily affairs at just the time when his unorthodox ideas had begun to meet with reservations in both the state and the Party apparatus.

The situation became worse the following year. Harvests were catastrophic. The Soviets decided on a drastic step to bring the Chinese back into their camp. In the summer of 1960 they recalled all of their experts (numbering about 1,390) without warning, stopped fulfilling supply contracts, and suspended the industrial projects that were under way. This was the end of privileged Sino-Soviet economic relations. China would in future have to seek its principal trading partners among the capitalist and Third World countries.

The Soviets' decision greatly exacerbated the disorganization of the economy. China's market for heavy industry had shut down; ties between the sectors were broken. Accustomed to looking to Moscow as the center of the socialist bloc, there was more and more doubt within the Party about the validity of the line adopted in 1958; the convictions of some members were shaken by Soviet criticism. Moreover the peasants at the base, whose standard of living had been cruelly lowered by the poor harvests, were being forced to resolve problems by methods which often bore no resemblance to collectivism.

Mao on the Sidelines

By 1960 Mao Tse-tung was no longer in a position to exert a decisive influence on all government decisions. In January when he made a five-point commentary on a report by the workers of Anshan (this was the "Charter of the Iron and Steel Combine of Anshan") and in the spirit of the Great Leap Forward laid down the principles which should govern administration and production in factories, his new directives met with silence. The Party secretariat felt that they were "not urgent" and that it would be better "to concentrate forces in the fight against revisionism." The charter was not discussed until five years later, and only with the coming of the Cultural Revolution did it reach the entire country. For several years Mao Tse-tung was obliged to back a policy of which he did not approve . Later, during the first months of the Cultural Revolution, he gave vent to a sort of self-criticism for having provoked a split in the Party leadership, into two fronts, and for having withdrawn to the second one—that of ideological questions.

Yet in the most important area of any socialist regime, political thought, the authority of the Chairman remained intact. None of his colleagues dared to challenge his ideas—at least not openly—concerning the larger strategic options. This is undoubtedly one of the aspects of the People's Republic during the sixties that is hardest to understand: Mao was certainly kept to the side, but at the same time, *he kept himself* to the side; people expressed reservations about his policies of the preceding years, but not about his ideas in general; some of them wondered if such a quick and radical break with Moscow was wise, but they allowed the Chairman's firmness and the strength of his conviction to carry them along the course he had planned.

Naturally there was talk against him: "To oppose the Chairman, after all, is only to oppose an individual," or again: "Even the sun has black spots." But when it came to settling an argument within the governmental team, people still appealed to Mao and sought guidance from him. Still, his opinion was asked less often than before, especially where domestic matters were involved.

In any case it is certain that economic policy concerned only
the first front and that the Chairman did not intervene in the daily
management of affairs. Perhaps it was even thought that he was
not the right man to organize modern China. Whichever, life in
China gradually became less political; the notion of class struggle
faded, as did that of the dictatorship of the proletariat. Here and
there in the rural areas the peasants engaged in price speculation,
taking advantage of the scarcity of provisions and fodder, or left
their villages to find employment in the city. Disguised forms
of interest loans began to appear; collective lands were sometimes
broken up into individual farms. At every echelon there were
cadres prepared to look the other way. The change was not widespread, but it existed everywhere to some degree.

The Party leader let the government and the Party secretariat
do what they pleased. In the early sixties Mao spent a large part
of his time in ideological dispute with the Soviet Union. As
chairman of the military commission of the Central Committee he
also kept close watch over the reforms that Lin Piao was intro-
ducing into the army. The new Minister of Defense was his ally
in the government: unlike the others, Lin Piao often came to ask
Mao's advice. The army was educated, reorganized, and changed
according to Maoist ideas, and in contrast with the Party—which,
after some extreme bursts of enthusiasm, was degenerating into
empiricism and even opportunism—it would soon give the impression of being an elite revolutionary corps. Lin Piao was the only
one to keep telling his subordinates that the political line determined everything, that a good army, like the Party, should fight
against egoism and personal interest. Year after year Mao's
thought, studied systematically in the barracks, alerted the soldiers to the dangers of revisionist backsliding. By 1964 the
People's Liberation Army had become "one large school for the
thought of Mao Tse-tung."

But though the army would play a decisive part during the Cultural Revolution, it would not be enough in itself to change the
course of events when Mao Tse-tung chose to criticize the new
team of leaders openly. To reaffirm the socialist way and a return to
it, a countermovement would have to be organized among the
people. During 1960 and 1961, which were bad harvest years,
Mao Tse-tung did not intervene on questions of policy. In
January 1961 the Central Committee spoke of starting a rectification movement, but the campaign never got off the ground. The
following year the harvest was better, famine was averted, and
Mao decided to plunge into the struggle. He felt the need for it

all the more urgently since, in the countryside, capitalist tendencies were stronger than ever.

Counterattack

In August 1962 at the Peitaiho work conference, and especially in the following month before the Central Committee, Mao reiterated and clarified his concepts of "the fundamental line of the Party throughout the history of socialism" and had them adopted. He revised the analysis he had proposed at the time of the Great Leap Forward: "Socialist society," he stated, "will exist for a relatively long period of history," and the transition to Communism should not be expected to take place in the near future. The class struggle would continue for a long time, always threatened by revisionist degeneration and the restoration of capitalism.It was and would remain the central problem, on which everyone should concentrate his energies. Mao launched the slogan, "Never forget the class struggle," which would later be found on walls throughout China; and to give the counterattack a concrete structure, he organized the Movement for Socialist Education.

This was primarily aimed at rural areas. Mao Tse-tung called for the revival of associations of poor peasants like those on which agrarian reform and the cooperative movement had been based. The rural poor, the peasant proletariat, should fight against all who were profiting from the current troubles. The movement, launched in 1963, soon ran into obstacles. The opposition resorted to its usual tactics: jumping on the train just to slow it down, stepping on the accelerator to derail the convoy. In 1964, excessive zeal sabotaged the campaign. Some of the rectification teams sent by conservative leaders attacked local cadres indiscriminately, organized general purges, and sowed trouble among the peasants; at the same time, directives from the top echelons asked the associations of poor peasants not to interfere with the work of the cadres.

Mao Tse-tung persisted, pushing the movement forward, taking note of the resistance, and drawing his own conclusions from it: part of the state apparatus was in the hands of Communists who had abandoned the socialist ideal. One day they would have to be stripped of power. For the moment, the movement would have to be extended from the peasantry to other sectors of society, activist militants would have to be trained everywhere to maintain the thrust of the revolution, young people would have to be given experience in political combat immediately so that they would be prepared to take the place of the older leaders. The country would have to make a final break with Soviet ideas, which Mao Tse-tung thought to be full of socialist decadence. And so the campaign for the study of Mao Tse-tung's thought gradually penetrated the barracks, schools, universities, and administrations.

> "In the past we took the struggle to the countrysides, the factories, and the cultural groups, and organized the Movement for Socialist Education, without resolving the problem, because we had not found a form, a method, that allowed us to mobilize the large masses openly, in all domains, starting from the bottom up, so that they would be able to denounce the darker side of our society."
>
> "February Interview," 1967

It was still necessary to take control of the whole area of culture, which was no longer supporting the revolution, or rather was neglecting it for an apolitical art or literature. As early as September 1962 Mao Tse-tung noted: "To resort to novels as a way of attacking the Party—there's a great discovery. Every time one wants to overthrow a political power, one must first form a political opinion and begin working out an ideology. This is just as true for the revolutionary class as for the counterrevolutionary classes." The art world had cut itself off from the working classes, he stated, whereas popular art was an art "created and used" by the workers and peasants. Theater was turning toward the past, was "showing dead people on the stage," and a number of Communist cadres were supporting this elitist and traditionalist art and rejecting revolutionary romanticism. "What a strange situation," he wrote in December 1963. "On the whole Party policy is no longer applied, people are no longer concerned with reflecting the socialist revolution and the building of socialism." And, in June 1964, "If we don't remedy this situation, a day will come when we will have an organization like the Petöfi Circle."[1]

[1] A Hungarian group of liberal intellectuals and adversaries of the Hungarian Communist regime active before the 1956 revolt. Named after a Hungarian nationalist poet who took part in the 1848 revolution.

That same year the Party leader, in agreement with Lin Piao, gave his wife Chiang Ch'ing the job of carrying out the revolution in this area, particularly in the Peking Opera, a bastion of traditional art. There was no doubt that Chiang Ch'ing conducted the reform in a spirit which Mao approved of, even if, as she said then, "My study of the works of Chairman Mao still leaves something to be desired, and my understanding of his thought is not profound." For four years she had been preparing for this crusade against the many literary and artistic associations which had reached "the brink of revisionism."

One Target: the State Leadership

Nevertheless, the movement for Socialist Education was already well under way by 1964. One million cadres had gone to the grass roots to work on rectification. At the end of the year Mao Tse-tung held a work session with the Central Committee to evaluate the movement. The 23-point document that resulted on January 14, 1965, bore his stamp and raised the tone of the campaign a great deal. Mao Tse-tung criticized those who wanted only to "correct the mistakes" without specifically stating that a struggle between two lines was involved, as well as a class struggle. He denounced those who would not distinguish clearly between ordinary mistakes and serious political mistakes and who, because of this, blunted the attack against capitalist elements. As it happened, the first figure to come under attack was none other than Liu Shao-ch'i, the Chief of State. Mao Tse-tung later confided that it was at about this time that he decided to get rid of the Chairman of the People's Republic, the front-ranking figure of the opposing line.

"The most important point of the movement is to oust those Party authorities who have gone the way of capitalism," the document asserted. "In some cases these figures have remained behind the scenes; in other cases they are out in front. Some of their support is from the bottom, and some is from the top . . . . These people are opposed to socialism—whether in the communes, the neighborhoods, the prefectures, the districts, or even the provinces and the *central departments.*"

But before a real cultural revolution could take place, the conflict had to become even more acute. It was in 1965 that the differences became more serious than ever, in the military as well as the cultural realm.

The incidents at Tonkin in August 1965—the American intervention and the new war in Vietnam—started a huge debate. What attitude should China adopt? Should it intervene as it had in Korea, or should it trust the Vietnamese to resist? Going against the opinions of some of the general staff, Mao Tse-tung and Lin Piao decided not to send in troops. They felt that, in the long run, a revolutionary war like the one they had conducted in China could be won against an enemy who was better equipped but weakened by its position as invader. In the little pamphlet "Long Live the Victorious People's War!" that appeared in September 1965, Lin Piao discussed and systematized the Chairman's theses. Shortly after publication of the pamphlet the Chief of Staff, Lo Jui-ch'ing, and the former Minister of Defense, P'eng Teh-huai (removed from office in 1959), were stripped of all responsibility in the Party and the state. At the same time China announced that there was no question of forming a United Front with the Soviet Union to help Vietnam; the Party leader had no intention of going along with those around him who were proposing a temporary compromise with the USSR for the sake of internationalism.

The fall of 1965 also marked the beginning of an attack against part of the state apparatus. From Shanghai, Mao Tse-tung started one of the most dangerous political battles of his career. He was aware of the risks involved and was diplomatic, even Machiavellian: to correct an unfortunate situation, he divided his adversaries and eliminated them one after the other, striking them in their weakest spots.

The first target was the intellectuals attached to the local government of Peking. The Shanghai newspaper *Wen-hui Pao* opened fire: it published a new critical piece on the play *Hai Jui Dismissed from Office,* written some years earlier by Wu Han, vice-mayor of Peking, which had hinted that P'eng Teh-huai should be rehabilitated. Three years before, Chiang Ch'ing had expressed reservations about the play, but with no result; now the debate started up again, in the very city where Chairman Mao's wife had already found solid support for her reform of the opera. Twenty days elapsed between publication of the article and its reprinting in the *People's Daily* of Peking—twenty days during which attempts were made to prevent its publication by the capital's mayor, P'eng Chen, whose ties with Wu Han were very close. P'eng Chen, in turn, was charged.

Relying on Lin Piao

So began a complex process whose history cannot be given here. What must be emphasized, however, is the strategy of the Party leader as he successively isolated his enemies before attacking them, without revealing his future targets. In May 1966 the Central Committee repudiated those of Mao Tse-tung's adversaries who had come "to the forefront." From that point on the Cultural Revolution was in full swing—at first through public address systems and wall newpapers, through articles in the national press and in countless meetings, then through the occupation of administrative offices and takeovers, and finally, from time to time, in more or less violent confrontations between opposing factions. The Cultural Revolution, properly speaking, lasted for three years, until the 9th Party Congress in April 1969.

Most people could not be aware of just how complex the struggle was—no more the participants than foreign observers. In fact the problems were becoming entangled. The aim of the "great strategic plan of Chairman Mao," as it was called at the time, was to maintain a continuing revolution through the settling of questions step by step. Here is one example of the complexity: Mao Tse-tung depended upon Lin Piao, one of the most active leaders in the fight against Liu Shao-ch'i and the only one who Mao could be sure was determined to fight, the only one who supported him unconditionally; and yet Lin Piao had not been among the most resolute during the controversy with the Soviets, and in the spring of 1966 he had begun talking in a clearly exaggerated way about the genius of Mao Tse-tung and the power of his thought—a new variety of "atomic bomb" which would put all the reactionaries to flight. The Party leader felt ill at ease: "No one, up to now, has spoken in such a way. Some of his ideas worry me deeply. I never thought my little books could harbor such a magical power . . . . They are forcing my hand." Mao Tse-tung sent these reflections to his wife in July 1966. But for the moment Liu Shao-ch'i was still in office and very powerful; it was necessary to let Lin Piao—head of the army, first Vice–Prime Minister since January 1965, spokesman for the Left within the government since the spring of 1966, and the man who had been proclaimed the Chairman's political heir and comrade-in-arms during the summer—pursue his campaign of propaganda and exaltation of the cult of personality. The cult was useful for the moment and, what was more, the revolutionary rebels were using it to dismantle the bastions of revisionism. The time had not yet come to cool off the enthusiasm of the "little generals"; later the situation would be corrected. But later, as it turned out, the problem of Lin Piao was to assume gigantic proportions.

In 1966 an unprecedented mass movement dominated everything—the "great revolutionary critique" begun by Mao Tse-tung. All the leaders, or almost all of them, came under fire from the people's critique (apparently one or two wall newspapers even attacked Mao Tse-tung). Most of the members of the Politburo vanished from the scene toward the end of the year, including Chief of State Liu Shao-ch'i, some of them to reappear only much later, after Lin Piao had been eliminated; 2 or 3 percent of the Party members had to turn in their cards. Meanwhile the Party admitted a number of young people who had shown revolutionary ardor and firmness.

One thing is certain: Mao Tse-tung alone decided to launch the Cultural Revolution. Yet even so one could hardly say that he had complete control over the course it took. According to his statements to the Central Committee in the summer of 1966, he had wanted it to be shorter and less violent than it turned out. The impression he gives is that he did not believe it should go on longer than about one year. But as it progressed from universities to secondary schools, from Peking to the provinces, from the lecture halls to the factories and villages, the revolution followed a tortuous path. After being held in reserve for a long time, the army had to be brought in. In several instances the verdicts had to be changed—to rehabilitate people who had been wrongly condemned.

"Difficult to See Things Clearly"

To bring about a revolution within a revolution is a delicate undertaking. The important thing, according to Mao, was to distinguish between "cases which result from ideological errors," that is, Communists who engaged in a revisionist line but who nevertheless supported revolution in principle, and "cases which result from contradictions between the enemy and us," that is, those who were anticipating a change of regime through the weakening of the popular and proletarian dictatorship. "For a time," Mao Tse-tung admitted, "we did not manage to see things clearly." Thus for a time many figures were freely called "renegades" and "counterrevolutionaries" who undoubtedly had supported some of Liu Shao-ch'i's moves but who were not that seriously and irretrievably guilty—many of them, in fact would become members of the 10th Central Committee in 1973.

In 1966 Mao Tse-tung felt it would be possible to hold the 9th Party Congress (the first since 1958) during the following year ; at the end of 1967 the Central Committee planned the Congress for the first half of 1968; it was finally held in April 1969. Normally, the National People's Congress would have met shortly afterward; but the struggle continued, new differences arose, and in 1970 the Central Committee divided on the question of this meeting; once again, the Politburo split in two and an abortive conspiracy postponed a return to political normalcy.

These delays were largely due to the skill of Mao's opponents and the diversity of their tactics—in some places encouraging wage demands, in others provoking strikes, invoking the authority of the Chairman to cover themselves; some slowed the movement down, others deflected it, and still others tried to take it over in order to assure themselves of rapid promotion in the hierarchy, each one using the brake, the accelerator or the steering wheel to obstruct the progress of the convoy. Clearly the increasing disorder served to encourage the ambitious and those who challenged the omnipotence of the Party.[1]

The best example is the case of the "May 16th Corps." In September 1967 *Red Flag* warned against a clandestine organization, full details of which were lacking: "Our comrades should be on their guard; there exists today a handful of counter-revolutionaries who are adopting the same tactics that we have. They are using slogans which seem to be extreme-Leftist—but which are actually far to the Right—in order to encourage the fatal tendency to 'distrust everyone,' and in order to attack the

---

[1]The French Revolution was also contested on two sides—not only by those who slowed the movement down, but also by those who tried to undermine it by going too far, as witness this speech of Couthon's before the Convention: "Some people, who are in continual dispute with their own consciences, secretly do all they can to hamper revolutionary measures for fear of being affected by them. And thus, without perhaps intending to be conspirators, these self-indulgent men in fact become true counterrevolutionaries . . . . Others constantly censure, condemn, attack, obstruct, and make trouble in the hope of somehow or other bringing about a new order, for example a legislature—if not worse—to which they expect to be elected to govern in their own way." This is strikingly similar to the denunciation of revisionist and extreme-Leftist tendencies in China.

proletarian headquarters they are sowing discord and fishing in troubled waters . . . . The people who created and who control the organization called the "May 16th Corps" form precisely this sort of counterrevolutionary group of conspirators . . . . [It] does not dare show itself in public. For the past few months, in Peking, it has remained clandestine. We are not yet very well informed about most of its members and leaders, and the people whom this organization assigns to post tracts and write slogans only come out in the dead of night. The masses are in the process of investigating, and we will soon know who we are dealing with."

The "May 16th Corps" was organized into eight armies corresponding to the eight sectors of the administration where it intended to seize power—"the present struggle consisting," they said, "of the new Central Group of the Cultural Revolution pitting itself against the old government." Actually they formed only a part of the extremist tendency. Those who systematically made sure that criticized Party leaders were kept inactive so as to ensure that the succession would be to their own advantage, found themselves in the following years behind Ch'en Po-ta, group leader of the Cultural Revolution, and behind Lin Piao, "Chairman Mao's best pupil—an example for all the people, the entire country, and the entire Army."

At the time of the death of Chairman Mao, it was still too early to describe with total assurance the history of the Cultural Revolution and the great crisis of 1970–71 which followed it. There is a good deal we do not know about Mao Tse-tung's relations with Lin Piao. In spite of the reservations which he had been expressing for several years, it seems that Mao's reasons for not choosing Lin Piao as his successor were purely tactical, that Mao trusted him—at least until 1969. It is also true, however, that in the months following Lin Piao's death, the Chinese people viewed the Vice-Chairman primarily as a man who had committed "Leftist" errors and therefore did not criticize—as they would soon afterward—his "far-Right" nature.

In fact, the belief that Lin Piao was "Leftist" stemmed from observations which must be characterized as fairly superficial: his continually renewed and intensified praise of the Chairman, the role played by the army in the power takeovers and the formation of revolutionary committees, the ousting of numerous Party leaders, and finally the official propaganda celebrating the Spartan virtues and the military genius of the Vice-Chairman. All this carries little weight in comparison with what is openly held against him today—and was implied from early in 1971—namely, his reservations about the Great Leap Forward and the great controversy with the Soviets, the priority he gave to production at the expense of the class struggle, his philosophical idealism, and, most recently, his desire for a "thaw" and for some sort of rehabilitation for the victims of earlier political struggles.

By the fall of 1970 Mao Tse-tung was faced with a serious problem: how to get rid of his designated successor, who had gradually turned into a rival.

Confrontation over a Constitution

A new Constitution was being drafted to be submitted to the next session of the National People's Congress for ratification. Should the position of Chairman of the Republic (occupied by Acting Chairman Tung Pi-wu since Liu Shao-ch'i's departure) be retained? Mao Tse-tung had caused Lin Piao's political report to be turned down at the Party's 9th Congress, in 1969, but had had to agree to the confirmation of the Minister of Defense as his successor. Mao was wary of the Vice-Chairman's growing power. He forced those drawing up the plan for the Constitution, one of whom was Ch'en Po-ta, to replace the position of Chairman of the Republic by a vague formula which would make Mao Tse-tung "Chief of State of the Proletarian Dictatorship." Lin Piao's position was no longer very precise: he was a designated successor but had to defer to the Chairman within the Party, and in the state had to take a back seat to the head of the government, Premier Chou En-lai.

Ch'en Po-ta and Lin Piao tried to obtain a different decision from the Central Committee. In the name of the theory of "fair denominations," derived from the tradition of Confucius, they wanted to reestablish the principle of a Chairman of the Republic, a more precise term than that of "Chief of State," which carried no special prerogatives. Their plan was to propose that the "genius" Mao Tse-tung be given the post of Chairman, knowing that he did not want it; the Central Committee would then have no choice but to give it to his "close comrade-in-arms," Lin Piao. Ch'en Po-ta, and then Lin Piao and his followers, abruptly broke in on the meeting of the Central Committee which had opened in Lushan in August 1970. The opposition of several leaders and the

personal intervention of Mao Tse-tung, who severely attacked
Ch'en Po-ta, put an end to their plan. After this open condemna-
tion of his undertaking before the Central Committee, Lin Piao's
hopes for the succession collapsed.

According to documents which are probably reliable the
Vice-Chairman in the spring of 1971 decided to risk everything
and attempted to save a hopeless situation by forcibly seizing
power. He outlined a political platform in which he revealed his
reservations about the Cultural Revolution and its accom-
plishments as well as his hostility toward Mao Tse-tung, the
"tyrant," the "Ch'in Shih Huang-ti of modern times."[1] On his
side, Mao Tse-tung set about destroying his adversary's positions.
During the summer of 1971, he set out into the countryside to
explain the shortcomings of Lin Piao, who, he believed, was not
very likely to redeem himself. He told about the Lushan debate in
detail, pointed out the seriousness of the mistakes that had been
made, and emphasized the need for the army to remain faithful,
whatever happened. Several weeks later came the assassination
attempts on Mao Tse-tung, under circumstances that are not
clear, then Lin Piao's flight and his death, reportedly in a plane
crash on the way to the Soviet Union.

We will probably never know all the details of the Lin Piao
affair. It came as a shock to the Party and to the entire country.
Mao Tse-tung himself seemed to be very affected by it, because
of the confidence he had placed in his Vice-Chairman for so
long. In some sense the two years that followed were largely devoted to repairing the damage caused by this unprecedented crisis
in the Party, and to drawing lessons from it.

After the 1973 10th Congress, though weakened by old age
and by the recent ordeals, Mao Tse-tung decided to start a new
rectification campaign which would be more extensive than any
of the previous campaigns. In the spring of 1974 he let loose a
"popular war" against the most illustrious Chinese philosopher.
The aim was no longer simply to criticize revisionism and denounce Soviet doctrines, as in the time of the Cultural Revolution; this time it was necessary to go back further in time, to the
very roots of Chinese feudal thinking or Confucianism, which, it
was said, had impregnated the mind of Lin Piao. In criticizing
Liu Shao-ch'i, Kruschev was mentioned; in denouncing Lin Piao,
Confucius and the principal philosophers of his school were
criticized. And as always the ideological problems were linked to

---

[1]Ch'in Shih Huang-ti, the "Yellow Emperor," was the founder of the Ch'in
dynasty (221-206 B.C.).

problems of the moment. The critique of Confucious was accompanied by a defense and intensification of the actions first undertaken during the Cultural Revolution, actions and notions which ran counter to the ideas of the theoretician of ancient times and of Mao's former successor. Young townspeople were sent into the country, leaders participated in manual work, the distinctions between leaders and followers were rejected, the necessity for a people's dictatorship and for the systematic reexamination of book learning were reaffirmed.

The following year saw the strong denunciation of all that remained of prerevolutionary China—salary scales, the importance of currency, inequalities deriving from the division of labor, and so on—all those elements which favor the creation of a new ruling class, a new class of exploiters. This campaign against the "bourgeois Right" developed throughout the year 1975 and led to the expulsion the next year of Teng Hsiao-p'ing, *de facto* head of government since the illness of Prime Minister Chou En-lai. The 1976 editorials attributed the following extremely harsh words to Mao, directed at the organization he headed: "They conduct a socialist revolution without even knowing where to find the bourgeoisie; this bourgeoisie is in the Communist Party itself; it is the leaders who are following in the capitalist road"

(Editorial of March 10, 1976).

Mao Tse-tung died without having found a successor. After ousting Liu Shao-ch'i and Lin Piao, he gave up the idea of officially designating his political heir. Chou En-lai was dead; Hua Kuo-feng, one was to believe, had been heading up the Politburo since January 1976. He became interim Prime Minister at the departure of Teng Hsiao-ping, and Prime Minister in his own right starting in April. The Central Committee also named him Vice-Chairman of the Party on this date, picking him over Wang Hong-wen, the leader who most embodied the idea of change. The choice of this administrator surely reflected tactical as much as ideological needs, and demonstrated the Party's anxiousness to preserve its own unity in the difficult period ahead. In fact the unceasing attacks of the radicals would have threatened national solidarity once the highest arbiter of conflicts had disappeared.

Mao, the man who had directed the Party for forty years, was struck down by illness in September 1976. His death followed closely the deaths of Chou En-lai, Prime Minister since 1949, and of Chu Teh, founder of the Red Army and Chairman of the National Assembly. The disappearance of these men imposed on China a dramatic renewal of its ruling team, a change in genera-

The Party's Ten Great Crises, According to Mao Tse-tung

During a tour of the countryside which he made in August and September of 1971, Mao Tse-tung stated that ten great crises had shaken the Party during its lifetime. This statement, and the specific details which accompanied it, can be seen as either contradicting or helping to complete the official history of the Chinese Communist Party. The following is a summary based on "secret" documents published by the Taiwan News Service:

1. "After the conference of August 7, 1927, at which Ch'en Tu-hsiu, the secretary-general, was deposed, he formed a 'faction in opposition to the Leftist Leninists,' and eighty-one of them published a declaration in which they made it known that they intended to try to divide the Party. After their attempt failed, they fled to join the Trotskyist faction.

2. "Ch'u Ch'iu-pai, who succeeded Ch'en Tu-hsiu, read one of my pamphlets from Hunan, in which I asserted that 'power comes from the barrel of a gun.' He and his clique, challenging the correctness of my ideas, forced me to resign my seat as alternate member of the Politburo. Later, Ch'u abandoned the fight.

3. "After the 6th Congress (1928), it was Li Li-san's turn. He was in favor of attacking large urban centers; he wanted to conquer one province before going on to seize another. I did not hesitate to make it known that I was against this line. Li Li-san was ousted from power by the Third plenum of the 6th Central Committee (September 1930).

4. "Luo Ch'ang-lun's Rightist faction formed a new Central Committee from 1930 to 1931, and tried unsuccessfully to impose a factionalist line.
   [In this little known incident, apparently Luo

Ch'ang-lun's faction was mainly opposed to the students who had just returned from Moscow. The incident did not pose a threat to the authority of Mao Tse-tung, who was still in the minority at that time.—Author's note.]

5. "Wang Ming's factionalist line survived longer. At the time of his visit to Moscow, he organized the "twenty-eight Bolsheviks," and with the support of the Third International usurped control of the Party for four years . . . . For four years, from 1931 to 1934, I could not make my point of view heard in the Central Committee. It was necessary to wait for the Tsunyi Conference of January 1935 to rectify the errors of Wang Ming and to overthrow him.

6. "During the Long March, Chang Kuo-t'ao also chose to follow a factionalist line, and tried to form a new Central Committee. But without success. He refused to go into North Shensi, though there was no other way out. How could we have extended our influence otherwise, established so many bases during the war against Japan? Chang Kuo-t'ao fled after we arrived in North Shensi.

7. "After the victory, it was Kao Kang's and Jao Shu-shih's turn to form an anti-party alliance; they failed.

8. "At Lushan, in 1959, P'eng Teh-huai—who had illicit contacts with foreign countries—tried to seize power . . . . P'eng Teh-huai wrote a letter in which he openly defied the Party. He failed in his attempt.

9. "Liu Shao-ch'i and his group wanted to divide the Party; their attempt failed.

10. "Finally, there was the crisis of the Lushan meeting in 1970, a theater for intrigues and surprise attacks. Lin Piao and Ch'en Po-ta decided to pounce . . . . Their plan included the establishment of a Chief of State, which the 9th Congress of the Chinese Communist Party was against . . . . [Lin] was clearly anxious to become the new Chief of State, to divide the Party, and to seize power.

tion and a true mutation. The country would have to fear for its unity and stability.

By October, 1976, the group of successors was split. A long-contained dispute reached full bloom with the sudden and simultaneous denunciation of Wang Hong-wen, the youngest member of the Politburo and Vice-Chairman of the Central Committee; Chang Chun-chiao, Shanghai Party Chief; Ch'iang Ching, widow of Mao Tse-tung; and Yao Wen-yuan, the brilliant polemicist of the "leftists." With them went the last representatives of those who had supported, encouraged, and organized the Cultural Revolution of 1966–68.

Both the deposed radicals and the centrists had based themselves on the thought of the deceased Party Chairman; but they disagreed on the practical conclusions implied by this thought, on Chou En-lai's policies, on how broad-ranging a revolution to pursue, on the dangers of bourgeois habits among Party leaders, on the urgency of economic growth. The radicals demanded a new cultural revolution, while the Centrists opposed all divisive moves and favored stability and unity, at least in the difficult moments of succession.

There was also the question of legitimacy. The radicals proclaimed that they alone represented the spirit of Maoist rebellion and the correct line of the Cultural Revolution. The powers who ousted them insisted that Hua Kuo-feng had already become the key figure in the transfer of power one year before the death of Mao. One could point to the importance of the proclamation/program announced by Hua Kuo-feng in October 1975 at the time of the National Conference on Agriculture. In this speech the future Party Chief spoke with authority and resolution about the large problems confronting the country. It was the only speech to be published from the conference, whereas the speeches of Teng Hsiao-ping (pushed from power in January 1976, though apparently making a comeback in 1977), and Ch'iang Ching (purged in October 1976), were barely mentioned.

Mao Tse-Tung was not there to confirm any of these assertions. No doubt he would have approved of the efforts at organization and economic development undertaken after his death; also he would certainly have found it correct to close ranks and forget differences for a while in this period. Nevertheless it remains true that the central idea of his thought was that revolt is justified, that revolution is inevitable and eternal. That however, would have to be left to future generations.

After 1975 Mao Tse-tung gradually withdrew from the scene;

the Chinese who had filed past him by the millions during the excitement of the Cultural Revolution became accustomed not to seeing him at all. Still, he would occasionally appear on television for a few brief seconds during receptions for dignitaries, his body appearing debilitated and his face wasted with age. In June 1976 the official visits were suspended. As he told friends, he had been preparing to "meet God" for a long time. He had fought his last battles, issued his last directives, conducted his last campaigns from the depths of his library, in silence and solitude.

2/Portrait of a Rebel

It is not easy to paint the portrait of a man whose career spanned so many years. It is not easy to choose among the many faces that his long history and complex personality evoke. The first picture, a little blurred by the haziness of childhood, is that of a defiant boy with an extremely questioning mind, a rebel in a rigidly hierarchical society. Even in primary school, say the old peasants of Shaoshan who knew him, he would refuse to stand when reciting his lessons. "Why," he would ask the old master, "must I stand up if you are sitting down?" He told Edgar Snow about his differences with his father, about how he threatened to commit suicide in order to force the old soldier to compromise. Hsiao San, a childhood friend, also reports that one day after his father had beaten Mao, demanding absolute obedience and citing Confucius, the impertinent boy had answered him by citing another passage from the *Analects,* in which it was said that a father should treat his son gently.

This same combative spirit filled the bold and individualistic young resident student at Changsha, who knew nothing about life but wanted to learn everything, who had an obscure presentiment of his future ordeals and would harden his body by splashing himself with cold water in the middle of January in the back courtyard of the Normal School. He was unselfconscious in front of his teachers and passionate about politics. He organized night school courses, founded reviews that were immediately banned, rejected the idea of marraige, and spent his evenings with his friends feverishly imagining the China of the future.

This student of 1917–18 is not an unfamiliar figure to us. The ideas which excited him are very much those of the most sincere "Leftist" students in the West, though he was also bitter about the humiliation of his country. There was perhaps a trace of anarchism in his thinking, certainly a desire to go out to the people, leave the classroom—and a ravenous hunger for all foreign literature, Marxist or not. Hu Shih, a philosopher and admirer of the West, who met Mao Tse-tung shortly after he arrived in Peking, told many years later in Taiwan how the strike in the universities and the students' efforts to continue their work gave Mao the idea of forming the first "university of self-education" in Hunan. This was how the New People's Study Society came into being, a society which was to become one of the first Communist cells in South China.

In Peking the life of a student was hard. Mao Tse-tung lived far from the university, in the "Three-Eyes Well" quarter, close to what is now the Hall of the People. He shared his room with seven other Hunanese students. They slept squeezed against one another on the *kang* (a brick bed heated from the inside), putting up with the lack of air as best they could. Clearly the conditions he lived in were much harsher than those faced by European or Chinese students today.

At that time he was too busy with politics to give any time to his love life. At least this is what he told Edgar Snow. But to understand Mao Tse-tung fully, we should remember the passion he felt for his first wife, Yang K'ai-hui. It was a deep, militant, tragic passion. Eight years younger than he, frail, very modern in appearance with her short hair, Yang K'ai-hui was part of the progressive youth of Changsha. Her father, an avant-garde intellectual had been Mao's teacher in Changsha before taking up a professorship at the University of Peking. Yang K'ai-hui had already been helping Mao Tse-tung in his political work for several years when they were married in the spring of 1921. That same year, soon after the Chinese Communist Party was founded, she became a member of the Party.

In 1927, fleeing from the Kuomintang massacres, the couple decided to separate. Yang K'ai-hui returned to Hunan with the children and went into hiding. Apparently she never saw her husband again. The Kuomintang arrested her in September 1930 and tortured her but she refused to reveal the whereabouts of her husband. They executed her in November; she was twenty-nine and left behind three children. In 1957 Mao Tse-tung sent to a friend a poem in memory of her husband, killed in battle in 1931, and his own dearly loved and well-remembered first wife:

> I lost my proud poplar and you your willow
> Willow and poplar soar up toward the heaven of heavens

(*Yang* means poplar, and *liu,* the name of his friend's husband, means willow.) The people of Hunan observe the anniversary of Yang K'ai-hui's death; even today, they still speak of her to visitors.

With the exception of a photograph taken at Changsha, the first picture we have of Mao Tse-tung dates from the late twenties. We cannot attach much significance to the family photograph from Shaoshan of the very young Mao, nor can we take very seriously the picture painted in 1968 by one Liu Ch'un-hua, which represents Mao Tse-tung in 1922 on the Anyuan road. The painter certainly took his inspiration from contemporary photographs, but his main purpose was to destroy the myth that Liu Shao-ch'i was the organizer of the miners' strike at Anyuan; he therefore tried to portray a figure which was resolute and angelical, the future savior of China. Mao Tse-tung's closed fist was intended to show a decisive spirit; the rising sun in the picture proclaimed the revolution. Even so, certain features seem authentic. The canvas, like the Changsha photograph, shows a very young man, tall and thin, with long, thick hair and a face that is still childlike, dressed in a long, traditional gray-blue robe. He is walking at a good pace, under the cloudy sky of South China, clutching at his side a precious oil-paper umbrella. But I need not dwell on a picture whose intention was more to glorify the personality of Mao Tse-tung than to depict it accurately.

A Fragile Young Man

Still, this image confirms portraits from the following years. In 1928 Mao's future bodyguard Chen Chang-feng met him for the first time in a Kiangsi village: "I looked at him curiously. His gray uniform was like ours. The only difference was that the pockets of his coat seemed particularly large. His black hair formed a vivid contrast to his light complexion. Perhaps he was a little too thin . . . ." This apparent fragility also struck English and American journalists when they made contact with the Communist forces in the thirties. Agnes Smedley, the biographer of Chu Teh, describes Mao Tse-tung as having astonishingly fine, almost feminine, features. In June 1936 Edgar Snow met the leader of the Party in the Red zone of Shensi. He was, wrote Snow, "a gaunt, rather Lincolnesque figure, above average height for a Chinese, somewhat stooped, with a head of thick black hair grown very long, and with large, searching eyes, a high-bridged nose and prominent cheekbones."

Mao Tse-tung adopted a Spartan way of life. Partly out of necessity, but also because he knew that the leader of the underground movement should embody the same virtues he demanded of his men. All he possessed at Kiangsi were the following: two blankets, a cotton sheet, two gray uniforms like those worn by the ordinary troops, a threadbare overcoat, a gray woolen sweater, a broken umbrella, a bowl to eat out of, and a rucksack in which he stuffed all his documents, maps, and books. Chen Chang-feng tells how Mao usually preferred to walk during the Long March, relinquishing his horse to exhausted combatants. At that time about ten people were attached to him: a few bodyguards, one or two secretaries, a porter, a doctor, and several young men assigned to deal with equipment.

This was hardly excessive for a man in charge of tens of thousands of his fellow countrymen.

It was during this period that Mao lived through his most difficult experiences. His comrades were falling one after the other at his side. He later said that of the 80,000 who had set out from Kiangsi on the Long March, only 8,000 survived. Every evening brought a new toll of losses and defections. When they halted there was often no water, no work table, no roof to provide shelter from the rain. Mao did not own a lined overcoat. His bodyguard describes him during the icy winter slipping in the snow and then advancing with difficulty in his soaked clothes, all the while affecting the good humor that was so indispensible to the morale of the troops. Chen Chang-feng says that at this time Mao was thinner than he had ever been.

Much later, in June, 1946, the writer Robert Payne met him in Yenan. "It was easy to recognize him, he had long black hair with blue highlights in it, delicate cheekbones, and an immense forehead." With his round glasses in their silver frames, his pursed and almost feminine lips, he seemed "like a university professor." "In most of the photographs," added Payne, "he is wearing a cloth cap, and one is struck by his round peasant's face, his short nose, his sleepy eyes; but the moment the cap is taken off, the peasant disappears . . . . He is fifty-five years old and looks thirty."

Foreigners did not see Mao Tse-tung when he was working. For that, one must read accounts by the men who traveled with him—Chen Chang-feng, who has already been mentioned, or Yen Chang-lin, who was with him in the North Shensi campaign, during the last years of the civil war. They portray a man subjected to the worst hardships, a man gifted with a great capacity for work (though perhaps not as great as that of Chou En-lai, which is famous). They tell of Mao at his radio set, listening to

news of the Kuomintang, fighting attacks of fever, walking in the
rain in shoes that gushed water at every step; Mao living from
one day to the next, not having a moment in which to read or
reflect, hastily searching for a route by which to escape his pur-
suers, getting lost in the dark because he had no guide, collecting
wood to make a fire to dry his clothes, going back and forth beside moving columns to talk to his soldiers, leading his horse by
the bridle over stony paths, emptying his bowl of rice with agile
chopsticks while poring over a map, looking for a flat rock on
which to spread his documents; Mao striding through the villages
plundered by the Kuomintang or laid waste by the war . . . It
was during these countless ordeals that his character was forged
and his prestige won.

Another of his guards, Chai Tse-chun, recalls the
Party Chairman in 1938 at work on the draft of "On
Protracted War," a long study which covers almost
one hundred pages of small print in the *Selected
Works:*

"It took him eight or nine days to finish it; he slept
very little, ate very little and at irregular hours; he
would not touch the food that was brought to him,
and if he was urged to eat, he would answer, 'In a
minute, in a minute,' but in fact would not eat any
more than he had before. His cloth shoes would be
damaged by fire and the soles burned before he
would notice it. When he finished, he called a guard
and asked him to send the manuscript to "Liberation," under the pen name of Hsu Pin, to be corrected. Several days later he sent it out in the form of
a booklet entitled 'On Protracted War.' And that was
how the guard learned that Mao had been busy, because he was writing a book. Afterwards he sent
copies to Liu Shao-ch'i, K'ang Sheng, and Chang
Wen-t'ien, for their comments. When it was finished,
he was ill with fatigue and had to rest for a day."

In Many-Sided China

The only time Mao Tse-tung left his country was to visit Moscow. He did not have a clear notion of the outside world. But then no one knew China better than he. Once in power, he spent several months—sometimes more than six months—every year visiting the provinces. But it was mainly during the civil war that he gained his experience. He must have traveled the entire continent of China, from the rice paddies of Hunan to the Peking plain, by way of Canton, Fukien, and the eleven provinces he crossed during the Long March. And there were the excursions he made into North China at the end of the civil war.

Still more important, Mao Tse-tung knew all levels of society at first hand. Chiang Kai-shek had never been able to understand the Communists but Mao was well-acquainted with the Kuomintang. He directed the Nationalists' propaganda and was secretary of the Kuomintang's daily newspaper at Canton. He lived in the clandestine workers' cells of Shanghai and took part in the solemn receptions of Chungking. He tramped through swamps and scaled icy peaks in flight from the enemy, and then later toasted that same enemy; he directed a night school and organized the underground; he held discussions with American diplomats before confronting the United States in Korea.[1] Few statesmen accumulated such rich and varied experience.

China after all is in itself an immense human and social laboratory, a sort of League of Nations: there is no province which does not have its national minorities. The biographies of Mao tell of his arrival, during the Long March, in the mountains peopled by the Yi. Mao Tse-tung did his best to communicate with his hosts, whose language he did not understand. He thanked them for their gifts, nodded his head, and imitated the gestures of the natives; his comrades did the same. The Yi, sensing his goodwill, ran up in crowds to salute this military leader who had not come to massacre them. One man in his entourage remarked: "Chairman, we are their brothers, but we do not understand anything they are saying. It is as if we were in a foreign country!" "That is not surprising," Mao answered. "You know how large our country is. You are from Kiangsi, and you can't even understand me, though I'm from Hunan. How could you possibly understand the language of the Yi?"

---

[1]There are contradictory stories about Mao's knowledge of foreign languages. Yen Chang-lin, one of the people close to him, asserts that during the civil war, Mao continuously studied one language which was not identified. Some of those who met Mao believe he knew no foreign languages. In Peking, in 1972, it was said that he was relearning English with Chou En-lai.

A Bungalow and Hawthorn Trees

What do we know about Mao Tse-tung today? Very little. As Edgar Snow regretfully notes, he was the least well known and the least accessible of all statesmen. Yet a few Chinese and some foreigners visited him in his residence in the Forbidden City. According to Edgar Faure (*le Figaro,* July 5, 1957), his home consisted of "a small Chinese courtyard, two Judas trees, some flowering hawthorns . . . . We enter something of a small palace, something of a bungalow; there is a fairly large room lighted by fluorescent lights and Chinese lamps, with carved wooden ornaments hanging from the ceiling. On one side is a conference table covered with red cloth, on the other a circle of club chairs."

A Family of Revolutionaries and Martyrs

Mao Tse-tung suffered the trials of war and revolution in his own life, and so did his family. Most of those close to him fell under the blows of the Kuomintang, the Japanese, or American troops during the Korean War. His wife, Yang K'ai-hui, died in Changsha in 1930, executed by the Kuomintang.

His brother, Mao Tse-min, entered the Party in 1922 and went to organize the workers of Anyuan and later, beginning in 1925, worked in Shanghai. At the time the Soviet Republic of Kiangsi was founded, he was managing the Party's bank. After taking part in the Long March, he became Minister of the Economy in the Yenan region. Two years later he left for Sinkiang. The Kuomintang captured him in 1942 and shot him the following year, in Urumchi. He was forty-seven years old.

Another brother, Mao Tse-t'an, first studied in Changsha in the school founded by his older brother, then, starting in 1923, worked in the workers' night schools. He took part in the Autumn Harvest Uprising and shortly afterward found himself in the Chingkang Mountains. He became a division head in the Red Army. He fell in battle, in 1935, at the age of thirty.

Although Mao's young cousin, Mao Tse-chian, is little known, she led the life of a true revolutionary. She joined the Communist Party in 1923, and she too. was involved in the workers' night schools. In 1926,

(continued)

she formed a small group of guerillas. In 1928, she was wounded, then captured by the Kuomintang, who executed her the following year. She was twenty-four years old.

Mao Tse-tung's oldest son, Mao An-ying, born in 1922, went to study in Moscow at the age of fourteen and remained in the Soviet Union during World War II. He died during the Korean War, in the fall of 1950, while commanding a division of Chinese volunteers. Mao's nephew Mao Chuh-siong, the son of Mao Tse-t'an, was buried alive by the Kuomintang at the age of nineteen.

Little is known about other members of Mao Tse-tung's family, except for Chiang Ch'ing, his last wife, and Ho Tzu-chen a member of the Communist Party since 1927, whom he married in 1928 according to some accounts. Ho Tzu-chen had studied in a Normal School. She took part in the Long March and lived with Mao Tse-tung in Yenan until 1937. She bore Mao five children. After several years, misunderstandings arose between the couple; Ho Tzu-chen became ill and left to seek medical treatment in Moscow, and from then on they lived apart.

Chiang Ch'ing, a former movie actress known by the name of Lan P'ing, arrived in Yenan at the end of 1939 and was apparently assigned to service in the military archives. She lived with Mao Tse-tung from 1940 on and bore him two daughters, Li Na and Mao Mao. Both of them were brought up in the family, at least until 1957. Li Na worked for a time at the Study Center of the Society of Writers and evidently took part in the Movement of the Hundred Flowers in 1957. The two young women were not inactive during the Cultural Revolution. Li Na was given certain positions of responsibility in the People's Army.

Almost nothing is known about Mao Tse-tung's other children. His second son, Mao An-ch'ing, apparently translated a number of works from Russian into Chinese on his return from Moscow University; there is still some doubt about the existence of a third son, Mao An-long who, according to certain sources, was a student at the university of Tsing-hua.

One of the soldiers who guarded Mao Tse-tung described the structure of the Chairman's life in the following way (*Chinese Youth,* February 1959): "Our leaders in the Central Committee have very frugal and very simple lives, particularly Chairman Mao, who is an excellent example. He lives in an old school building. In the small courtyard stands a bungalow surrounded by a few pine trees. In front of the house there are four pots of flowering chrysanthemums and a curtain of reeds. The room is furnished in a very simple way too: there is nothing but a set of bookshelves, a bed, a work table, and a few chairs."

The following is an account of a visit in 1952 by the official formerly responsible for Chairman Mao's security: "It is Saturday today, the Chairman's two daughters, Li Na and Mao Mao, have come home from school; Mao's wife, Chiang Ch'ing, is here too, and there is a boy sitting beside her [the son of Tse-min—Author's Note]; a few men are playing cards . . . . In the livingroom there are three sofas, one large and two small, seating only one person, a low tea table, and a single bed. Chiang Ch'ing and the children are wearing quilted clothes of blue cotton and cloth shoes."

Of course as he grew older, Mao Tse-tung gained weight. His rheumatism began to bother him, and he exercised less than before. A little swimming and ping-pong, people said. No more of those solitary excursions on foot or on horseback into the hills of Yenan that had so upset his guards, who were afraid of Kuomintang agents. He had to watch his health, smoke less. His last tour of the provinces took place in the summer of 1971, in the weeks before the denouement of the Lin Piao crisis. Until the end of the sixties he had regularly watched the millions demonstrating in T'ien An Men Square; but starting in the fall of 1971 he was apparently confined to his rooms. Instead of entertaining in the drawing rooms of the nearby National Assembly, as he used to, he received visitors in his library. It was in this setting, stripped of all majesty, with books piled in disorder on the pedestal tables, that he appeared to his fellow countrymen on television or in the newsreels during his last years.

These three- or four-minute-long sequences seemed much alike, especially since there was no sound track. It was a strange spectacle, in which you might see figures engaged in a dialogue about the great problems of the world, but could hear only soft music, sometimes the sound of a lullaby, sometimes a pastoral melody, with soaring flights of strings and woodwinds evoking the quiet harmony of a world without conflicts. Ensconsed in a vast armchair, Mao Tse-tung would turn his age-worn face alternately right then left, looking first at the person he was talking to and then at his interpreter; he would emphasize his remarks with energetic movements of his hands, his finger pointing at his visitor as though to support an argument. But mainly you would see him posing questions, asking for details. Sometimes his face would light up mischievously, as when he was astonished by the height and the fur-covered caps of visitors from Zaire, or the jewels and the curtseys of the women from the Zambian delegation—he curtseyed back, bursting with laughter. Before long he would get up from his chair, accompany his guests to the door, slowly wave goodbye and return to the shadows.

Everyone who was close to Mao Tse-tung agrees about the simplicity of his habits and his nature. Apparently power did not go to his head. Hs clothes were made out of ordinary cloth and worn a long time. His shoes of discolored leather did not shine any more than they once had. In 1959, he was still wearing a patched bathing suit, according to one soldier. His family also dressed modestly; when they lived with their father, his two daughters were said to look like young country girls. His simple fare did not vary from year to year. It consisted of fried soy noodles, beef, red pepper—until late in his life he thought it an effective stimulant—and various common Chinese vegetables.

In 1954, the New China News Agency printed the accounts of sailors who had descended the Yangtze with Mao from Hankow to Shanghai—including these remarks about food:

"At every meal he has two dishes and a soup: the dishes consist of vegetables, very little meat, and some peppered soy noodles. He drinks plain water. As for his shoes, I heard that he bought them at the time the People's Republic was founded; that means he has been wearing them for four years now."

His official image was hardly flattering: he often looked stiff and priestly, as though immobilized by the camera. In films about the Cultural Revolution, Mao Tse-tung seems like a sort of rigid god in T'ien An Men Square, his gaze lost above the crowd that is cheering him and that he does not see. The film of the 9th Congress on the other hand portrays another figure—one that is powerful, full of life and humor—and it is undoubtedly much more accurate. Perhaps the detachment shown on the grandstand, was useful to his policies—grandeur requires distance, and at that time Mao Tse-tung needed the fervor of the crowds to win the battle. Then again, perhaps that reserve expressed the resignation of a man who would have preferred not to resort to such demonstrations, or who wished to dissociate himself from an entourage who were past masters in the art of using flattery for their own purposes.

Not much is known about the way Mao Tse-tung spent his time once he was in his eighties, except that in the last years he gave up the duties of daily administration to dedicate himself to what was most important: thinking over the larger strategic decisions. In February 1972 he followed very closely the drafting of the Chinese-American joint communiqué which was signed at Shanghai, and after the 10th Congress in 1973 he took charge of the rectification movement called the "Critique of Lin Piao and Confucious." Many of his writings have not been published, or at least not under his name; he often wrote the editorials in the *People's Daily,* drawing attention to the "typical experiences," or to the successful achievements of one or another model unit which the rest of the country should be aware of.

Mao Tse-tung held the country together; he was the guide and teacher, a man of reflection, who studied and read but did not lose himself in the culture of the past: he combined study and action. In the early seventies for instance, when China was about to emerge on the international stage, he examined and analyzed what he called "the reference works on world affairs."

He was unique among Communist leaders of his time for two character traits: his revolutionary optimism—a patient optimism—and his rejection of conformity. He undoubtedly owed a large part of his prestige and the trust and affection Chinese crowds felt for him to these qualities. At the same time, they answered the needs of the national revolution perfectly: in a China marked by so many conservative traditions, it was necessary to be enterprising, to dare to violate the taboos.

A Feather Flies All the Way up to Heaven

"Who says a chicken's feather can't fly all the way up to heaven?" Mao Tse-tung asked in 1955, during the cooperative movement. In one Hunan village the well-to-do peasants were saying of the poorer ones: "They have less money than an egg has fur, and they think they can start a cooperative. Can a feather fly up to heaven?" But, said Mao, that is precisely what happened: "People have debated about whether a chicken's feather could rise all the way up to heaven. It is evidently an important question. In thousands of years has such a thing ever been seen? This impossibility has become a truism. But if the Party does not criticize this old idea, the poor peasants will be completely at a loss." The reason for such rumors was that the cooperatives had not yet increased their production and the Party had not explained the advantages of cooperation, it had not yet shown why "in a socialist period, the ancient truism—'chicken feathers cannot fly up to heaven'—is no longer true."

"The poor want to change their lives. The old system is dying. Feathers are flying towards heaven. In the Soviet Union they have already arrived. In China, they have just taken off. The feathers are going to glide over the whole world."

Mao's lyricism is characteristic. "A single spark can start a prairie fire." The following phrase (1971) no doubt also belongs to him: "Countries want independence, nations want freedom, and people want revolution"—a summary of China's international strategy.

Socialism will inevitably replace capitalism and bury imperialism. That society should establish its own laws, that collectivism should reject individual power and organize itself in a collective manner is the normal course of events as Mao Tse-tung saw it, like the succession of the seasons and the rotation of the stars. Man, who is a social being, cannot help but desire socialism—perhaps only dimly, but nevertheless profoundly. That is why he first of all needs the confidence, the hope, and the will to accomplish his destiny. To dare to think, to dare to act, to dare to fight.

"There is nothing terrifying about these difficulties," he told his bodyguard. "The only thing to dread is the fear of them. They are truly terrifying if one dreads them. But they are not in the least terrifying if one does not become alarmed." Stubbornness, the spirit of sacrifice, the support which the people inevitably bring to a just cause, will ensure victory, as long as one accepts the notion of a "a protracted war."

"Chairman Mao is a force, a creator, an activist; his strategy involves surprise, tension, and relaxation. He is wary of calm periods that go on for too long. Nothing, for him, changes very fast. But he is prudent, pragmatic, and capable of extended patience in order to attain his goal by stages. There are proofs that as early as 1959, Chairman Mao was outlining the strategy for the Cultural Revolution and the purges whose result, among other things, was to carry Chou En-lai to the top."

Edgar Snow, l'Express, August 2, 1971

Mao Tse-tung's optimism was also based on this profound conviction: Marxism is the only philosophy through which one can understand the world; it is nothing other than the concrete analysis of the dialectical nature of phenomena. Idealism is "subjectivism," or class oppression imposed on and deforming reality: deforming it and so preventing effective action. Idealism, a "bourgeois philosophy," gradually becomes the philosophy of impotence. The Marxists see the world without blinders and are the only ones who can liberate it.

In general, Mao Tse-tung also believed, "what succeeds is right, what fails is wrong." The first criterion by which to judge an idea, a political line, is to analyze its concrete effects—not to turn on the "record players," that is, the intellectuals with their stuffed heads who know nothing of the world. Mao Tse-tung never acknowledged any authority a priori. He always asked for proof in terms of the facts. Such a man was needed if China was to learn to reject the burden of a tradition many thousands of years old.

A Horror of Word Battles

Nonconformism, antiauthoritarianism, the critical reexamination of clichés—this is what characterized Mao Tse-tung who as a seventy-year-old fastened the armband of the Red Guard to his sleeve just as the young schoolteacher of Changsha might have done. Long before he controlled the Party, the "authorities" kept this unpedigreed provincial, who had never been approved by Moscow, out of the most important positions. The professors and young militants freshly molded by Bolshevik universities looked with suspicion on this peasant with the strong Hunanese accent, who was as interested in the peasants as in the workers. Though Mao Tse-tung took care what he said, whatever he did or suggested doing was a challenge to the *a priori* reasoning of the Communist International and the Chinese Party.

It was during this period that he realized that theoretical knowledge and book learning were not worth much when it came to carrying out a complex and urgent task successfully. "All true knowledge," he declared, "is based upon direct experience." To everyone—and there were many—who praised or condemned what they had not taken the trouble to observe for themselves, he said: if you do not investigate, you have no right to speak! Mao had a horror of dogmatism, which flourished in China as it does among all extreme Leftists in the world before they seriously undertake to transform their own societies from the ground up.

As for the Party, Mao Tse-tung was constantly vigilant. He criticized its instructions, first from the inside, then by disobeying—refusing to follow Li Li-san's orders to attack the cities. Later he urged the people to criticize the Party; then he called upon the army to join in the criticism, and finally the young people. Mao Tse-tung was not an organization man. Of all Communist leaders, he is probably the only one who was never secretary-general of the Party. Because of this he could keep his distance, avoid the daily routine, guarantee that a spirit of opposition would be maintained and that a variety of theories would continue to compete with one another.

"We must remain in touch with all sorts of people," he said in 1967 to leaders of the Cultural Revolution, "the Left, the middle of the road, and the Right. I have never believed that an organization should be completely 'pure.' It is good, it is desirable, for there to be lively debate within the Party: yes, there must be some Rightists!" In July 1966 he spelled it out even more clearly: "Do not arrest people carrying reactionary wall newspapers and slogans. Some people are writing, 'Support the Center of the Party. Down with Mao Tse-tung!' Why arrest them? They are still supporting the Center of the Party! . . . Don't be frightened by a few reactionary wall newspapers and slogans!"

Important members of the Party always conspired to prevent

debates. In 1954 Mao Tse-tung took up the cause of two young mothers who could not find a newspaper that would print their criticism of an essay on the famous novel *The Dream of the Red Chamber*. The debate began. Mao Tse-tung noted: "The controversy was sparked off by two 'illustrious unknowns' and as could be predicted, the 'prominent figures' hardly paid attention, and even obstructed it; they formed a united front of idealism with the bourgeois writers and voluntarily made themselves the prisoners of the bourgeoisie."

He believed in challenging important members of the Party, distrusting platitudes, and scorning book learning. His irony was cutting: "Books do not move. You can open and close them. Nothing is easier. It is harder for a cook to prepare meals or for a butcher to kill a pig. Pigs run when you want to catch them. They squeal when they are killed. But a book lying on a table neither moves nor cries out. You can do whatever you want with it. Is there anything in the world easier to do than read a book?"

In February 1964 he devoted a long interview to the question of teaching. "One should not read too much. Some of Marx's books should be read, but not too many. A few dozen would be enough. When you read too much you achieve just the opposite of what you wanted: you become a bookworm, a dogmatist, a revisionist. Often the greatest men did not study at a university. Gorky had only two years of school; he taught himself. Franklin, the American, sold newspapers. Watt, the inventor of the steam engine, was a worker."

That same year, he mercilessly criticized the national system of education before a delegation from Nepal: "School goes on too long, there are too many courses, and the teachers inject knowledge instead of appealing to the imagination. At examinations they treat candidates like enemies, and try to trap them . . . . Many children do not know what cows, horses, chickens, dogs or pigs are; they cannot recognize rice, millet, corn, wheat, sorghum, or Indian millet."

The West has heard only vague rumors about Mao's disputes with intellectuals. This is not surprising. Many of the authors who wrote about Mao Tse-tung avoided discussing this aspect of his character precisely because they felt themselves under attack. They continued to believe in the ascendancy of innate intelligence. Sacrilegiously, Mao Tse-tung, who believed only in the validity of experience, accused them of not knowing anything important—not knowing how to cultivate the earth, forge a tool, shape a mind, kill an enemy, nor even organize themselves enough to settle a problem as a group. For him, these men had neither hands nor brains; they were only "semi-intellectuals."

Against the Current!

Mao Tse-tung spoke for our own societies and their values as well, if only implicitly. Here in the West, engineering courses never compete in prestige and dignity with linguistics, though no one needs linguistics to express himself; and inexperienced graduates, fresh out of the examination room, are put in positions of power over the people who are feeding the country, making its tools, and building its machines. When Mao Tse-tung urged his fellow countrymen to criticize the pedants and professional writers, many "sensitive souls" outside China might well have felt they too were under attack.

And so nonconformity and rejection of authority are coupled with good sense and a respect for popular knowledge. Anarchism is not a question here: Mao Tse-tung was attacking something that seemed to him to embody bourgeois thought and bourgeois customs. He wanted to accept all the challenges of the bourgeoisie, but no others. He fought the enemies of Marxism with integrity, invoking revolutionary discipline. Only in the last years of his life, particularly after the 1973 10th Congress, did he specifically outline his ideas about this, in connection with the famous directive "go against the current"—one of the most original and dramatic aspects of his thought.

One must dare to go against the current. "To go against the current is one of the principles of Marxism-Leninism," Mao Tse-tung asserted, and he was quoted accordingly by Chou En-lai in his speech to the 10th Congress. The directive was obviously a response to the problems of the preceding years. Lin Piao had succeeded in imposing some of his views on a Central Committee that was too docile, that had not been able to identify the old-style conspirator lurking behind the man with immoderate praise for his Chairman: Lin Piao's accession to power, following the elimination of the leader, would undoubtedly have led to the repression of all elements loyal to the Chairman. Mao evidently wondered how many of them would have dared to stand fast and face up to the new authority.

The Lin Piao affair cast a gloom over political thinking in China. It revealed the possibility of a sudden and rapid loss of power. This idea was not entirely new to Mao Tse-tung. In a letter to Chiang Ch'ing in 1966 he had foreseen that "the Right will start an anti-Communist *coup d'etat* in China [and] for a time [it will] use what I say to gain power." But he remained optimistic. Concerning the Right he wrote that "its regime will probably be shortlived, because the revolutionaries representing the interests of the people, who constitute more than 90 percent of the population, will not let it take over." But the bitter experience of 1971 and the stabilization of a "revisionist" power in the Soviet Union and in Eastern Europe led him to take the possibility of a "restoration" very seriously and to prepare the militants without further delay to form a future opposition if such a change made it necessary.

Wang Hong-wen's report on the Party statutes, at the 1973 Congress, includes a quotation which some people attribute to Mao (his 1958 speech at Chengtu): "When the line is at stake, when the situation as a whole is in question, a true Communist must act without any selfish considerations, must dare to go against the current, without fear of being discharged, expelled from the Party, thrown into prison, obliged to get a divorce, or shot." These carefully chosen phrases—which we have no reason to believe were exaggerated—show how seriously the Chinese Party felt about threats pressing on the socialist regime.

"Go against the current!": the expression itself shows that Mao did not believe that the path to socialism was lined with triumphs. He believed that a majority in the Party could go off in a mistaken direction, not simply because it had been forced to, but because it had not been able to distinguish between "true and false Marxism." If there were such a thing as a triumphal way where progress was smooth, it would have to be the path to revisionism.

This is why Mao Tse-tung ended his directive by stating that "Marxism is a fighting philosophy." It is not simply a rigid set of permanent formulas to be applied. "Marxism can only develop within the struggle; it has been that way in the past, it is that way now, it will continue to be that way in the future." Even more forceful is the phrase that was so often repeated after the 10th Congress and which is typical of him: "Not to fight is to retreat; not to fight is to change; not to fight is to be defeated; not to fight is to become revisionist."

Thus Mao Tse-tung saw the possibility, even the likelihood, that the Party leader would revert to an erroneous line. He urged the Communists, and all the people, to rise up, do away with the errors, and drive out the traitors. To take up arms in the name of loyalty to Marxism and to the revolution.

Starting in the fall of 1973 the slogan ''Go against the current!'' became yet another exhortation to day-by-day revolutionary vigilance and to the challenging of the lower authorities— particularly the factory managers and the teachers—in order to destroy the ''four old things'' (old principles, old customs, old ideas, and old habits).

All this was directly in the tradition of the Cultural Revolution. Young people were consistently urged to take responsibility for the sharpening of intellectual habits. ''In our society, the youth is the most active and dynamic force. Young people are eager to study and have fewer conservative ideas than other people. This is particularly true during a period of socialism.'' Mao Tse-tung sided with the young rebels, particularly those who had the courage to go into the countryside and live with the peasants and for the peasants, and who were the objects of criticism and mockery on the part of city cadres and their families. For Mao Tse-tung the watchword ''Go against the current!'' was a way to cross the barriers separating the different social classes; it was a way of remaining true to himself: of keeping in touch with what he was sixty years before, when he traveled the countryside on foot with his umbrella and a little bundle on his shoulder.

God and Allah

''Do you believe there is a God?'' Edgar Snow asked him. No, he did not believe there was, but people who claimed to be well informed were certain that there was a God. It seemed that there were many gods and it so happened that the same God supported all sides at once. During the European wars, the Christian God had taken the side of the English, the French, the Germans, etc.—even though they were fighting one another. During the Suez crisis, God was with the French and the English, but then Allah was supporting the other side.

Reported by Edgar Snow in *le Nouveau Candide,* December 11, 1965

No Gilding the Lily

Mao Tse-tung was one of a small number of empire builders and founders of civilizations in the history of mankind. This in itself makes him a great figure. There is no need to gild the lily, proclaiming or pretending to believe he was infallible. As if without a pedestal he would not seem big enough.

Several of his plans failed of course, several of his expectations were not fulfilled. Who in 1974 talked any longer about the 1958 plan to catch up with Great Britain and outstrip it within fifteen years? The program of agricultural development which was started in 1955 and intended to take twelve years had achieved only half of its goals by 1973. For a few months in 1958, Mao Tse-tung thought that some sort of economic miracle was possible and envisaged "leaps" in agricultural production that no experienced agronomist would have credited. Perhaps he should have foreseen that in 1960 Krushchev would recall his technicians and throw industry into confusion, instead of being so completely caught off guard. Nor, if we are to believe Krushchev's memoirs, did Mao Tse-tung expect the United States to intervene in Korea in 1950. And so on.

The Cultural Revolution, which did a great deal for his fame, abroad as well as in China, was a much more difficult enterprise than Mao's flatterers would have us believe. The Chairman's "great strategic plan" went on much longer than he had at first envisaged. Mao Tse-tung had insisted on the need to refrain from violence or armed struggle; but the 16-point decision of 1966 was hardly followed. Slogans like "revolution is not a banquet" and "without destruction there can be no construction" stirred up the Red Guards and served to excuse confrontations between different factions. "For a while, one had the feeling the country was in total chaos," admits an editorial dated July 1, 1971. Initially, Mao thought the Cultural Revolution launched in 1966 would last one or two years at the very most; yet more than five years later it came to life again over the Lin Piao affair.

Mao Tse-tung was not lucky in his choice of successors either. Liu Shao-ch'i wanted to nibble away at his authority little by little; a revolution was needed to drive him out, as well as some rather inglorious allusions to his dubious compromises with the Kuomintang in the past. Lin Piao sang the praises of the Chairman so loudly that Mao himself could not be heard. Liu Shao-ch'i ended up as a "renegade, enemy agent, and traitor of the working class," Lin Piao as "a bourgeois careerist, conspirator, two-faced individual, renegade and traitor.'' Obviously since Mao Tse-tung had the means of getting rid of them even after they were in power, he could also have prevented their rise in the first place. If he did not, it was because he had let himself be fooled by them, particularly in the case of Lin Piao. He had not had enough foresight and had not been able to prevent a temporary weakening of the Party leadership.

But however serious were these shortcomings and their consequences, they could not be called inexcusable blunders. No statesman ever completely accomplishes what he sets out to do; every expectation carries with it the risk of disappointment; no government can avoid personal quarrels and political divisions. Besides, in a system of collective leadership, Mao Tse-tung's mistakes were shared by the Politiburo and the Central Committee. Among the two hundred or so members of the Central Committee especially, there were many followers of Liu Shao-ch'i, and then of Lin Piao, or at least many who agreed with their positions. This complicated Mao Tse-tung's task in a singular way as he tried to make his views dominant and then oust his two opponents. It even appears that several times Mao Tse-tung did not succeed in rallying the Central Committee behind him, that he was isolated, and that in obedience to Lenin's dictum—"If one does not have the majority, one must be content with unanimity''—he had to go along with the decisions of the greater number, against his will.

But praise, too, should be fairly attributed. Not all the successes of the Chinese Communist Party were due to Mao Tse-tung, despite the obvious importance of his leadership. In his interviews with Edgar Snow, published in the revised and enlarged edition of *Red Star over China,* Mao was anxious to emphasize the excellence of his colleagues: he named several leaders who later fell into the category of ''renegade''—like Liu Shao-ch'i, Wang Ming, P'eng Teh-huai, and Lin Piao—and an even larger number of men who remained loyal to him.

Some academics, confining themselves to Mao's books, accuse him of having created an infallible image of himself. It is true that Mao Tse-tung polished his image, that in the Peking Editions of his selected works he left out the less orthodox passages and the more dubious opinions. But these slight changes are not as striking as the fact that there are so few of them. And who blames a writer for taking up his work again and cutting out what he now believes to be inexact? Especially since Mao's writings are first and foremost a tool for political education: wasn't his *first* concern to provide his fellow citizens with a correct analysis, rather than an original text? Mao's aim seemed to be to provide his hundreds of millions of fellow countrymen with the lessons he learned both from his experiences and from the country's struggles—not to make the historians' work easier. Besides, the significance of the changes should not be exaggerated. A few sentences were rewritten, others were deleted. Most often it was a matter of cutting out expressions that were too direct, too familiar, almost vulgar—the kinds of things people say in the heat of battle but which do not belong in a collection of selected works destined for posterity.

Mao Tse-tung does not move through the history of China like a political comet in a sky without clouds or stars. The fact that his history is also a human adventure in no way diminishes it. Some people—quite a few in the lecture halls—criticize him in the name of Marxism and deplore his "low theoretical level;" others complain about his inability to understand present-day military problems; still others, though they concede that he had some talent on the battlefield, deny that he had any skill as a chief of state. And there are those who feel sorry for him and wish he had remained a poet and calligrapher. Why be surprised at these reservations? It is an old truth that the virtues of a great man are seldom recognized during his lifetime. Even Seneca fumed about it: "If the names of the most excellent men are referred to, you do what little dogs do before strangers—you bark; the fact is that no one seems good to you; it is as if you saw in the goodness of another man a reproach for all your faults." The people who attack Mao are aiming at the broken branches in order not to have to talk about the forest.

3/Cult
and Countermyth

Any book about Mao Tse-tung must touch on the question of his "personality cult." First of all because a cult did exist and second because it alarmed people in the West, where detractors of the People's Republic referred to it extensively. In the final years before Mao's death, the official personality cult disappeared. For the Chinese, Mao Tse-tung was by then the foremost political philosopher of his country, a shrewd leader, and a renowned historical character. And this is a judgment with which most foreigners would agree.

The disappearance of the most conspicuous forms of the personality cult between the 9th and 10th Party Congresses (1969 to 1973) obviously had something to do with the elimination of Lin Piao and his followers who, according to Chou En-lai, "always kept the book of quotations at hand and never stopped singing his praises" in order to ensure their own positions in the Party. Yet no one can deny the extreme personalization of political life during the Cultural Revolution, and this included forms of a cult—in other words, an irrational, almost mystical attitude on the part of a part of the population, particularly the young people.

If we go by the letter he wrote to Chiang Ch'ing in July 1966, Mao Tse-tung did not approve of the extremism of the propaganda services nor the fact that the *Little Red Book* was being used as a sort of magic wand. But he accepted the situation. It was not the right moment to curb people's enthusiasm—not only because of the difficult struggle being waged against prominent members of the Party but also because the immeasurable enthusiasm of the young was a valuable asset. (A short time before, in Edgar Snow's presence, he had posed the question: "Would Krushchev have been driven out of power if he had encouraged a cult of personality to develop around himself?") A fight for political power was taking place in China, and Mao Tse-tung no doubt intended to use his assets to his advantage.

When Mao therefore appealed to the people to help him rid the country of a burden grown too heavy and to regenerate the Party, the crowds, carried away by enthusiasm and constantly stimulated by the propaganda services, lavished him with praise. To read him brought illumination, to see him was a joy, to speak to him transfigured one; love for Chairman Mao was deeper than love for one's father and mother. His sayings pervaded revolutionary publications. Every speech was packed with them: "Chairman Mao is our great guide, our great leader, our great commander-in-chief and our great helmsman. Chairman Mao is the bright red sun in the hearts of the Chinese people and revolutionary people all over the world."

Naturally, such a deluge ran the risk of drowning the revolutionary movement in words, banners, cries of joy, and sincere or simulated enthusiasm. People tried to outdo one another: the "best" students of the Chairman would be the ones who praised him the most often and the most lavishly, in the hope of gaining the crowds' confidence or of averting suspicion. During the summer of 1967, Chief of Staff Yang Ch'eng-wu strove to have his extravagant article on Chairman Mao published: "Comrade Lin Piao said that there hasn't been a genius like Chairman Mao in the world for several hundred years and in China for several thousand. Chairman Mao is the greatest genius in the whole world." Everyone knew about the plaster statues, the shoddy color prints with their artistic pretensions, the use of the Chairman's quotations for every purpose—not just to discuss socialist thought, but to cure disease, and to solve any and all of the problems of everyday life.

A personality cult is a complex phenomenon. For a time Mao Tse-tung made use of it, though he was under no illusions about it. ("Of all those who cry 'Long live Mao Tse-tung'," he said to Edgar Snow, "one third are sincere, one third are going along with the majority, and the rest are hypocrites.") The people who surrounded him used the cult to secure their positions, to pose as the official spokesmen of the master, or sometimes to cover their tracks when they were suspected of belonging to the other side. On the other hand some people sang his praises quite spontaneously, out of love for a leader who had given them so much and who, in the end, no longer seemed to them simply a man among others.

Three thousand years of feudalism cannot be wiped out in one

stroke. On September 28, 1969 in the *Kansas City Star* Edgar
Snow told how on the first anniversary of the Republic, in T'ien
An Men Square, thousands of peasants wanted to show their respect for Mao Tse-tung the same way they had once shown their
respect for the emperor—by touching their foreheads to the
ground in front of him. Soldiers had had to stop them from pros-
trating themselves.

But the personality cult of Mao Tse-tung did not assume the
same form nor have the same significance as the cult of Stalin.
Its object during the Cultural Revolution was not to establish the
power of one man nor to create an omnipotent state machinery.
On the contrary, the point was to encourage debate, to induce the
people to take an interest in the affairs of state and to criticize
leaders who were following an "erroneous" path. What is more,
the cult never touched on the private life of Mao Tse-tung, about
which citizens knew very little. It was primarily an exaltation of
his thought, which took on the aspect of a weapon in the fight
against political degeneration.

Also the personality cult spread beyond the borders of China,
and this shows that it was to some degree spontaneous. In the
West, for example, many on the extreme Left bought the *Little
Red Book* and singled out those passages which supported their
opinions of the moment. In October 1969 the New China News
Agency reported with some pride that there existed "according to
incomplete statistics, more than 1,100 editions of the works of
Chairman Mao, published in seventy languages in sixty countries
and territories."

The gradual disappearance of the badges and statues, the sup-
pression of incorrect sayings (for example, "impose the absolute
authority of Mao Tse-tung's thought"), the termination of the
great parades through T'ien An Men Square, the elimination of
the Chairman's most rabid flatterers and advocates of "red
ocean" tactics, and lastly the nonobservance of Mao's birthday
on December 26, formerly noted in red letters on all the calen-
dars, signaled the end of the official personality cult. Of course
not all traces vanished immediately: in China as in other countries
there undoubtedly existed naive and credulous people who endowed the supreme leader with magical powers. And there were
many songs and poems extolling the boundless love uniting the
people and the Chairman, though the most idealistic songs were
replaced by workers' songs. In any event the tone in the press
and in official documents became rational rather than lyrical.

Mao Tse-tung's Reaction

In 1966 Mao Tse-tung criticized Lin Piao's campaign for a broad distribution of the *Little Red Book,* or rather, expressed doubts about the intentions of the Minister of Defense:

"Some of his views trouble me. I never thought that the few small books I wrote would have such a magical effect; anyway, ever since he made them seem like important works, the whole country has followed his example, which reminds me of the fable about Grandmother Wang, who always boasted about the sweetness of the melons she sold. In effect, I have been forced to join the bandits of Liang Shan P'o;[1] apparently I have no choice but to go along with them."

> Excerpts from a letter to Chiang Ch'ing, July 8, 1966, published in Taiwan.

During a tour of the country in July 1971, he rebelled against the "genius theory":

"As for the concept of genius, I think this a purely theoretical question; when they alluded to genius, they actually meant me. I am not a genius. I studied the works of Confucius for six years, then capitalist books for seven years, and it was only in 1918 that I began to study Marxist-Leninist works. Then how can I be called a genius? Again and again, I have cut the words 'with vast and creative genius out of the preface Lin Piao wrote for the second edition of my quotations . . . .

"Lenin's articles and the words of the International reflect the Marxist point of view. They urge the slaves to revolt out of love for the truth. There is no savior, no God, everything depends on us alone. Who creates the world of men, if not the working masses?"

> Summary of Mao's conversations with various comrades during his tour of inspection (August–September 1971), published by the Taiwan News Service.

---

[1] An expression taken from the classic Chinese novel *Water Margin* and meaning "to act against one's will."

The Countermyth

As mentioned earlier, the West did not escape the personality cult of Mao Tse-tung, nor was its effect confined to Maoist circles. In anti-Communist circles a morbid legend developed during Mao's lifetime, the legend of a mysterious figure who was always either sick or at the edge of death. The following are a few examples of this:

Reports of Serious Illness

"Mao Tse-tung is stricken with Parkinson's disease—a terrible illness that is incurable even today . . . . The rigid look of his body, a certain trembling, the muscular stiffness observable in his left arm, as well as his hesitation, are clear signs to a doctor: This is akinesia—or, the loss of motor control characteristic of the 'paralysis agitans' of Parkinson's.''

Minute, January 8, 1965

"According to the Hong Kong *Times,* a pro-Nationalist China newspaper, Chairman Mao Tse-tung must undergo a serious brain operation, and an American cardiologist, Dr. Dudley White, 85, is in Peking to treat him in case of heart failure . . . .

"As for the Hong Kong *Star*, it reports that according to its own sources inside China, Chairman Mao had a heart attack on September 9th during a violent debate in the Politburo.

(Associated Press), Hong Kong, September 24, 1971

"It is considered just as possible that Mao is either actually very ill, or that he has been marked for liquidation. Mao has tuberculosis, and he has had several very severe heart attacks. His death of natural causes would therefore not be surprising. But neither would it be surprising if he suffered the kind of convenient 'heart attack' which has ended the careers of numerous European Communists.''

Stewart Alsop, *New York Herald Tribune,* March 18, 1951.

"Last December Mao mysteriously vanished from the public eye, and rumors cropped up that Peking was concealing news of his death. There was even one report that Mao, 63, had died following an operation for cancer . . . . The Chinese Communist press, naturally, ignores such rumors.''

Time, April 12, 1954

"Mao Tse-tung is known to be in failing health with his mental powers faltering. There are surely cleavages in the Chinese Communist leadership as between the moderates and the extremists that could burst into a struggle for control when Mao dies."

Tilman Durdin, *New York Times*, May 27, 1962

"While Mao alternated between coma and consciousness, decision making in Peking was being handled by a triumvirate; Defense Minister Lin Piao, officially designated by the Party last spring as Mao's heir; Premier Chou En-lai; and ideologue Ch'en Po-ta, one of the main figures in the Cultural Revolution."

Jerold Schechter,[1] *Time*, September 26, 1969

Chairman Mao said to have at least four doubles

"Quoting travelers from China, the anti-Communist newspaper *Kuong Sheung Man Po* stated Wednesday that during the last few months at least four doubles of Chairman Mao have made public appearances as the real Mao. The newspaper added that this was particularly true at the time of the famous swim across the Yangtze several years ago, when photographs of the swimmer clearly showed, because of certain details of the face, that it was not the Chairman but simply a double."

Associated Press, Hong Kong, September 24, 1969

Did Krushchev try to poison Mao?

"In Peking, there are rumors that Soviet agents started a vast project to get rid of Mao's whole team by gradual food poisoning. This is why Mao and his principal colleagues are presently being subjected to strict medical surveillance . . . . As a consequence, there will soon be sensational new developments in the conflict between China and the Soviet Union."

Aux Ecoutes, September 25, 1964

Reports Embodying the Myth

"Every time he dives into the Blue River, something happens . . . ."

"A god called Mao . . . ."

---

[1]Director of the magazine's Moscow office, who was informed by a dependable Communist source that Mao Tse-tung had suffered a stroke on September 2.

"700 million men idolize or fear him . . . ."

"Mao: This is the story of a man who had become God, who was hurled off his Red Olympus in 1958, and who is now regaining its summit . . . . For five years, Mao waited in silence. And now, suddenly, during these past few weeks, he has reappeared . . . like the exterminating angel of the wicked."

Lucien Bodard, *Le Journal du dimanche,* September 11, 1966

"He prefers to live in the shadows . . . . No one has ever seen a child in his house . . . . His wardrobe seems to consist of no more than two plain jackets without lapels and two pairs of pants without creases . . . . His only weakness appears to be that he lies down on his bed and reads poetry."

Roy MacGregor-Hastie, *Candide,* January 11, 1962

"Being against any form of coexistence with the capitalist world, the man who calls himself 'the bridegroom of revolution' seems to be the most troublesome threat to the West. He is a reincarnation—and with how much more power!—of the famous 'yellow peril' which haunted our ancestors . . . . He is the man without a face—and apparently without a past—of the new China."

Candide, December 28, 1961

"The Red Dragon has dug his claws into the oldest empire in the world."

Paroles, November 11, 1949

"Emperor of the Blue Ants"
Title of a book by Gyorgy Paloczi-Horvath

"The red war lord."
Une Semaine dans le monde, February 7, 1948

"They say his wardrobe consists only of two cotton robes . . ."
Informations militaires, November 23, 1945

Chronology

Mao Tse-tung's Life	Chinese Politics	International Affairs
1893 Mao Tse-tung is born in the village of Shaoshan (Hunan province).		Laos becomes a French protectorate. The Second International holds its Congress in Zurich.
	1894 Japan declares war on China and wins a quick victory. Sun Yat-sen founds the Society for a New China.	
	1895 In the Treaty of Shimonoseki, China loses Korea, a part of Manchuria, and Taiwan.	Russia finishes the first section of the Trans-Siberian Railway. Death of Engels.
	1898 K'ang Yu-wei's attempts at reform fail.	Philippine national resistance is crushed by the American army.
	1900 The Great Powers put down the Boxer Rebellion.	
1901 Mao attends primary school.		
		1904 War between Russia and Japan. *Entente cordiale.*

Mao Tse-tung's Life	Chinese Politics	International Affairs
	1905 Sun Yat-sen forms the Revolutionary Alliance to fight the Manchu Dynasty and establish a republic.	
1906 Mao in conflict with his father.		
1907 His family marries him to a girl four years his senior. Marriage never consummated.		
	1908 Death of the Empress Tz'u Hsi.	Revolution of the Young Turks.
1909 Famine in Hunan province. Mao leaves his family in search of a modern education.		
		1910 Japan annexes Korea.
1911 Mao joins the Republican army and remains in it for six months.	Wuhan uprising spreads and overthrows the Manchu Dynasty.	
	1912 Sun Yat-sen hands over the leadership of the Republic to Yuan Shih-k'ai. Sun founds the Kuomintang.	Balkan War.
1913 Mao studies at the First Normal School in Changsha.		
	1914 Part of Tibet comes under British influence.	World War I begins; it stimulates Japan's ambitions.
1915 Secretary of the Students' Association, Mao becomes a faithful reader of *New Youth*, founded by Ch'en Tu-hsiu.		The Czar establishes ascendancy over Mongolia.
	1916 Death of Yuan Shih-k'ai and beginning of struggles among local warlords.	Ireland rebels against the British.

Mao Tse-tung's Life	Chinese Politics	International Affairs
1917 Mao publishes his study of physical education in *New Youth*.		The October revolution in Russia opens up new perspectives for the socialist movement.
1918 Graduating from the Normal School in Changsha, Mao goes to Peking and works in the university library. There he meets the future leaders of the Communist movement , Li Ta-chao, Ch'en Tu-hsiu, and Chang Kuo-t'ao.	Appearance of the first Marxist study societies at the university of Peking.	Japan and Britain occupy Vladivostok. German revolutionaries proclaim the Republic of the Soviets.
1919 In July, he founds the *Hsiang River Review* to spread the ideas of the May 4th Movement.	On May 4, students, soon joined by workers, protest foreign encroachments. The protest turns into a literary and intellectual revival movement.	The German and Hungarian Communists are crushed. 1st Congress of the Third International. The Paris Peace Conference awards Germany's concessions in China, including the Shantung Peninsula, to Japan.
1920 Mao organizes a Communist group in Hunan province.	Socialist cells multiply in the country.	The 1st Congress of Oriental Peoples is held in Baku.
1921 In July, Mao takes part in the founding of the Party in Shanghai. Three months later, he becomes secretary of the Communist Party of Hunan.	In Canton, Sun Yat-sen is president of a socialist government.	
1922 With Liu Shao-ch'i, Mao organizes the strike of the Anyuan miners, and becomes president of the province's trade union federation.	P'eng P'ai organizes peasant soviets in South China.	Stalin becomes Secretary-General of the Communist Party of the Soviet Union. Mussolini takes power in Italy.
1923 Mao is elected to the Central Committee of the Party.		The Bulgarian uprising is crushed. The USSR decides to support Sun Yat-sen.

Mao Tse-tung's Life	Chinese Politics	International Affairs
1924 Mao is elected to the Central Executive Committee of the Kuomintang.	The Kuomintang allows Communists to join.	Lenin dies. The Soviet advisers of the Kuomintang take part in the founding of the Whampoa Military Academy.
1925 Mao organizes peasant agitation in Hunan. Then, threatened with arrest, leaves for Canton. He becomes one of the officials in charge of peasant affairs in the Kuomintang.	Sun Yat-sen dies. In May, workers' agitation in Shanghai, Canton, and Hongkong. The Kuomintang divides into three groups.	War of the Rif: Berbers subdued by France and Spain.
1926 Mao is deputy director of the Peasant Movement Training Institute, and realizes the importance of peasant rebellions in the south of the country.	Certain incidents turn Chiang Kai-shek against the Communists, whose influence in the Kuomintang declines. Together, they embark on the expedition to the north for the political unification of the country.	Hirohito becomes emperor in Japan.
1927 Mao emphasizes the need to rely on the peasant movement. In August, he leaves for Changsha to organize the "Autumn Harvest Uprising." He then establishes a revolutionary base in Hunan-Kiangsi. The survivors of other uprisings join him.	In April, Chiang breaks with the workers' movements and massacres the Communists of Shanghai. In August, the Nanchang uprising takes place, marking the beginning of the Red Army. The Party condemns its leadership for not having supported the peasants. In November, the Party censures Mao Tse-tung for his "military opportunism." The Canton commune is crushed by the Nationalists.	Japanese land on the Shantung Peninsula. A conflict develops between Stalin and Trotsky, who is finally ousted.
1928 Chu Teh and Lin Piao join Mao in the Chingkangshan. Chu takes charge of military operations. Mao assumes responsibility for politics.	The Kuomintang seizes Peking. Chiang asserts his authority. The Nationalist regime is recognized by foreign powers.	First Soviet five-year plan.

Mao Tse-tung's Life	Chinese Politics	International Affairs
1929 With the Red Army, Mao leaves the Chingkangshan and establishes a new base in Kiangsi, at Juichin.		Beginning of the great economic crisis in capitalist countries.
	1930 First "encirclement and annihilation" campaign launched by Chiang Kai-shek against the Red Army. Founding of the League of Leftist Writers.	Communist Parties are formed in the Philippines, Indochina, and Malaysia. The Communist International condemns Li Li-san's line as adventurist.
1931 In November, Mao becomes Chairman of the Chinese Soviet Republic proclaimed at Juichin.	Second and third encirclement and annihilation campaigns. In November, First All-China Soviet Congress held at Juichin.	Japan enters Manchuria. Spain becomes a republic.
	1932 The Chinese Soviet Republic declares war on Japan. The Nationalists sign a truce with Japan. They launch their fourth campaign against the Communists.	Roosevelt becomes President of the United States. Japan attacks Shanghai and threatens North China.
	1933 Fifth campaign against the Communists.	Hitler comes to power.
	1934 Beginning of the Long March north.	
1935 The Tsunyi Conference gives Mao control of the Party. In June, a dispute breaks out with Chang Kuo-t'ao.	The first detachments arrive in the northwest. The Communists prepare a United Front against Japan.	Italy attacks Ethiopia.
	1936 The Chinese Communist Party proposes to the Kuomintang that they fight Japan together. Captured in Sian, Chiang agrees to fight the Japanese invaders.	Spanish Civil War begins. Popular Fronts in France and Spain. Moscow trials.

Mao Tse-tung's Life	Chinese Politics	International Affairs
	1937 The Communists sign an agreement with Chiang. The Republic becomes an autonomous regional regime. The Red Army is reorganized.	Japan launches a full-scale attack on China, seizes Shanghai and Nanking.
1939 Mao works out his theory of the new democracy, a transitory stage on the way to socialism.		End of the Spanish Civil War. Hitler occupies Czechoslovakia. World War II begins. Japan occupies Hainan.
		1940 Japan occupies Indochina.
	1941 The Nationalists attack the Communist troops again.	Hitler attacks the Soviet Union. After the bombing of Pearl Harbor, the United States enters the war.
1942 Mao begins an ideological rectification campaign in the Party.		
		1943 German assault on Stalingrad fails—the turning point of the war. The Cairo Conference: Taiwan to be returned to China after the defeat of Japan.
1945 Mao goes to Chungking to negotiate with Chiang. Agreement without lasting effect is signed on October 10.	Hostilities with the Kuomintang resume in late October. Truman assigns General Marshall to negotiate a truce between the two parties.	The Yalta Conference. End of World War II. Soviet troops enter Manchuria. Moscow signs treaty of alliance with the Kuomintang. Korea is liberated. Vietnam proclaims its independence. Colonial independence movement grows.
	1946 In January, a temporary cease-fire. In April: seizure of Changchun by Communist troops.	Civil war in Greece. French bomb Haiphong; beginning of the French-Indochina war. Founding of the Republic of the Philippines.

Mao Tse-tung's Life	Chinese Politics	International Affairs
	1947 Communist advances in Manchuria. American military deplores the corruption of the Nationalist regime.	Beginning of the Cold War. India gains independence. Pakistan established.
		1948 Burma becomes independent. State of Israel established.
1949 Mao becomes Chairman of the People's Republic, proclaimed on October 1. He leaves for Moscow to negotiate an alliance.	Having conquered North China, the Communist troops cross the Yangtze. The Nationalist government leaves for Taiwan.	First atomic bomb exploded in Soviet Union.
1950 In June, Mao announces the beginning of agrarian reform and an austerity budget.	Marriage law passed. In Ocotober, Chinese troops drive back the American forces that have entered North Korea. Tibet is incorporated into the People's Republic.	Beginning of the Korean War. The U.S. 7th Fleet occupies the Straits of Taiwan. The United States supports the French in Indochina.
1951 Mao undertakes to reorganize the Party by ideological rectification campaigns and a struggle against bureaucratization.		Japan signs the San Francisco peace treaty. The United Nations condemns China as an aggressor in Korea. Truman dismisses MacArthur for his Korean policy.
	1953 First five-year plan.	Stalin dies. Krushchev becomes First Secretary of the Soviet Party. Signing of the Panmunjom armistice in Korea. Revolt in East Germany.
	1954 Adoption of a Constitution. Chou En-lai becomes Prime Minister. First crisis over the Straits of Taiwan.	China and India define principles for peaceful coexistence. French defeat at Dienbienphu. France withdraws from Indochina after the Geneva Conference. Nasser comes to power in Egypt. Beginning of the Algerian revolution.

Mao Tse-tung's Life	Chinese Politics	International Affairs
1955 Mao urges an acceleration of collectivization of the countryside.	The army reestablishes a system of ranks.	Bandung Conference.
1956 Mao disapproves of the way Krushchev criticizes Stalin, and launches the Campaign of the Hundred Flowers against bureaucratic excesses.	The socialist transformation of the economy has for the most part been achieved. New Party statutes omit reference to Mao Tse-tung's thought.	Suez crisis. Hungarian uprising. In Poland, return of Gomulka to power.
1957 Mao insists that it is impossible to settle the "contradictions among the people" by violence. In November he makes his second trip to Moscow.	Beginning of the second five-year plan.	The Treaty of Rome establishes the Common Market. First Soviet satellite (Sputnik) launched. Ghana the first African country to achieve independence.
1958 In January, he announces his intention not to seek reelection as Chairman of the Republic.	In May, the Party Congress adopts the principle of the "Great Leap Forward." During the fall, people's communes multiply in the countrysides.	Revolution in Iraq. Second crisis over the Straits of Taiwan. The Soviet Union does not support the Chinese position.
1959 Mao is strongly attacked by P'eng Te-huai for the difficulties experienced as a result of the Great Leap Forward.	Lin Piao becomes Minister of Defense. Liu Shao-ch'i is elected Chief of State. Bad harvests.	Fidel Castro takes power in Cuba. The Soviet Union refuses to help China build nuclear arms. Rebellion in Tibet.
1960 Mao engages in sharper and sharper criticism of "revisionism" and of the Soviet Union.	Departure of Soviet technicians from China and termination of supply contracts. Industrial troubles.	Nigeria gains independence (many African countries follow suit in the ensuing decade).
1962 In September, Mao urges a resumption of the class struggle.	China easily wins out over India in a border conflict in the Himalayas.	End of the Algerian War. Geneva Conference on Laos.
1963 Mao makes public the conflict with Moscow. The Third World countries are in the "storm zone" of the world revolution, he asserts.	Production begins to increase little by little. The Movement for Socialist Education prepares for the Cultural Revolution but encounters resistance.	Chou En-lai undertakes an extensive journey through Africa and Asia.

Mao Tse-tung's Life	Chinese Politics	International Affairs
1964 Mao calls on the country to follow the example of the army and to form the relief force of the revolutionaries.	First atomic explosion in China. Reform of the Chinese theater and opera.	U.S. Bombing of North Vietnam. Fall of Krushchev. Death of Nehru.
1965 Mao denounces the existence of counter-revolutionaries in the central structures of the Party.	Lin Piao advocates people's war. First attacks by the press on the town council of Peking.	Massacre of the Indonesian Communist Party.
1966 In May, the Cultural Revolution begins under the direct control of Mao Tse-tung. Mao becomes a member of the Red Guard. He urges a "bombing of the general staff."	Ousting of the Peking town council, the propaganda officials, and the Chief of Staff. Attacks on the Chief of State. The enlarged Central Committee decides upon the principles and procedures for the Cultural Revolution.	
1967 Several times, Mao investigates the progress of the revolution in the provinces.	Revolutionary committees gradually replace the Party apparatus. The press denounces Liu Shao-ch'i. China explodes an H-bomb.	The 6-day War in the Middle East.
1968 Mao states that "the working class must take control" throughout the country.	The Central Committee decides to expel Liu Shao-ch'i from the Party.	
1969 Mao presides over the 9th Party Congress, which adopts new statutes and accepts Mao Tse-tung's thought as the theoretical basis of the Chinese Communist Party.	Lin Piao becomes Mao's official successor. Serious border incidents on the Amur and the Ussuri rivers and in Sinkiang.	President Nixon announces his intention to withdraw American troops from Asia. Opening of negotiations with the Soviets in Peking.
1970 Mao comes into conflict with Lin Piao. He is prepared to meet with Richard Nixon.	The Party forms provincial bureaus. The state reconstitutes its ministries.	The United Nations votes in favor of admitting China.

Mao Tse-tung's Life	Chinese Politics	International Affairs
1971 After sharp conflict with Lin Piao, Mao eliminates him. He accelerates the campaign against the personality cult.	Little by little, the army gives way to the civilians. Cultural and intellectual renaissance.	Kissinger goes to Peking. China becomes a member of the United Nations. War between India and Pakistan ending in secession of Bangladesh (January 1972).
1972 Mao meets with Nixon at Peking, then with Kakuei Tanaka, Prime Minister of Japan.	Foreign policy is increasingly centered upon the Third World. Japan normalizes its relations with Peking.	
1973 In August, Mao presides over the 10th Congress of the Chinese Communist Party, of which he is reelected Chairman. He meets with many statesmen, including Georges Pompidou.	The country opens itself to the outside. The Party pursues and intensifies its criticism of Lin Piao. It prepares for the movement called the "critique of Lin Piao and Confucius." Return of figures ousted during the Cultural Revolution.	Signing of the Paris agreement on Vietnam and the Vientiane agreement on Laos. "Yom Kippur" War in the Middle East. Overthrow of Allende in Chile.
1974 Mao makes a mass movement out of the critique of Lin Piao and Confucius.	The larger themes of the Cultural Revolution reappear. The critique intensifies in the higher echelons.	End of Caetano regime in Portugal. Death of Georges Pompidou. Formation in Laos of a temporary National Union Government. First nuclear explosion in India.
1975 Mao launches his critique of the "bourgeois Right"—the bourgeois state without a bourgeoisie.	Meeting of the 4th National People's Congress. Adoption of an ambitious economic program. Teng Hsiao-p'ing heads the government during Chou En-lai's illness.	Guerillas triumph in Indochina. The USSR and Cuba intervene in independent Angola. Intensification of the Lebanese Civil War.
1976 Mao denounces the bourgeoisie within the Party and the errors of Teng Hsiao-p'ing. He dies September 9.	Death of Chou En-lai. Hua Kuo-feng replaces Teng. In April, incidents in T'ien An Men Square. In October, Hua becomes Party Chairman; Ch'iang Ching and three "leftists" ousted from Politburo.	Syrian intervention in Lebanon. The white government in Rhodesia promises to accept black majority rule. Jimmy Carter is elected President of the United States.

two/
Mao Tse-tung:
His Thought

Though in the end men are forgotten, their ideas live on. A scholarly presentation of Mao Tse-tung's thought would fill several exhaustive and rather tedious volumes. My purpose here is to show in what ways his theories are significant, to China and especially to the West.

Though Mao Tse-tung's reflections are theoretical, they are rarely abstract. Usually his doctrinal statements are closely linked with efforts to resolve immediate problems. Nothing in his writings is reminiscent of the great abstract constructions of Marx or the philosophical preoccupations of Lenin.

Mao Tse-tung might set out to explain a strategy, citing the example of one village; he might compose a directive for a three-month period; he might suggest how to hold a meeting or how to contend with hostile opinions. From time to time, he would systematize his general reflections in a slim pamphlet. Mao wrote to be read, and so he is brief; he intended his writings to be used, and so he is clear. With rare exceptions the theory is not called theory; but it has the value of theory because of the richness of experience it contains.

Mao Tse-tung's ideas evolved over time. At the time of his earliest writings he knew nothing about Marxism. When he first became a Communist he accepted Moscow's theses, dazzled like all his friends by the success of the Bolsheviks. But a short time later he realized that revolution in China had to take its own independent course. His thinking grew more precise from one period to the next, moving from the discovery of the essential role of the peasantry to the principles of people's war; from the strategy of a United Front with the Kuomintang to the definition of a new transitional phase on the way to socialism ("the new democracy"), from criticism of Stalin's mistakes to the Great Leap Forward; from repudiation of Soviet "revisionism" to the organizing of the Cultural Revolution.

In spite of this evolution there is a remarkable consistency to his thinking, a consistency further emphasized by the Peking Editions, which have slightly modified the original texts to increase the homogeneity of the writings. This official edition, certainly examined by Mao, contains what could be called Mao Tse-tung's thought—in other words, the most important of the principles he formulated during his maturity. It is necessarily our main reference; other, more personal writings allow us to understand more clearly the foundations of his thinking.

Before reviewing the principal subjects of Mao Tse-tung's thought, I have two remarks to make about Mao's basic position.

Mao Tse-tung always belonged to China's extreme Left. But he never belonged to the most "extremist" groups within this extreme Left except, perhaps, during the summer of 1927, when he was attempting to stir up the peasants. He always had enemies both on the "Right" and on the "Left." His confidence in the people's latent revolutionary potential led him to seek bold solutions; but his sense of responsibility obliged him to distinguish carefully between his hopes for the future and the actual situation at a given moment. In jest he once situated himself at the "left center" of the revolution—and, joking aside, this seems to me correct.

Second, Mao Tse-tung always believed that the soundness of the line taken is a more likely guarantee of success, in a prolonged struggle, than wealth or military strength. The Communists will win, in his opinion, because they represent the most vital part of their society. The proletariat is not only larger than the bourgeoisie, but—even more important he believed—it is healthier. Isn't one of the great lessons of history the victory of ill-equipped underground forces against powerful armies—the definitive success of a Party that was unknown in foreign countries over a powerful administration that had outside support but was undermined by corruption, by the absence of any national ideal, by a lack of sincerity, and above all by the unspoken hostility of the people? Human quality determines everything.

Here, Mao Tse-tung would no doubt agree with the following comparison, made by the great 8th century thinker, Han Yu:

"A good doctor does not look to see if a man is fat or thin. He wants to know if the internal organs are healthy, and that is enough for him. In the same way, anyone who is acquainted with the functioning of the Empire is not anxious to know whether the country is agitated or at peace. He examines the foundation to see if they are sound or corrupt, and that is enough for him.

"The Empire is like a man. Prosperity and adversity are like stoutness and leanness. The foundations are like the internal organs.

"If the latter are not diseased, there is nothing wrong with the man's being thin. On the other hand if the internal organs are infected, the man will die even if he is stout."

1/Fundamental Concepts

The wind will not cease, even if the trees wish to rest.

—Chinese proverb

The Class Struggle after the Taking of Power

The internal threat comes from the bourgeoisie, the people must be won over . . . . Arms must be found for the sans-culottes, they must be angered, enlightened, republican enthusiasm must be aroused by all possible means.

—Robespierre

One class takes power and drives out another. But the struggle continues and victory has not yet been won. According to Mao Tse-tung the main conflict in China since the founding of the People's Republic has always been "the contradiction between the working class and the bourgeoisie."

In 1949 the Liberation Army drove out the Kuomintang and Communist leaders founded the People's Republic; the following year the important landowners lost their property; by 1956 there were no longer any independent peasants or capitalist industrial enterprises: the whole activity of production was carried out in collective structures. Some of the leaders declared that capitalism had been eliminated, that exploitation of labor no longer existed, that the socialists had won a definitive victory. Mao Tse-tung rejected this idea.

The distinction was crucial and the stakes were enormous: if it

84

were simply a matter of ousting the bourgeoisie from power at one go and of collectivizing production, commerce, and finance, it would not be hard to achieve socialism. It would be enough for the Communists to take the country in hand for about ten years and set an irreversible process in motion. If this were not the case however, the animal thought dead—but in fact only wounded—might rise up and devour his recent conqueror. The conqueror must therefore stay on guard and strike as soon as the beast begins to growl.

In 1957 Mao Tse-tung stated: "Marxists are still a minority, both of the population in general and of the intellectuals." Furthermore, he said, "vestiges of the overthrown classes (landowners and compradors) are still present, the bourgeoisie still exists, and the petit bourgeoisie is only beginning to reeducate itself." Since each was pursuing its own objectives, the struggle would continue "and from time to time it could even become very intense."

It was therefore necessary, he said, to remain vigilant, to be ready to fight. Certain portions of the socialist movement claimed that Mao Tse-tung was giving in to "Leftist opportunism;" he was overestimating the enemy, his thesis was too extreme.

What real importance did the opposition to the regime have? It is difficult to answer: in all countries the problems of security are a matter of state secrecy. Still, we can attempt to list the social categories which the Communists did not trust.

First there were those who had suffered from the change of regime, who had lost their lands, their houses, their servants, their fortunes. Among them were former landlords and, more numerous, rich peasants, who were disliked by the population and who undoubtedly missed the comfort of their former life.

Another category consisted of those who had been defeated by the regime, those who had fought wholeheartedly with the Kuomintang. Some were former soldiers (the Nationalist army numbered 8 million men). Though most of the rank and file had gone over to the Communists, the Nationalist officers—beginning with company commanders—were apparently still suspect. The same was true of the highest-ranking officers in the old police apparatus and state police force. Lastly, those who headed the *pao-chia*—the local organizations set up by the Kuomintang to control rebellious peasants—had not been pleased by the arrival of the Communists. Also, it was clear that the Kuomintang had its agents in every part of the continent. Sufficient proof of this was the number of top secret official documents that Taipei was

A good idea of the dangers which threaten a socialist regime once it has taken power can be seen in the large-scale investigation of 1955 into "The Socialist Upsurge in China's Countryside." The subject was eighteen cooperatives in a district of the province of Kweichow, in the prefecture of Duyun.

The report, published in 1955 in *Work in Kweichow*, noted twenty-six serious political incidents since the beginning of the cooperative movement, namely: 2 cases of destroyed livestock, 2 cases of destroyed hydraulic installations, 4 cases of sabotage of production plans, 1 case of destroyed manure, 9 thefts, 3 corruption schemes, 4 cases of spreading false rumors, and one act of violence.

Another investigation revealed that 49 people, or only .24 percent of the population of these eighteen groups, were "bad elements"—vestiges of the old society of the Kuomintang. They were identified as 3 local gangsters, 4 Nationalist army officers, 2 members of the Kuomintang's youth league, 2 Kuomintang functionaries, 7 local Kuomintang authorities, 2 suspected counterrevolutionaries, 1 habitual thief, 3 roving bandits, 17 Kuomintang block authorities, 4 local agents who also represented the Kuomintang, 2 freed convicts, and 2 sorcerers.

What has to be pointed out is the astonishingly high position which these people had managed to reach. Nineteen of them became leaders in the organization of the cooperatives: 4 were presidents or vice-presidents of cooperatives, 2 were bookkeepers, 6 administrative officials, 5 heads of production teams, and 2 labor managers.

It is easy to see that enemies of the regime who succeeded in occupying positions of control could undermine things to a great extent, taking advantage of the upheaval and uncertainty caused by agrarian reform. In fact, though agrarian reform managed to drive out the landowners, it was not able to eliminate Kuomintang elements.

able to get hold of shortly after their being issued.

There were still other real or potential enemies of the regime. Secret societies had been disbanded during the first years after the Communist take-over, but apparently the old ties in these organizations were still strong in certain areas. Also, some of the leaders of former political parties opposed to the Communists were still alive.

During the Great Leap Forward, or more precisely during the difficult years of 1959 to 1962, the reappearance of speculative practices (money lending, the hiring out of labor, the squandering of public funds) showed that in parts of China capitalist tendencies were still alive, even if they were not openly expressed.

But hostility to a regime is not always—perhaps not even most of the time—the result of the personal suffering of individuals. The families of all those who were in one way or another hurt by the regime may have made up so many more pockets of secret resistance.

Too many tales came from the Chinese mainland—taking every form, from short stories to comic strips—describing acts of sabotage in the coastal regions and near Hong Kong, for one to underestimate the activities of the regime's enemies.

"In what ways do the counterrevolutionaries play their double game? How do they deceive us with their disguises, doing in the dark that which we do not even begin to suspect? This is what thousands and thousands of honest people do not know. And this is why many counterrevolutionaries have succeeded in infiltrating our ranks. Our eyes are not experienced enough to distinguish good men from bad. We can distinguish them when they carry out their activities under normal circumstances, but we are incapable of recognizing certain individuals who are doing things under unusual circumstances."

Preface to material for the critique of Hu Feng's counterrevolutionary group, *People's Daily*, June 15, 1955

It was obvious that the opposition did not have the strength to fight the government openly. It would therefore attempt to weaken it from within, encouraging a slackening of ideological tension and a relaxation of the authority exercised by security forces and a fraction of the population. In this respect Liu Shao-ch'i's statement in 1956 that the class struggle had "practically ended" in China only served to reassure adversaries of the regime (whatever Liu's intentions might have been at the time). That is why the following year Mao was anxious to declare that "the question of which will win out, socialism or capitalism, has not really been settled yet."

Mao Tse-tung was well aware that the regime's adversaries had attempted to change the course of events to their own advantage several times. The campaign against corruption and misappropriation of funds (1952–53), the agitation of the intellectuals who sided with Hu Feng, the deflection of the movement of the Hundred Flowers towards a campaign against the regime, the disguised acts of sabotage during the Great Leap Forward, the deliberate waste during the lean years, the gradual change in the behavior of certain leaders, the secret opposition of part of the Central Committee and of its general secretariat, the "thaw" advocated by Lin Piao—all these were evidence to Party leaders that their opponents had no lack of resources.

Confirmed enemies of the regime were not the only ones implicated. The goal of socialism was collectivization, but it continued to make use of personal motivation ("to each according to his work"). These ambiguities left room for antisocialist behavior. Throughout the period of transition to Communism unequal remuneration continued to exist, as well as material incentives (in the broad sense of the term). Private markets and plots of land brought in revenues not available in the socialist sector. And of course here as elsewhere, administrative and political power could be used to serve individual ends. The rules could be bent, accounts falsified, production turned to the profit of private interests. No written law could prevent the degeneration of socialism.[1]

Aware of this problem, Mao Tse-tung confided to one of his compatriots in 1965: "The bureucrats on one side and the workers and poor peasants on the other are violently antagonistic classes. In the eyes of the workers the bureaucrats are already— or soon become—capitalist vampires . . . . They are the target of

---

[1]In *Mémoires d'outre-tombe,* Chateaubriand wrote: "When one shares the sufferings of the poor, one is aware of inequality; no sooner has one stepped up into a carriage than one scorns the people on foot."

our struggle and of the revolution.''[1] To prevent the formation of
new exploitative ruling classes, the workers' level of consciousness had to be raised; they had to take real control of the management of the factories. Such a radical change could not be accomplished in a few days.

"Socialism is something new. A difficult fight must be waged
against the old ways of behaving before it can be put into practice," Mao Tse-tung stated in 1955. "Old ideas, which reflect
the old system, remain in people's minds for a long time. They
do not go away easily."

Surprising as it may seem, Mao Tse-tung was one of the only
leaders of the socialist movement to maintain that the class struggle continues after the taking of power. Lenin had been aware of
the possibility of a rebirth of capitalism out of the ruins of a
socialist system and denounced the "new bourgeoisie [that was]
coming into being . . . among our Soviet functionaries." But his
time in power was too short for him to learn all the possible lessons. Stalin, like many other leaders, considered internal opposition to the regime either a legacy from the capitalist past which
would be absorbed with the passing of time, or the result of outside subversion. The North Korean Chief of State, Marshal Kim
il Sung, whose analyses are very close to those of Mao Tse-tung,
strongly condemns "revisionism" but does not go so far as to
state that a return of the bourgeoisie is possible.

Naturally Moscow rejects this idea of class struggle within a
socialist regime, preferring Stalin's 1939 analysis: "What is u-
nique in today's Soviet society, unlike any capitalist society, is
that there are no antagonistic or enemy classes in it, that the
exploitative classes have been eliminated." Ever since the thirties, when this elimination took place, the dictatorship of the proletariat has theoretically ceased to exist in the Soviet Union; a
state of "all the people" is supposed to have been achieved.

Mao Tse-tung strongly denounces these Soviet theses. The society without antagonistic classes, the society of "all the people"
is actually as dictatorial as Chinese society, if not more so. The

---

[1]Robespierre, in a speech before the Constituent Assembly on August 22, 1791,
showed similar understanding about the need for a popular dictatorship over the
state apparatus: "If you do not provide some means for watching over public
functionaries in order to stop whatever culpable designs they might have, you
have not in the least overthrown despotism. Who will dare to denounce a
functionary if he is obliged to fight him? Isn't it clear in this case that the man
backed by great power has the advantage?"

dictatorship is merely disguised: "A privileged segment of the bourgeoisie opposed to the Soviet people now occupies the dominant place within the Party and the government, and in the economy, the culture, and other areas."

Prolonging the Dictatorship of the Proletariat

There is the struggle, but there is also the dream. When the militant Communist dreams, he foresees a classless, egalitarian society, in which the peasant is not distinguished from the industrial worker by his work, his intellect, or his wages; a society which is not split up into different factions on the basis of work; a society in which—miracle of miracles—the opposition between manual workers and intellectuals has been abolished. Some go so far as to imagine that men, no longer having any deep reason to quarrel, would no longer fight among themselves and instead devote all their energy to the common good. In this history at a stand still, "all would be intelligent and objective. Mutual support and brotherhood would prevail."

Mao Tse-tung disliked utopias because they are false. Paradise had hardly any attraction for him. He did not develop his ideas about the Communism of the future except to say that the world will remain dominated by contradictions. A society without classes is also a society without wars. But it is not a world without struggle: evolution continues, technical innovations meet with resistance, attachment to the past slows progress, errors appear and spread through society. In any case that stage has not yet been reached.

We are still very far from the classless world foreseen by Marx. Mao Tse-tung predicted that in China, as in all socialist countries, the bourgeoisie would try to take power again. The people might very well let themselves be won over. After all as Lenin said, "the force of habit in tens of thousands is the most irresistible force." The Communist Party and the proletariat should keep tight control over "the instruments of the dictatorship."

For how long? Mao Tse-tung did not say. Jokingly he told Kosygin that China was prepared for ten thousand years of ideological struggle with the USSR. More temperately he said in 1962 that "socialist society will continue over quite a long period of history." The following year he implied that the restoration of capitalism was possible even after "several decades." In 1968 he repeated: "We cannot relax our vigilance, even during the coming decades." Mao specifies that the final victory of socialism in China depends on the victory of socialism in other countries, on the elimination of capitalism throughout the entire world. This will not happen in the near future. It will be necessary to do away with imperialism before the bourgeoisie can be eliminated. "The era which we are entering," he declared in 1962, "will last for fifty, even one hundred, years."

Mao Tse-tung retains the essentials of Marx's analysis, and accepts his sequence of events: the taking of power followed by the dictatorship of the proletariat, followed in turn by Communism. But he differs from Marx in his emphasis on the need to continue the revolution after the taking of power, to continue it "under the dictatorship of the proletariat" and for "a long period of history." He rejects 19th-century utopias: today's socialists will not live to see Communism, nor is it likely that their children will. But do true militants need visions of paradise?

Democracy within the Dictatorship

We have two different systems of weights and measures: what we approve for one idea, one system, one interest, one man, we condemn for another idea, another system, another interest, another man.

—Chateaubriand

The mind can only consent to what seems true to it; the heart can only love what seems good to it. Coercion makes a hypocrite of a man if he is weak, a martyr if he is courageous. Weak or brave, he will feel the injustice of the persecution, and he will be indignant . . . . If your truth condemns me, my error, which I take to be the truth, will condemn you.

—Diderot, *Letter to My Brother*

Once power has been taken and the cities have been conquered, another struggle begins. The new society struggles to defend itself, to transform itself. All the while building up its strength, China has charged off in pursuit of progress. Visitors in 1955 no longer recognized the country: the looks, the language, the very physique of the people had changed, as had the streets, the neighborhoods, the government, and, of course, many aspects of daily life. All this implies organization, a system.

Marx spoke of a dictatorship of the proletariat, but Mao was more precise, he termed it the people's democratic dictatorship. Against the regime's enemies he called for an inflexible dictatorship, a "democratic centralism." This formula is not new, though it is usually applied to the Party rather than to the regime itself.

Though in many "socialist" countries this formula is meaningless, Mao Tse-tung took it seriously. One could even say that from 1949 on all his energy was devoted to this, to giving China a true democratic centralism. Centralism was necessary, democracy was indispensable. Here again Mao's contribution has been to take one of the theoretical reflections of his Marxist precursors and carry it to its limit on a practical level.

As early as 1955, in other words before Krushchev criticized the excesses of Stalin's dictatorship, Mao Tse-tung made his position clear: "In dealing with the people it is a crime to apply constraints, to obstruct their liberty, to block them when they criticize the errors and weaknesses of the Party and the government, to forbid free discussions in universities. That is our system. But in dealing with the enemies of the people, it is a crime to allow counterrevolutionaries to say or do what they please; it is legitimate to apply the dictatorship."

Mao Tse-tung took these ideas up again and gave them their most systematic expression in 1957, in his study of "contradictions among the people." It would be necessary, he said, to rely on gradual education, on persuasion, on the force of truth to bring the people to the point of rejecting their illusions and commiting themselves to the Communist way.

Practically speaking this meant: "if you have some reservations about us, express them. You cannot challenge the principles of socialism except in your own hearts, but regarding the functioning of this particular regime we will listen to you, you should fear nothing." Evidence shows that Mao Tse-tung deeply believed in this principle and that a large number of leaders agreed with him. If the regime has no critics, it will lose its popular support. The people will be disillusioned, the leaders will be living in isolation. The Party must therefore seek criticism. Little children in nursery school recite these words: "We are at the service of the people, and if we have shortcomings we are not afraid if you call attention to them and criticize them. Anyone may call attention to them. If he is right, we will correct them."

As might be imagined, the principle is not easy to apply. But there is no question about Mao Tse-tung's sincerity. He demonstrated it on two occasions, during the period of the Hundred Flowers and during the Cultural Revolution.

A number of leaders around him feared that a campaign of free criticism would weaken the Party—not to speak of their own positions. In February 1957—with the painful experience of the Hungarian uprising fresh in his mind—Mao Tse-tung asserted that on the contrary, the Party would emerge from it stronger, more vital, and would avoid degenerating into "a new religion and a new source of restriction."

He went far. On February 27, 1957, Mao Tse-tung delivered a four-hour speech which was published in June after some slight changes as the pamphlet "The Correct Handling of Contradictions among the People":[1] "We need not fear," Mao Tse-tung declared, "that the policy of the Hundred Flowers will bear poisoned fruit. Besides, sometimes it is necessary to have these poisoned fruits in order to know what we are fighting against. This is why we have decided to publish the complete works of Chiang Kai-shek and even a collection of broadcasts from the Voice of America."

It is necessary to know one's enemy, perhaps even more necessary to test the strength of the regime: "The young people do not understand the object of our struggle today. One cannot grow flowers in a hothouse. They would never be beautiful or vigorous. We must strengthen them and make them hardy if we want them to bear fruit."

Even political strikes can have positive effects. "In one sense, small strikes are beneficial: they point to the mistakes that have been made." In the June pamphlet he is more precise: "In 1956 small numbers of workers or students in certain places went on strike. The immediate cause of these disturbances was the failure to satisfy certain of their demands for material benefits, of which some should and could have been met, while others were out of place and excessive . . . . But a more important cause was bureaucracy on the part of the leadership."

It has often been said that the freedom to criticize advocated by Mao Tse-tung was only a trap, that the only aim of the Hundred Flowers, for example, was to induce the enemies of the regime to

---

[1]Extracts of the speech appeared in *The New York Times* in June 1957, transmitted by the paper's Warsaw correspondent.

show themselves—in short, that the Hundred Flowers had been urged to bloom just to make it easier to pick them. It is certainly true that the large campaign of criticism that took place then— and also later, during the Cultural Revolution—made it possible to spot antisocialist elements, who were treated without indulgence. Yet that was not the main object of these campaigns.

The great danger to socialist regimes is enforced silence. The state has a monopoly over the press. Party members have a tendency to reserve examination of the more delicate questions for cell discussions. As far as they are concerned the people have no say in the matter. Mao Tse-tung was aware of this risk and tried to save China from it.

A dictatorship presupposes a directorate; a directorate implies a center. But there is no point to centralization if it is not accompanied by democracy. Mao Tse-tung stated it formally: "Without democracy, there can be no correct centralism: because people's opinions differ, the absence of unity makes it impossible to establish centralism . . . Our directing bodies play the role of a transforming station defining the correct line, the appropriate methods and policies of both a specific and general nature. If a factory lacks primary materials, it cannot transform anything; if the primary materials are lacking in quantity or quality, it will not produce a good final product. Without democracy we cannot understand what is happening at the ground level and the situation will be confused; we will be unable to collect enough opinions from all sides; the summit and the base will be cut off one from the other; the upper bodies of direction will decide matters on the basis of unilateral and incorrect materials and so it will be difficult to avoid falling into subjectivism; we will not be able to arrive at a unity of conception and action, a true centralism will be impossible."

During the first phase of the Cultural Revolution Mao Tse-tung's convictions were asserted with great firmness, though several members of the Party had quite different opinions. He attacked leaders who were afraid of criticism: "Just because you let the people speak, the sky is not going to collapse, and you won't fall down either. On the other hand if you deprive other people of the chance to speak, then sooner or later you will inevitably fall." Before another assembly he said "What are you afraid of? Those who are bad will show it. But why be afraid of the good elements? Replace your fear by daring. You must show that in the end you are capable of passing the test of socialism."

Not all his comrades went along with him. Mao was not able

to persuade every member of his entourage to share his ideas. During the Cultural Revolution his enemies counterattacked by voicing general criticisms, spreading confusion. This was not what the Chairman had asked for either. He wanted the Party and the people to obey these simple precepts of Chinese tradition, which he was fond of quoting:

> "Do not remain quiet about anything you know
> Do not keep anything to yourself which you have to say
> No one is guilty for having spoken
> It is up to him who hears you to draw the lesson
> If you have faults, correct them
> If you have none, keep a sharp eye on yourself."

This desire to make the fullest possible use of open dialogue to prevent a gap from growing between the people and the Party, between the Chinese masses and their leaders, was apparent during the last phase of the Cultural Revolution, at the time of the reconstruction of the Party. The so-called rectification movement was supposed to be carried out "openly," in other words under the control of the people. In a speech which was probably given before the 9th Congress (April 1969), Mao formulated the following directive: "Each cell of the Party must work towards a new cohesion, in the presence of the masses." This should be done with the participation of the masses and not only with the few cell members—the masses of non-Party members will be present at the meetings and will voice their opinions."

In this respect Mao was a great innovator. No other Communist leader has dared to invite the people in such a direct way to be involved in the affairs of the country. In typical Party cells only Party membership gives a person the right to speak. Mao Tse-tung wanted to do away with this kind of rigidity. In fact his attitude grew naturally out of the idea he had formed of what a leader should be, and can be explained by the extreme importance he attached to the latent revolutionary potential which he believed existed outside the Party.

Which is why we should now turn to his conception of the "mass line."

The People: The Main Strength of the Revolution

China's strength depends on the the daily efforts of several hundreds of million of peasants, several tens of millions of workers and craftsmen. It was these same Chinese masses who more or less consciously wanted the revolution and in the end allowed it to come about. These are the two basic ideas of Mao Tse-tung: he has never questioned them. Even at the end of his life, he expressed them more systematically than ever.

What the people want, hope for, demand, believe possible to obtain, even what they dream about determines the strength of the revolutionary movement. What the people know, what they know how to do forms the essence of the national "stock" of intelligence. But what about the great figures of history, the clever statesmen and Machiavellian strategists like the legendary Chuke Liang? "Three shoemakers are equal to one Chuke Liang," he answers. "The masses contain enormous forces for creativity. There are thousands of Chuke Liangs among the Chinese people; there are some in every small market town." These statements were made in 1943. In 1968, Mao Tse-tung was even more emphatic: "Humble people are the most intelligent and prominent people the most idiotic."

Here again Mao turns Western ideas on end, as he does Chinese tradition. Isn't knowledge picked up in the cultured world, by associating with teachers, with people who speak in an authoritative manner about the great affairs of state, who know how to address a select audience in a florid style, with ringing phrases? It is an old debate. Mao Tse-tung felt the revolution was heavily burdened by an elitist tradition of knowledge and the conservatism of the intellectuals, so he decided to support the other side, the people who know how to do things, but not how to speak or read.

Many thinkers of the Enlightenment, and especially the French Encyclopedists, had a similar point of view. They were amazed by the multitude of trades in France. The Encyclopedists undertook to make a list of all the techniques that had been brought to perfection over the course of the centuries. The system of trade guilds and freemasonry handed down a wealth of indispensable techniques from generation to generation; as for the peasants, their knowledge of soil, cultivation, and the seasons, enabled them to produce food for the country. Economic theories of the 18th century held (as did Marx) that the ruling classes—the so-called nonproductive classes—were almost totally useless. But little by little over the next century idealism prevailed, the age appointed its "leading lights" and dreamed of "philosopher kings;" many intellectuals, as well as many in the merchant classes, set themselves up as superior. Book learning became the rule everywhere. The centuries-old familiarity with natural herbs and drugs disappeared from the countrysides, industry displaced the traditional crafts, technical knowledge was transmitted by textbooks in schools, taking the place of the skills gained at first hand in workshops. In this way Western economic development was accompanied by the destruction of large areas of popular knowledge.

Mao Tse-tung deplored this loss, partly for economic reasons, but also because he felt socialism could not be built by repudiating or scorning the people. Like many other Third World countries, China had to begin by getting to know itself, by reverting to the age-old skills and rationalizing them: pharmacists went roaming the hillsides, in search of medicinal herbs that could replace industrial medicines.

Mao Tse-tung was convinced that the popular masses who were the basis of the regime wanted socialism—or would want it sooner or later. This conviction went back to the first years of his political career, when he observed the peasants of Hunan revolting against the local potentates and reorganizing village life together. Thirty years later, he noted how readily and enthusiastically people in the country gave up individual farming and joined together in cooperatives. "The masses have an immense force of enthusiasm for socialism . . . (they) are endowed with an unlimited creative power."

This optimism may be a little more exaggerated than what Mao really believed. His thinking here is more subtle than might appear. Mao was well aware that education and enlightenment are indispensable—and that they require work. He did not believe in spontaneity. But it is also true that the Party could at times underestimate the people's desire for progress. Part of the population "lags behind," but another part leads the way. It was up to the Party to encourage the movement as a whole, in accordance with the principle of the "mass line."

Mao Tse-tung often specified what he meant by that expression: a two-way dialogue between the Party and the population. He described it in the following way: "We must go among the masses, enroll in their school, derive general ideas from their experience, draw from that experience better and more systematic principles and methods, then communicate these principles and

methods to the masses (through propaganda), urging them to follow if they want to solve their problems."

As we shall see later, Mao Tse-tung did not merely formulate
this idea. He urged China and its leaders to put the idea into
practice. The mass line is not a magic formula. Of course it has
its limits, and they involve more than secrets of state or national
defense. Not everyone discusses everything. There are special
structures for dealing with collective problems. The larger
questions or national policies cannot be discussed on a local
level. From what we can see, concerted action on these questions
takes place as far down as the level of the canton, but hardly de-
scends any lower. Conversely, individual decisions are not under
the jurisdiction of the collective.

Though this is obvious, Chinese "Leftists" have sometimes
misunderstood it. Within the collective are individuals, each with
his own personal characteristics. Mao Tse-tung took the trouble
to remind people of this in phrases that are full of obvious good
sense: "Everything has its shared aspects and its individual aspects, is both the same and different. It is impossible to have
everything in common. For example, what we have in common is
the fact that we are meeting together here. After the meeting, our
own personal behavior will prevail again: some of us will take a
walk, others will read, still others will have something to
eat . . . . So that every production unit or individual must have
his own motivations and his own character, in conjunction with
what he has in common with others."

One must not pull too hard on the rope, for fear of breaking it.
Too much tension is harmful to the undertaking. We must remain
reasonable towards the rural areas says Mao Tse-tung, "We must
be careful not to ask too much of the peasants, not to make their
life too hard. Except in the case of serious natural disasters, we
must ensure as far as possible that the peasants' income increases
every year."

These reflections about the mass line and democratic centralism
have to do with relations between the Party and the people. The
question of how to deal with elements hostile to socialism is resolved differently. Here we should be more precise about the notion of "people," and of the distinction between "antagonistic"
contradictions and "nonantagonistic" contradictions.

The People and Social Contradictions

One should know that war is universal, that justice is a struggle
and that all things are born from struggle and necessity.
                                                    —Heraclitus

Who are the people? They are the great body of all those who
support the regime, who accept its principles, who do not try to
challenge it. Earlier I identified the categories of society reputed
to be dangerous. Everyone else belongs to "the people" and is
not subject to the dictatorship. According to Mao Tse-tung, what
we are defining is a fundamental political category, even more
important than that of the proletariat. The dictatorship of the proletariat is in fact exercised by the "people's democratic dictatorship."

By definition, "the people" is made up of the majority of the
population. But each regime has its supporters and its enemies,
and the notion of the people changes with the nature of the
power. During a fight against an invader, "the people" is comprised of everyone who is defending national independence; it
therefore includes part of the upper middle class; it excludes only
"traitors." This concept becomes narrower during a civil war:
the landowners who supported the Kuomintang, the financial and
commercial circles with foreign ties, an entire section of the
bourgeoisie which rejected the revolution and took up arms
against it placed themselves *ipso facto* outside "the people."
With the taking of power the situation changed again. The permanent core of "the people" consists of the workers and peasants, as in the formulations of Lenin or Stalin. But the petite
bourgeoisie, and even the national bourgeoisie, also participate
alongside them in the building of socialism. Here is where Mao
Tse-tung departs from European ideas. He believes that capitalists
can accept the socialist regime; they must be given the right to
vote.

The people's democratic dictatorship, therefore, is based on
four classes and not two. The bourgeoisie and the petite
bourgeoisie have a place in this dictatorship.

The powers of the bourgeoisie have nevertheless been eroded
steadily. The state, which controls the machine and is also the
supplier and main consumer, has restricted the economic liberty
of the capitalists, limited them in their production and sale of
consumer goods, and forestalled price speculation. Little by little,
it transformed the status of the capitalists and made them into

fixed salary-workers. After a few years, the "national capitalists" hardly deserved to be called that any more, except that they were still receiving some money without having to work for it.

Yet there has been a change in terminology: the dictatorship of the proletariat is mentioned more and more often, the people's democratic dictatorship less and less. In this respect, it seems that the Cultural Revolution marked a new stage in Chinese life, the elimination of the bourgeoisie as such. This elimination has taken place without serious conflict. The economic development of China allowed the capitalists to pass through this transitional phase without too many problems, before finally losing their privileges.

Mao Tse-tung and the Death Sentence

Though he allowed capitol punishment to exist, Mao Tse-tung proposed a system which would reduce the number of executions. It is known as "the policy of the sixteen characters":

The man condemned to death is given a stay of execution lasting two years; he engages in forced labor, and at the expiration of this period the results and effectiveness of this reeducation are reviewed.

This system is now widely used, so that the number of executions is much lower than the number of death sentences. As he often said, Mao Tse-tung thought it better to kill ideas than to kill people. His method was certainly humanitarian, but it was also highly effective: being lenient with his enemies and giving them a chance to redeem themselves was another way of dividing them.

Mao Tse-tung's analyses of the conflicts in Chinese society are extremely flexible, so flexible that they sometimes seem contradictory. On a political level the main conflict—the main contradiction—is between the proletariat and the bourgeoisie, says Mao. This "antagonistic" contradiction is resolved by the disappearance of one of the adversaries. As a consequence, socialism condemns the bourgeoisie to death. But it does not condemn bourgeois people to death. The bourgeois—as opposed to the bourgeoisie—are part of the people. "The contradictions between the working class and the nation's bourgeoisie are among the contradictions which appear within the people . . . . Certainly these contradictions are antagonistic . . . but they can be changed into nonantagonistic contradictions and be resolved peacefully if they are handled in a judicious manner." As far as that goes, the bourgeois have no choice: they must accept the regime and the change of status mentioned above. Otherwise open battle will be declared and blood may flow.

If they accept the regime the bourgeois become part of the people, and they escape the dictatorship. In effect, "the dictatorship is not imposed on the people. There is no way that the people could impose the dictatorship on themselves, and one part of the people could not oppress the other."

In less theoretical language this means that if the bourgeoisie does not resist too much, at least a section of it will be able to retain its advantages for some time. Society will not reject it; but of course society will not put it in a position of control, either. In any case, the lot of the bourgeoisie will be better than the proletariat's was when it was under the bourgeoisie. The people will not seek revenge.

Here Mao Tse-tung is applying a very subtle social dialectic. If the capitalists rebel they will be treated as enemies, but the doors of socialism are being opened wide to them, they are being urged to accept the inevitable, to take their place in the ranks of the people. The bourgeoisie will not be able to enter the Party, but it will be able to occupy a small place in the state. It will support the state's anti-imperialist policy, even if it is not in favor of collectivism.

Mao Tse-tung gave evidence of his remarkable skill in handling transitions from 1950 to 1956, while rural areas were being transformed. Almost everywhere the eviction of landlords was the result of a true *coup d'état*—often a brutal one—at the village level. Then, once the former agricultural workers, the "poor or moderately poor peasants," had become small landowners, they would engage in collectivism without much hesitation. This was because the Party and Mao Tse-tung made an effort to arrange the transitions for them. Progressing from temporary to permanent mutual aid teams, from semisocialist to socialist cooperatives, the peasants discovered little by little how the collective effort could help them, was even necessary to them. Besides, peasants the world over are aware of the advantages of working with one another. Mao Tse-tung knew how to help them to realize this

and to forestall the spread of privatist tendencies. The collectivization of the rural world was accomplished more quickly, was
more thorough and less brutal than in the Soviet Union.

Should the credit for this success be given to the whole Party
or to Mao Tse-tung alone? Actually the credit goes to both, but
the personal convictions of the Party leader determined the direction taken. The people want socialism; mistakes made in the past
were made by leaders ignorant of specific situations and distrust-
ful of the masses: on this subject Mao formed a notion of the
relations between the people and their leaders which may not be
new, but is at least very systematic.

The Leader: A Man on the People's Own Level

In order to do great things, it is not necessary to be superior to
other men but to be with them.

—Montesquieu

A cadre must remain one of the people, he must come out of
his office. Mao Tse-tung defended this idea all his life, and
he managed to imbue the Party with it: "However high one's
position, one must remain one of the people—an ordinary
worker. Let us not act high and mighty; let us free ourselves of
the bureaucracy. Let us listen patiently to everything and pay attention to ideas that come from the lower echelons."

Is this modesty based on strategic considerations? Absolutely
not. It is necessary to the leader, Mao says, for while he is aware
of the role he has taken on because of his skills and other positive qualities, he also knows that the place the masses hold is far
more important. Second, Mao Tse-tung continues, the leader
must be aware that his skills and his actions are only a small drop
in the ocean: "The individual horizon is limited and narrow; the
horizon of revolutionary knowledge and action is vast, and what
it encompasses is rich and complex . . . . An individual is only a
small cog in the revolutionary process. We are taught this by
Marxism-Leninism: all success is a result of collective power; no
individual can separate himself from a collectivity; without a
Party to guide him, without an organization to support him, and
without the masses to sustain him, an individual cannot accomplish anything. If we truly understand the part played by the masses and by the individual in history, and their mutual relations,

then we will remain unpretentious."

This idea guided Mao Tse-tung throughout his political career. After accepting the development of a personality cult which sustained him in his fight against Liu Shao-ch'i, Mao Tse-tung went to work to destroy it in 1970. His flatterers, including Lin Piao, were driven out in 1971 by the movement for the intensification of Marxism and by the campaign to reflect on the meaning of history.

All of China has memorized the second verse of the "International":

> We want no condescending saviors,
> To rule us from a judgment hall;
> We workers ask not for their favors;
> Let us consult for all.

For Mao Tse-tung, the myth of the leader does not exist. Not, at least, in the same way it did for De Gaulle. Of course, Mao developed "a certain idea" of China over a long period of time; like De Gaulle, he knew that power involves cunning, perhaps a certain cynicism; he also knew how to isolate himself, keep aloof from everyday affairs, and maintain his prestige. But the reason he did not lose himself in government meetings and large national committees was more than anything else so that he could work in greater depth and closer association with the people. Mao Tse-tung had his own idea of what the work of a Communist leader should be, and no one can doubt his originality on this subject.

Work Methods

Mao Tse-tung considered himself to be primarily an instructor, a professor—most of all, a teacher. This was the way he wanted posterity to think of him. He wanted to teach Communists how to think and how to work.

This was a constant preoccupation. In 1930 he attacked "book worship" and commented on the methods used in his "Investigation of the Peasant Movement in Hunan." In 1941 he urged China to "Reform our Study," then wrote "Rectify the Party's Style of Work." In 1943, he brought out "Some Questions Concerning Methods of Leadership." At the end of the civil war, he elaborated on the "Methods of Work of Party Committees" (1949). In

1958, he proposed a 60-point resolution on "Work Methods." Ten years later, the Chinese press published "Twelve Points Relating to Work Methods," an article directly inspired by the Party leader. And these are only a few examples.

What kinds of ideas does he develop in these texts? Mao Tse-tung was the opposite of an armchair ideologist or parlor doctrinaire. Until late in life, according to Edgar Snow, he was still spending six months out of every year touring the countryside. He wanted to be on the spot, to short-circuit the official network of information. At the end of 1959 he urged leaders of production teams not to mistake their own desires for the real situation, not to inflate the harvest figures. The real situation is in the fields, not in your enthusiastic imaginations, he told them.

On-the-spot investigation is the leader's basis for work. The best example, which came at the very beginning of Mao's career, is the famous investigation of the peasant movement in Hunan. Thirty years later Mao edited and wrote a commentary on a series of investigations entitled "The Socialist Upsurge in China's Countryside." These case studies, which were written by the peasants themselves, are undoubtedly models for the socialist movement, not only because of the frankness with which they tackle problems but also because of the directness and specificity of their objectives, and because of the simplicity of the language and brevity of the texts—which make popular readership more possible.

A visit to the spot and a good monograph, says Mao, are worth more than all the tedious volumes full of nothingness hatched by professional theoreticians—there are as many in China as anywhere else. On this subject Mao does not mince words: "Many of our comrades love to work subtle variations on the Party jargon in their articles. Their writings are dead; they do not solve anything. It gives one a headache to read them. They do not bother with either grammar or sentence structure; they create a hybrid of literary style and common speech which is sometimes loquacious and redundant, and sometimes obscure and archaic, as if they were deliberately trying to make the reader suffer . . . . How many years will we have to wait for there to be an end to this Party jargon which makes our heads feel dull and heavy?"

If the leaders make mistakes it is because they mistake their own ideas for reality or, as May Tse-tung says, because they decide in a "subjective" manner what line to follow. His optimism led him to sum up the correct procedure for leadership in two equations: familiarity with the real situation = the right political line; the right political line = success.

Books are full of ideas, but the ideas are not worth anything until one tests their validity by applying them. The same is true of Marxism. It cannot be taken for granted that all of Marx's or Lenin's thoughts are applicable to China. It is even likely that they will be found not suited to such a different society—once we abandon abstractions and begin to adopt practical directives. Marx, Engels, and Lenin outlined general laws, but not one of their principles can be accepted in China without changes.

Of all Marxist leaders Mao Tse-tung was undoubtedly the only one who asserted his independence from the founders of Marxism. This allowed him to emphasize the "universal value" of the doctrine. Marxism-Leninism, he said, "should not be considered a dogma; it is a guide for action." It has no interest until you try to apply it: to study Marxism is to try to use it and to succeed in using it.

Mao Tse-tung had only sarcastic, almost vicious things to say about armchair theoreticians. After all, the graduates returning from Moscow shared responsibility for the massacre of tens of thousands of militants—bent as they were upon defending principles formulated in faraway cities and on battlefields in the West. He once said that this form of Marxism, which comes out of textbooks and hours of student discussions in the evenings and which does not lead to anything, is worth no more than "dog dung." Even that is useful for fertilizer, he remarked, but what use are empty ideas?

Party militants who came from poor backgrounds needed practical advice on a thousand matters which the decadent system of education had not taught them in their youth—how to study a problem, how to write, how to hold a meeting, how to get everyone to participate, and so on. Mao Tse-tung made an effort to answer these questions. He insistently urged his comrades to "get the questions out into the open" during meetings. Everyone ought to be informed in advance which subjects are going to be discussed and should prepare to take part. Some believed they were saving time by leaving the decisions to the authorities, but they were actually losing time; "commandism" can ruin a revolution, leave it in isolation, denying it the indispensable nourishment of the people's support.

Mao Tse-tung outlined several work methods which are interesting because of their psychological implications—they are strategies transposed from the battlefield to the individual project or village. I will mention three:

1. *Take control of one-third.* An absolute majority is not at all necessary to dominate a situation. In a committee the Communists can impose their points of view with only one-third of the seats: because of the excellence of their work and their arguments they should have no trouble convincing the centrist third, which is uncertain but open-minded; the rightist third will remain isolated and in the minority. This formula permits a larger participation by the popular masses and a form of Party control which is more extensive but less evident.

In 1959, at the Lushan conference of the Central Committee, Mao Tse-tung applied the same idea to mass dynamics:

"At least 30% of the people are activists, another 30% is made up of pessimists, landlords, former rich peasants, counterrevolutionaries, bad elements, bureaucrats, middle peasants and some poor peasants; as for the remaining 40%, it consists of those who follow the trend. 30%—how many people is that? 150 million. These people want people's communes and refectories, they throw themselves into cooperation on a large scale and display great enthusiasm. They want all this. Can anyone say this is petit bourgeois fanaticism? No. These are the poor and the fairly poor peasants, the proletariat and the semiproletariat. As for those who follow the trend, it hardly matters to them whether or not this program is carried out. Those who do not want it make up 30%. In short, add 30% and 40% and you get 70%" (unofficial text published in a Red Guard newspaper).

This principle can be applied to other areas, for example, when a social experiment or an economic innovation must be extended to a whole region, or to the whole country. One starts by applying it to one-third of the districts in depth, taking note of the difficulties encountered and drawing a lesson from them before going on to generalize. Mao Tse-tung attached extreme importance to this technique for spreading progress: a model is perfected and then gradually extended to the whole. Progress does not happen suddenly, it develops in an uneven way. Small people's pamphlets attempt to convince the militants of the value of model experiments.

2. *It is necessary to provide a margin for failure.* In combat, a prudent strategist will not send all his men into the first round of fire; he keeps some troops in reserve, to avoid being caught unprepared. The same is true in civilian matters. One must

make sure of the result before playing all one's cards. If an enterprise hopes to raise production from 100 to 150, it will provide itself with a margin for failure. The objective becomes two-pronged: it guarantees a production of 125, in conformance with the national plan, but it tries to go beyond that to 150. If it does not reach the higher objective it will at least be congratulated for having fulfilled the plan, and the morale of the workers will benefit.

Mao seemed anxious to keep China in an ideal state of tension. You must aim high, he said, but if you pull too hard on the bowstring it will break and you will fall back, as happened during the Great Leap Forward. Tension and relaxation must alternate to keep the country alert. It seems a mistake often made by bottom echelon cadres is that they ask too much, and for too long a period from a peasant population just recently dominated by superstition and fatalism. One must not try to resolve everything at once. "A meal is eaten bite by bite, a war is won battle by battle."

3. *Take both ends of the spectrum into account.* How does one size up a situation? Do you look for the average? No, said Mao. Within a group of people there are always some advanced elements, some in the middle, some in the rear guard. Instead of working out a line for the average people to follow, hoping that the other two categories will join in, he believed it better to look into the reasons why the more advanced people are so successful and the backward elements so hesitant. Successes and hesitations have their own profound causes, and these must be discovered. Then one can formulate a more ambitious policy for the people as a whole.

Because of the care he devoted to his trial runs and for many more reasons, Mao Tse-tung's policy could be called experimental. He tracked down a problem, straightened it out, reoriented the project. His methods became indispensable to all the Chinese leaders. They probably contribute a great deal to maintaining the unity of the country in spite of all the tensions resulting from economic changes and political differences in various parts of China.

Mao Tse-tung the Moralist

Marxism is supposed to be scientific, and in the West Marxists
have deliberately set aside moral considerations for political
analyses. Mao Tse-tung, on the other hand, emphasized the importance of morals to a Communist. Here again he was the only
socialist leader to do this. This Communist morality holds true
"among the people," it does not apply to class enemies. But in
many ways it resembles Christian morality. It is summed up in
three texts called "the three texts most widely read" or, in
Chinese, "the three old articles." Lin Piao, who was very aware
of this idealistic side of Mao Tse-tung, gathered these three small
pieces, each several pages long, into a thin pamphlet which was
distributed first in the army, then in the schools, and then
throughout the country.

This is in some sense the gospel, and Christians at least can
hardly remain insensitive to it. What is preached is love of the
people, self-denial, modesty, and industry. Mao lets himself go
here more than elsewhere, undoubtedly because he was moved
at the time these texts were composed—two out of the three
speeches were given on the occasion of the death of a revolutionary. Through the sadness we can discern a discreet but profound
romanticism.

What is the meaning of life, wonders Mao Tse-tung, reflecting
on the passing of an obscure militant crushed to death under a
wood pile. Not all lives and deaths have the same significance.
To quote the historian Ssu-ma Ch'ien: "Of course men are mor-
tal, but some deaths are heavier than Mount Tai while others are
lighter than a feather." "To die for the people," Mao Tse-tung
continues, "is weightier than Mount Tai. The Chinese people are
suffering; it is our duty to save them and we must exert ourselves
in struggle. Wherever there is struggle there is sacrifice, and
death is a common occurrence. But we have the interests of the
people and the sufferings of the great majority at heart, and when
we die for the people it is a worthy death."

Thus the basis of socialist morality is to serve the people. An
internationalist imperative is involved here: not just the Chinese
people, but all the peoples of the world deserve to be helped, as
the Canadian surgeon Dr. Norman Bethune showed when he
came into the liberated regions of the northwest to help the
Communist forces in their fight against the Japanese Army.

"Comrade Bethune's spirit, his utter devotion to others without any thought of self, was shown in the boundless sense of re-

sponsibility in his work and his boundless warm-heartedness towards all comrades and the people . . . . What kind of spirit is
this that makes a foreigner selflessly adopt the cause of the
Chinese people's liberation as his own? It is the spirit of internationalism, the spirit of Communism, from which every Communist must learn . . . . I am deeply grieved over his
death . . . . We must all learn the spirit of absolute selflessness
from him. With this spirit everyone can be very useful to the
people. A man's ability may be great or small, but if he has this
spirit, he is already noble-minded and pure, a man of moral integrity and above vulgar interests, a man who is of value to the
people.''

Several years later the civil war started up again. Wasn't the
Communists' task too overwhelming? Would they be able to
change their country's fate, cure the sick man? In 1945 many
foreign observers were doubtful. The Kuomintang seemed
stronger than ever; the war had restored its prestige. As for the
Communists, in twenty years they had hardly advanced at all.
Wasn't their task as hopeless as the task of Sisyphus? Before the
7th Party Congress Mao Tse-tung explained why there was hope,
why victory was close at hand.

He repeated the old fable of Yu Kong, the peasant who wanted
to move the mountains with his pick and the help of his sons.
High as the mountains are, said Yu Kong, they are not growing;
every blow of the pick reduces their mass; after my death, my
sons will take over; then, there will be my grandsons. And he
continued to work with his pick day after day.

In recounting how the old man arrived at his goal, Mao reveals
one of the keys to his philosophy. ''God was moved,'' he says,
''and sent down two angels, who carried the mountains away on
their backs . . . . We must persevere and work unceasingly,
and we too will touch God's heart. Our God is none other than
the masses of the Chinese people. If they stand up and dig together with us, why can't these two mountains [imperialism and
feudalism] be cleared away?''

To touch the feelings of heaven, to touch the feelings of the
people—the conviction that truth and justice will sooner or later
win over the masses and take the place of lies and oppression—is
one of the pivots of Mao Tse-tung's political thinking. If a cause
is just it will win out in the end, because it will capture the hearts
of the people, and then their minds. Oppression on the other hand
can last only a short time. The great political decisions of Mao
are based on this confidence in the awakening of the people, on

this certainty that a day will come when the people will recognize the superiority of Communism. A cause is strong, therefore, because it is just. Morality is the basis of politics. As we shall see, Mao and the philosophical tradition of China share a common ground here.

Mao Tse-tung and Classical Philosophy

Everything is both an extension of some other thing and at the same time distinct from it; every man both continues a tradition and at the same time breaks away from it. Mao Tse-tung is no exception. Though what follows is in no way a detailed explanation of the national origins of Mao Tse-tung's thought, I want to call attention to several points:

1. *The Importance of Political Morality.* Throughout China's history, political thought has been one of the essential branches of literature. The political man, the civil servant, is also a scholar. Mao Tse-tung himself wrote poems and studied calligraphy.

   Political thought is always based on moral—or more generally philosophical—meditation. For Westerners, state morality has never been more than a by-product of religion; secular morality is seen as laughable, ineptly trying to copy Christian precepts. In the West, the source of morality is the individual conscience. Church and state remain separate.

   The situation in China is very different. Since there is no religion, morality belongs to the secular world; it does not emanate from heaven but is established by men in a rational way. Morality fixes social norms but also individual codes of behavior, and in doing that it plays the role that religion does in the West. So there is nothing surprising in the fact that Mao Tse-tung formulated moral principles: this is one of the functions of the head of a regime. Moreover, most of the great Chinese thinkers have held high administrative posts, starting with Confucius himself.

   Because there is no God in Marxist materialism, it automatically conforms in some sense to this tradition. The absence of a transcendental being puts the problem of human relations into the foreground. Chinese society is traditionally more politicized than Western society. For us, politics remains a minor aspect of our lives and we do not expect it to change us in any profound way. In China, politics is the expression of a particular concept of the world, a notion of man and even of the universe. It can therefore mobilize people's energies much more than it can in our society. At the end of his life Mao did not want to be called a helmsman any more; but in China the responsibilities of a teacher and philosopher are certainly as great as those of one at the helm.

In the West this idea is sometimes shocking; but it is common in the East. For instance, morality impregnates political life in Japan. Year after year Chiang Kai-shek called upon the people of Taiwan to reform their way of life and bring about a national renaissance. In North Korea, according to the press, Kim il Sung embodies the most noble ideals of Korea, while in South Korea each of the successive leaders has relentlessly issued moral exhortations. Of course these moralities all differ from one another. But whether revolutionary or reactionary, they arise from a shared tradition.

2. *Dialectic is Natural to China.* The concepts of alternation, opposition, and synthesis have been part of Chinese philosophy for a long time. Three centuries before Christ, Chuang-Tzu wrote: "Beginning and ending, fullness and emptiness, the revolutions of the stars, the phases of the sun and the moon, all these are brought about by that unique cause, which is invisible but always present . . . . Beginning and end perpetuate themselves without beginning or end."

There will be no twilight of the gods, no last judgment. History will continue to flow on, like the Heraclitean river. As we have seen, Mao Tse-tung had some reservations about the Marxist concept of Communism: without definitively rejecting it, he deferred it to a period far in the future. He emphasized that whatever happens history will not stop, that one will always have to fight against mistakes and attachment to the past. In his speech at Chengtu, in 1958, he went so far as to say that in the end the Communist system itself would yield to a more progressive social organization.

The idea of contradiction is even older than the idea of alternation. Everyone knows that Chinese philosophy began with reflection on the *yin* and the *yang*—the female principle and the male principle—which in combination formed the elements and then the entire world. This "uniting of opposites" is certainly closer to Plato's idealistic dialectic than to Marxist concepts. Yet it explains why the penetration of Marxism into China

evoked a response in the hearts and minds of the people that
was very deep and many thousands of years old.

3. *The Contribution of Chinese Tradition to the Dialectic.* Mao
Tse-tung pursued the analysis of contradictions further than any
other Marxist. He did not confine himself to demonstrating the
unity of opposites in all things; he classified contradictions as
primary and secondary; he made them dynamic by showing
that one of the opposed elements is always predominant; he
made them flexible by showing that "in different circumstances the primary aspect of the contradiction may become secondary, and contradictions which were secondary before may become primary." (For example: in a capitalist regime, the main contradiction is between the bourgeoisie and
the proletariat; but in specific circumstances, this contradiction
can yield to antagonism toward a foreigner—resistance to Hitler for example. In a normal situation, the dominant element
is the bourgeoisie, but in a prerevolutionary period, a united
front could supplant the bourgeoisie.)

No doubt Mao Tse-tung owed the great flexibility in his
dialectical analysis to the multiplicity of combinations of the
ancient *yin* and *yang*, in which there is an entire gradation between the male principle and the female principle, each intermediate stage being characterized by new *yin-yang* relations
and new characteristics. In other words, the quantitative
changes are expressed directly in qualitative terms. As late as
1957 Mao Tse-tung quoted Lao-tze, the father of Taoism:
"Happiness depends upon unhappiness and unhappiness is
concealed within happiness." And, he asserted, "A bad thing
can be changed into a good thing."

This interpenetration of two opposite principles explains the
subtlety of Mao Tse-tung's analyses, particularly where his
enemies are concerned. This is why he was able to cement an
alliance with Chiang Kai-shek in 1936, in spite of the Kuomintang massacres which had decimated the Communist Party; this
is why, to the end, he asserted that the Soviet Party is mainly
composed of authentic Communists, in spite of the vast differences of opinion between the two countries and the exchanges of gunfire at the border; this is why Mao Tse-tung received President Nixon in spite of the intensification of the war
in Indochina, making a distinction between "an elected president" of the people, and the "head of the monopolies;" this is
why he was always prepared, if need be, to make a new compromise with Chiang Kai-shek, if the agreement could be to

his advantage.

In the West, these "reversals" are sometimes taken to indicate a lack of principle. The Left sees them as manifestations of "opportunism." But the Chinese people, always sensitive to nuance, see in them only a very understandable skill in strategy.

4. *The Prominent Position of the Leader.* In ancient China the emperor, who was both political leader and the son of Heaven, served as the model for the nation. Everything depended on him, as the poet Tsao Ye wrote in the 9th century:

> If the emperor loves war and fighting,
> The people no longer work the land, the mulberry trees
>   are neglected.
> If the emperor prefers young people,
> No one will recommend deserving old people any more.
> If he likes pretty women,
> Husbands and wives will part.

I do not mean to suggest that Mao Tse-tung simply took the place of the emperor. Yet as Party leaders have acknowledged many times, the people retain certain traditional attitudes, particularly regarding their leaders and the most prestigious among them. In the 9th century the great philosopher Han Yu said: "Heaven chooses men who thunder and it makes them thunder." For many Chinese, Mao Tse-tung was the spokesman of the nation. Until his death he safeguarded the transition from ancient China to the China of today. His successors will undoubtedly not be able to continue to fill this role of charismatic leader, and a tradition will die.

I have pointed out several of the links between Chinese tradition and Mao Tse-tung's political thought. There are many more, but to list them would require a book in itself. Confucius himself can be cited, among others: more than two thousand years ago, he too said that one's attitude toward the people was the ultimate referent; "When Fan Ch'ih asked him what goodness was, the Master replied: 'It is loving the people.' Asked about intelligence, he said: 'It is knowing the people.' "[1]

---

[1]Recent analyses of Confucius's thought, however, have somewhat weakened these hypotheses. They put the abstract aphorisms back into the historic context of a transitional society. According to interpretations that are popular today, the term "people" did not in fact refer to the large popular masses, the slaves, but

It was natural that Mao Tse-tung, the son of a peasant, should feel this respect for the people. The dignity of the peasant has long been celebrated in China, as in a poem by Hi K'ang (3rd century), where a peasant answers someone who is praising the emperor: "I start work at daybreak, I rest at dusk. To drink, I dig a well; to eat, I work the earth. How is the emperor better than me?"

Even the challenging of tradition has deep roots in the past. Lao-tze asserts: "When intellectuals appear, artifice is soon to follow . . . . Let us renounce wisdom, let us reject knowlege, the people will be a hundred times better off."

In the 14th century the emperor Hung Wu attacked the scholars: "Their style is diffuse and inflated, they drown a thought in floods of words. If there exists an obscure or ambiguous expression, this is precisely the one they will choose: one would think they were writing in order not to be understood at all." These phrases are irresistibly reminiscent of the criticisms Mao Tse-tung addressed to those obsessed with Party Jargon. The emperor also urged the scholars to leave their books and "go read the great book of society, to know everything that happens in it, so that you can serve it according to its needs." Mao says the same.

Another parallel should be drawn between Mao Tse-tung's notion of love of the people and the concept of "the all-embracing love" formulated by Mo Tzu, a philosopher of the 5th century before Christ. No one emphasized the need to subordinate individual interest to the general interest as well as Mo Tzu, who criticized egotism and petty-mindedness. Mo Tzu, like Mao Tse-tung, also preached frugality and simplicity of habits; he attacked the family for being an obstacle to that universal love which could raise society in a great surge towards the good. I have remarked upon the echoes of Christianity in Mao Tse-tung: actually, they come to him from Mo Tzu.

The fact that he shares certain qualities with ancient Chinese thought should not be interpreted as proof that Mao Tse-tung is primarily an heir to Chinese tradition, that he is "more Chinese than Marxist." As a revolutionary, a materialist, an organizer of the class struggle, an admirer of Western socialists, Mao Tse-tung broke with the prevailing ideas as early as 1919 to join in

---

to the class of slave owners, in the same way that the philosophies of ancient Greece were meant only for the "citizens," the free men. Apparently the meaning of the term "people" gradually changed and narrowed between the 8th and the 5th centuries before Christ.

China's great movement toward cultural renaissance. The policies which he would later put into practice opened an ever-widening gap between him and the past which no one would ever cross again.

Yet it was only in his last years that he began to feel that a radical break with Confucian tradition was essential. Not that he had earlier defended this tradition—in 1919 he had participated in the May 4th Movement, with its clearly anti-Confucian orientation; he had been pleased by the boldness of the Hunan peasants when they violated temples and burned statues in 1927; in 1940 at the time of the "new democracy," he had said that it was necessary to fight the semifeudal culture which had allied itself with imperialism, and he included "everyone who praises the cult of Confucius, the study of the Confucian doctrine, ancient morality and the old ideas;" two years later, in his Yenan Interviews," he denounced the traditional concepts of love and human nature, which transcended social class divisions and seemed to him to help the ruling classes consolidate their power.

Yet Confucius had not yet become that pernicious, hypocritical, and violent character portrayed in the campaign of 1974. Mao Tse-tung occasionally quoted Confucius's aphorisms, and in his poem "Swimming," written in 1956, Mao referred to him as an authority; later, in Lushan, when accused by P'eng Teh-huai, Mao retorted: "Everyone has his faults; even Confucius made mistakes," which shows how much he respected him.

But he did not believe Confucius should be looked to as the ultimate teacher, as did Liu Shao-ch'i (cf. "To be a good Communist") and Lin Piao, who used the old philosopher to help him challenge the intensity and bitterness of class struggle in a socialist regime. After this experience Mao realized that it was not only imperative to denounce the Chinese conservative tradition, but that in a socialist society this denunciation would have to continue for a long period. This was the reason for the offensive launched after the 10th Congress. There was a total break with Confucian philosophy. All its fundamental concepts were analyzed, turned around, measured against the real historical situations, and rejected as "poisonous plants": human nature, love, the happy medium, virtue, goodwill, fairness, loyalty, the ability "to control oneself and go back to the rituals," and so on.

There is no question that Mao Tse-tung was in charge of this denunciation campaign. His earlier analyses were brought into full force. Conservatism in China seemed to him even more deeply ingrained than he had thought; he saw it in the very heart of the Communist Party, among the ranks of the Politburo. He knew that its theoretical origins lay in the doctrines of Confucius, and he undertook to extirpate them from the socialist ideology.

This attack did not simply amount to a denigration of Chinese culture or scorn for the past. On the contrary, since the Marxist dialectic on whch it was based required the precise analysis of texts and descriptions of historical circumstances, the attack was accompanied by a massive (and critical) publication of the works of Confucius and his philosophical followers. It would not be an exaggeration to say that large sections of the Chinese people discovered Confucius during a campaign which was intended to destroy his influence.

2/Foreign Policy and the Priority of the Fight against Imperialism

Foreign policy is not one of Mao Tse-tung's major concerns, at least in his writings. He is first and foremost a man of China, the man who led the Chinese in the conquest of their own country. The great enemies at the time of the underground—the Japanese and the Kuomintang—had to be eliminated, driven out; before the liberation, the guerillas were hardly concerned with diplomatic affairs.

In 1949 Mao Tse-tung became a head of state. His entry into the socialist camp excused him from forming—or did not allow him to form—an original foreign policy. The Party leader confined himself to laying down a few principles which were never afterward contradicted and which seem strangely up to date even now, in the seventies—since they were the basis of the decisive diplomatic breakthrough which took place between 1970 and 1972.

"We are ready to open negotiations based on principles of equality and reciprocal advantage, as well as the mutual respect of sovereignty and territorial integrity . . . . The Chinese people are disposed to cooperate in a friendly way with the people of all other countries, and to reestablish and develop commerce abroad in order to encourage production and develop the economy."

In this speech given in June 1949 Mao Tse-tung laid down the most important of the principles of peaceful coexistence as they would be specifically established five years later by the Chinese and Indian governments. He also separated relations between peoples from relations between states. He was aware that the latter were more difficult to establish; he said this before the Central Committee in March: "As for the question of China being recognized by imperialist countries, we must not be in a hurry to settle that now. The countries which have always been hostile to the Chinese people will certainly not treat us as equals in the near future.''

Another permanent principle of foreign policy was that every country should determine its own affairs freely. In a speech delivered on June 28, 1950, three days after the beginning of the Korean War, Mao Tse-tung laid down the principle of nonintervention which he would later develop into a hostility toward politico-military ''blocs'': ''The affairs of different countries in the world should be regulated by the peoples of those countries; the affairs of Asia should be settled by the peoples of Asia and not by the United States.''

It was not until the sixties and the official break with the Soviet Union that Mao and his comrades in arms expressed their own views about world affairs. In the years that followed Mao Tse-tung made a series of statements: against racial discrimination in the United States (August 8, 1963), in support of the struggle of the people of Panama (January 12, 1964), in support of the struggle of the Japanese people (January 27, 1964), in support of the people of Leopoldville in the Congo (November 28, 1964), in support of the resistance of the Dominican people against American aggression (May 12, 1965), in support of the struggle of black Americans again, after the death of Martin Luther King (April 16, 1968), and then the great May 20, 1970, declaration which showed the Soviet Union replacing the United States as China's principal adversary and marked a tactical turning point in Chinese foreign policy.

No doubt we should add to this list of statements the audiences Mao Tse-tung held with different political figures, especially a delegation from the Japanese Socialist Party (August 1964), and with the American journalist Edgar Snow (December 18, 1970). Finally, we must assume that most of the documents relating to the great polemic with the Soviet Union, particularly the June 14, 1963, ''Letter in 25 points,'' were drawn up by Mao, or at least with his full approval.

As Mao Tse-tung defined it, China's foreign policy had to serve the cause of socialism. It would do this first of all by serving the interests of the Chinese socialist state and second by supporting the struggle of other peoples against imperialism and their efforts to achieve socialism. There is nothing surprising in these principles. But they are limited in their application.

Mao Tse-tung believed that each people must basically find its own forces for the struggles it faces. Weapons can be taken from the enemy; strategy does not come from the outside, but is worked out in discussions within the revolutionary organization. A revolution cannot be exported, it must develop its roots deep inside the nation. Guerillas who rely on support from a distance by foreigners are doomed.

Consequently China should engage in proletarian internationalism only where authentic revolutionary movements are concerned, that is, movements deeply rooted in the people, which follow a proletarian, not an intellectualist line, identifying themselves with socialism and accepting the principle of revolutionary violence. Furthermore, the aid which China gives should be only a contribution—a large one, perhaps, but never the main one.

A third limitation has to be added, one which is not based on political principle: the poverty of China does not allow it to give effective support to more than a very small number of revolutionary struggles in the world, beyond its large gifts to the Vietnamese and Cambodian people. China's rapid economic progress after the Cultural Revolution has led to a considerable development of exchanges with Third World countries, but their volume is still small in absolute terms. Nevertheless when there is aid, the aid is truly helpful: the loans do not carry any interest and need not be paid back for more than twenty years. Finally, arms furnished to a revolutionary organization are free. Mao Tse-tung often said: "We are not in the business of selling weapons."

At the end of his life, Mao Tse-tung was the leader of the greatest power in the Third World—the only great power in the Third World. He had foreseen China's preeminent position for a long time; but he formed a theory for it only at a late date, once Peking had freed itself of Soviet guardianship. This theory, called the theory of intermediate zones, is not only original, but also clearly explains the different tactical phases of Chinese foreign policy since 1960.

Four Zones

In the years before he formulated his thesis dividing the world into four great areas, Mao had already developed modifications of a more classical, primarily dualistic conception. In 1939, on the occasion of Stalin's sixtieth birthday, he said: "The world today is divided into two antagonistic fronts—the imperialist front which oppresses humanity and the socialist front which fights this oppression. Some people think the revolutionary national front in the colonies and semicolonies lies somewhere between the two. However, since its enemies are imperalist, it must be on the side of socialism and fall into the category of a revolutionary front against oppression.''

Yet at the end of World War II, Mao realized that the situation had changed. Forces wanting independence were emerging in the Third World. He anticipated that in a few years China would have driven out the Kuomintang. What was more, Chinese Communist leaders did not in the least approve of Stalin's policy towards other Communist parties. The Yalta agreements—which unilaterally decided the fate of the world—and the dismantling of Manchurian factories by a Soviet Red Army reimbursing itself for its lightning war against Japan, had not been well received. Neither had the Kremlin's encroachments on several East European countries.

So that in August 1946, in an interview with Anna-Louise Strong, a progressive American journalist, Mao Tse-tung modified his earlier dualism: he introduced the concept of an intermediate zone. ''The United States and the Soviet Union,'' he said, ''are separated by a very large zone which includes many capitalist, colonial, and semicolonial countries in Europe, Asia, and Africa. Before the American reactionaries subjugate these countries, an attack against the Soviet Union is out of the question.'' With its military bases the United States was trying to control the Far East, the British Empire, and Western Europe, as it had Latin America. ''At the moment it is not the Soviet Union but rather the countries where these military bases have been established that will be the first to suffer from the aggression of the United States.''

Mao Tse-tung was not yet revealing everything he thought. Up to 1960 he agreed that the Soviet Union should lead the socialist camp—at least he agreed to this in public. But for a long time the Chinese leaders had realized that it was better to act independently from the Soviet Union.

Mao Tse-tung's only hope, disappointed as he was by the evolution of the socialist bloc, lay in the Third World countries, which at the beginning of the sixties were throwing off the colonialist yoke and asserting their independence. The struggle against imperialism would sooner or later lead to socialism, he believed. In any case this struggle was more promising than than the workers' movements in capitalist industrial regions, ravaged as they were by "revisionism" and "parliamentarianism." This was why the true "storm zone," the crux of all the modern world's contradictions, was in the countries of the Third World—in Asia, Africa, and Latin America.

Actually, apart from the Indochinese and Palestinian resistance movements, there did not seem to be any clearly antiimperialist storm zone in the Third World during the sixties. But during that period a second element emerged which supported Mao Tse-tung's thesis and also made it more complicated: this was the slowly changing relations among industrial nations, particularly in Western Europe. The smaller countries were no longer eager to invade the socialist camp; the bourgeoisie in power wanted above all else to protect itself from the threat of America and from the rivalry of neighboring countries. De Gaulle's France was primarily trying to resist America, trying to dominate by containing West Germany's political ambitions and keeping Britain out of the Common Market.

The very concentration of industry, the growing power of what Western Communists called "the great monopolies," reinforced the tendency of industrial societies toward autonomy, worried as they were about American pressures. The revolutionary movement in these countries, surprised to find itself face to face with a dynamic bourgeoisie—very different from the one it expected—ran out of steam and was broken up by reformism and "putsch-ism." The dominant element, therefore, the element on which Chinese foreign policy was based, was the assertion of national will—a will that was sometimes hesitant and sometimes aggressive, but always troublesome to imperialism.

It was at this time that Mao Tse-tung explained his theory of intermediate zones, which was at first completely anti-American. In 1963 he wrote: "American imperialism has one consistent aim, and that is to commit aggressions in the intermediate zone between the United States and the socialist camp, in order to control this zone, quelling the revolutions of oppressed peoples and nations, liquidating the socialist states, and enslaving and putting under the control of American monopolies all the peoples and countries of the world, including the allies of the United States."

The following year, in an audience with several Japanese socialists, Mao Tse-tung went into more detail. There were two intermediate zones, he said. The first was comprised of Asia, Africa, and Latin America: here the independent countries were trying to assert their independence, and the colonies were trying to become independent. The second intermediate zone comprised

Europe, Canada, the South Sea islands, and Japan. Several of these countries were imperialist—France and Great Britain for example—but they could not continue to maintain control because America was taking too active an interest. These regimes manifested a split personality: they institutionalized domestic exploitation on the one hand, and at the same time they stood in the way of American expansion. It was therefore possible sometimes to bring them into a worldwide anti-imperialist front.[1]

In 1964 Mao Tse-tung had not defined what he meant by the socialist camp. Prominent figures in the Party were opposed to excluding the Soviet Union and its satellites. The border incidents had already claimed several victims, but Peking did not yet dare take the final step, which would also have antagonized many Parties in other countries, anxious as they were to see the ties between China and the USSR maintained.

The Two Superpowers

Later the situation changed. The United States committed itself completely to the war in Vietnam, but during the fighting it became clear that this would be America's last colonial venture—and that it would fail. During the years of the Cultural Revolution, while Chinese activity in foreign affairs came to a standstill, American society became divided and questioned its own values: American currency weakened, and foreign exchanges showed growing instability. While the United States succeeded in its daring moon project, the Soviet Union built up its defense, increasing the number of intercontinental rockets, rivaling and then surpassing American forces. In competition with America all over the world, the USSR advanced every time its enemy retreated, and square by square, pawn by pawn, it nibbled away at Ameri-

---

[1]On April 10, 1974, Vice–Prime Minister T-eng Hsiao-p'ing presented an analysis to the United Nations that was considerably different. In it there were only three zones ("three parties, three worlds"), the socialist bloc having ceased to exist. According to this analysis, China, North Korea, North Vietnam, and Albania are part of the Third World. The validity of such an analysis, which makes no distinction between poor countries that remain economically and politically dominated and sometimes suffer from famine and those which are their own masters, could be open to question. But certainly such a speech could not have been made without Mao Tse-tung having first read it, agreed with it, and approved it.

ca's positions.

The spring of 1969 had not yet thawed the Ussuri River nor had the Chinese Party, shaken as it was by the Cultural Revolution, yet been able to convene its Congress, when fighting broke out on the banks of the border streams. The Soviet Union brought in troops; China braced itself; the threat from the north became a reality, and in Moscow there was talk of preventive raids on Sinkiang. The Soviets, at the very gates of the country, began to seem more menacing than the Americans, who at least were not contemplating an attack against China.

In 1969 China protested against the "new Czars." The following year, after the opening of border negotiations and the resulting improvement in the situation, the slogans became less emotional and more political. Mao decided to launch a systematic campaign against the "two superpowers." The last long text by the Chairman—his May 20, 1970, declaration—was still entirely aimed against America, which had just entered Cambodia, but already Mao portrayed America as weaker. "Who is really afraid of whom in the world nowadays? . . . Actually, American imperialism is afraid of the peoples of the world. At the slightest sign of unrest, it panics." Mao Tse-tung and Chou En-lai both saw a new kind of imperialism appearing beyond America, a more subtle and more vigorous imperialism that had not yet suffered defeat, the imperialism of "the weaker of the two superpowers"—the Soviet Union.

From that point on Mao made no more statements; in concert with Chou En-lai, he acted. He knew that the United States was trying to withdraw from Asia and that it no longer hoped for a military victory in Vietnam. He told this to Edgar Snow. He said that he was ready to meet with President Nixon, on condition that concessions were made about Taiwan, the territory still held by his Nationalist adversary under American military protection. First Chou En-lai saw Secretary of State Kissinger. Eight months later, Mao Tse-tung shook hands with Richard Nixon.

Mao explained his reasons for holding this meeting in terms of a 1945 text justifying his interviews with Chiang Kai-shek. This document, which was studied throughout China in 1971, clarified the basis for the interview: "Our policy, which was decided upon long ago, consists in giving tit for tat . . . . The manner of giving tit for tat depends upon the situation. Sometimes, not to negotiate is a way of giving tit for tat; then again, to negotiate can also be a way of giving tit for tat. Before, we were right not to negotiate, but now it is right for us to negotiate; in both cases, we are giving tit for tat.''

It was under the same circumstances that Mao Tse-tung agreed to meet with Prime Minister Tanaka of Japan, in September 1972, to put an end to a state of war which had officially been going on since 1932, when the Chinese Soviet Republic—of which Mao was Chairman—had declared war on the invader. The Party leader took it upon himself to invite the President of the United States and the head of the Japanese government. These were his last great diplomatic strokes. If anything could guarantee their success it would be the twenty years of strict principles and proud yet necessary isolation which had created favorable conditions for them.

After requesting an audience, the Americans came to Peking, met Mao and formally recognized the Chinese regime. China had regained its place in the world. As for the subtle diplomatic moves surrounding these encounters, the credit goes essentially to Chou En-lai. At this late point in his life Mao clearly preferred to confine himself to outlining strategy and defining the larger principles.

All Mao's great statements of the sixties and seventies have one thing in common: the appeal for unity, unity in the fight against imperialism. Mao Tse-tung believed absolutely that every people would one day feel the urge to free itself of the foreigner's yoke and form a socialist regime. "The peoples of all countries, who make up 90% of the population, will eventually want revolution and will support Marxism-Leninism. They are not in favor of revisionism. Even though some of them may support it at the moment, they will abandon it in the end. One by one they will awaken, begin fighting imperialism and the reactionaries of all countries, and oppose revisionism."

Unfortunately, he points out, this desire to fight does not immediately result in action: all popular movements are divided— the American Left, the European Left, the Palestinian movement, the Arab states, the African countries. Even in Indochina Mao continually had to urge the underground forces of the four territories to cooperate in their struggles against adverse forces.

Another principle is the rejection of "great power chauvinism." Mao Tse-tung probably has not directly inspired the decisions made by the Chinese delegation since its entry into the United Nations in 1971. But the struggle against the "superpowers," the rejection of military blocs, the support which Peking gives to the little countries that suffer from extortion by the big countries, arise from principles which have evolved over a long time and which occupy a prominent place in the *Little Red Book*.

"China should contribute more to humanity" he wrote in November 1956. "For a long time our contribution has been very small and this is regrettable. We should be unpretentious—not only now, but also forty-five years from now and forever. We Chinese must completely, radically, and resolutely wipe out great power chauvinism in international relations." Every country has its strong points and its weak points, he has said again and again. And in 1966 he attacked those who did not respect the Party's position on this point:

"We have proposed the following slogan: let us learn from other countries. I believe this is right. But some of the leaders of our country do not dare or do not want to go along with that slogan. They must become courageous—they are capable of it—and drop these grand airs which have no place outside the theater."

As he neared the end of his life, Mao Tse-tung was very aware of China's growing power. He wanted to make China the first great power that was not in the least imperialistic, the first country which would not put pressure on the smaller nations around it. No one would dare suggest that Peking's policy will always be guided by this idealistic notion. But one thing is certain: Mao really wanted it that way.

3/The Peasants' War

Revolutionary war is the only kind of war whose
ends may be achieved without making the world go
up in flames.

—André Chamson

In dominated countries of the Third World, revolutionary war is
often the first form of political struggle. The guerilla forces of
black Africa, the Arab peninsula, or the jungles of the Far East
learned strategic principles and tactics from Mao Tse-tung. In industrialized countries on the other hand, there is little interest in
revolutionary war. And so the main object of this chapter is to
show the spirit in which Mao Tse-tung approaches the subject of
war.

Before taking power, Mao Tse-tung was a member of the underground for twenty-two years. It would be an understatement to
say that this experience made a deep impression on him: the fact
is that the idea of war structured his entire thinking; civilian
struggles, for him, mirrored military combat; after 1949 he led
the Chinese people in a war against underdevelopment; he
launched a number of ideological "campaigns" and directed operations on the "production front" and the "cultural front;" later, he perfected "a great strategic plan" for the Cultural Revolution, and eliminated the "class enemies" in several "engagements."

Mao Tse-tung was the first to define the principles of people's
war in the 20th century. By 1928 his ideas were already firmly
established, well before the Communist International abandoned
the 1917 Bolshevik model. During the ten years that followed the
October revolution, the uprisings of urban proletariats or-

ganized in various parts of Europe and China were all brutally quelled. There was not a single success; the revolution lost its momentum. It was recovered in China, as revolution spread through the poverty-striken countrysides.

"Red power can exist in China," Mao Tse-tung said in October 1928. After a year of resisting the Kuomintang, he saw new revolutionary possibilities in places far from the cities. After the bloody failure of April 1927 in Shanghai, the peasants rose in the south of China. They seized power in the provinces of Kwangtung, Hunan, and Hupei, and remained in power for several months. The fires had been smoldering for a long time in that region; at the beginning of 1927, Mao Tse-tung had delivered an eloquent eulogy to the rebels of Hunan.

The Communist International hesitated: it conceded the peasants an important role in the revolution, but only a supporting one. It was the workers who were supposed to play the most important part. Of course, in a nonindustrialized country the part played by the rural population would be necessarily greater; but it should not push urban militants into a subordinate position; otherwise the revolution would lose its proletarian character and would not lead to soviets.

Mao Tse-tung did not want to break with the International, so he made his doctrine more flexible: our soldiers will be peasants, and our strategies will derive from the proletariat. "In semicolonial China, the revolution will fail if the peasant struggle does not have working class leadership; but it will hardly suffer from the fact that in the course of their struggle the peasants have become more powerful than the workers."

Everyone Can Fight

The fighters in the people's war would be primarily peasants, and because of this from 1927 to 1949 the revolutionary army was a mirror image of the Chinese people. Everyone could fight; there were a thousand ways of killing an enemy when one had no guns: everyone owned a knife, the peasants had picks, acts of sabotage could be performed by everyone. "There is a certain distance between the civilian and the military," said Mao Tse-tung in 1936, "but they are not separated by the Great Wall: the distance can be quickly crossed . . . . Our chief method is to learn warfare through warfare. A person who has no opportunity to go to school can also learn warfare—he can learn through fighting in war."

Under circumstances as difficult as those endured by the earliest underground forces, all or almost all applications were accepted. There were many peasants, some workers, some down-and-outs, even some vagabonds. One could not be choosy: "These people know how to fight, and since we have to fight every day, suffering heavy losses in dead and wounded, we should be glad that these elements can help us replace the men we are losing," Mao Tse-tung acknowledged in 1928. "Most of the soldiers have come to us from mercenary armies."

In spite of its disparate elements, the Red Army remained unified. Intensive political instruction helped, but a more important source of unity was oppression by the common enemy—the corrupt administration supported by local potentates and urban employers. "There is dry wood scattered all over China which will soon flare up. One has only to look at the student strikes to understand that it will not be long before a spark will set the whole prairie on fire." Even heavy defeats would not change the situation, because in China, which was so vast, "the forest will continue to provide wood," according to Mao Tse-tung.

In a people's war the weak conquer the strong. In 1930, 40,000 men in the mountains of Kiangsi resisted 100,000 of Chiang Kai-shek's soldiers; in May 1931 the government doubled its troops, but 30,000 underground fighters succeeded in driving them back; in June of the same year, when the third campaign began, the balance of forces was even more unfavorable: 30,000 Red Army soliders against three strong columns numbering 300,000 in all. The Reds fled, stole away, but managed to destroy isolated forces and break the encirclement. The ratio had been one to ten.

Actually it had been ten to one, because when each battle took place, the balance was reversed: there were more underground troops, because they concentrated their forces and struck at a divided army. People's war, according to Mao, was based on a fundamental distinction between strategy and tactics: you can destroy forces that are superior on a strategic level, as long as you are stronger in tactical engagements.

Mao Tse-tung applied this distinction not only to war, but also to ideological struggles, to political combat within the Party. It was also an entire method of looking at international politics and its evolution: the socialist camp may be weaker, but it can accumulate tactical successes and ruin the adversary's positions. In the long run, imperialism and capitalism will crumble, the paper tiger will be reduced to ashes. Everything breaks up, as the old Chinese dialectic teaches, everything proceeds from a dual nature. The reactionaries are powerful, but they are weak. It is up to the underground forces to take advantage of their weaknesses.

People's war, as Mao Tse-tung defined it, is based on contradictions. In its general strategy it is a defensive war, fought by the people on their own terrain. But on a tactical level it is actually an offensive war: only an offensive war can destroy the enemy; the enemy is attacked in its own positions, away from the guerilla base. Another contradiction is that though the people's war lasts a long time, the tactical offensive depends upon quick decisions. It is imperative to maintain these contradictions, and the only way to be successful. One formulation of Mao's sums up this unity of opposites, this dialectic of people's war: one must combine "offensive operations in a defensive war, operations involving rapid decisions in a war that will last a long time, and operations outside the lines in a war that takes place within the lines."

First, the war will be a long one. In the beginning, the positions occupied by the revolutionaries will be very precarious, they will not be able to bring about a rapid victory. The enemy, whether foreign or domestic, can make use of the state and its troops; it has more money, and it can claim legitimacy. The revolutionary army must withdraw. This is the first phase of the hostilities: strategic offense by the enemy, strategic defense by the revolutionaries. Some African guerillas are still at this stage.

After a while the situation changes. The enemy, thwarted in its advance, consolidates its positions. The guerillas, better armed, more numerous, and with more help from the population, prepare a counteroffensive from their bases. This is the second stage. Finally, the counteroffensive takes place. The enemy is forced into a strategic retreat. The triumphal march of the People's Liberation Army toward the south, in 1949, is an example of this last phase of the protracted war.

What causes this reversal of the situation? According to Mao it is caused by the gradual annihilation of the enemy's forces during brief, carefully planned, and deadly operations.

Techniques for Annihilation

For the weak to triumph over the strong, they must concentrate forces in the attack and attack only where the enemy is weak. They must strike only with the certainty of success, without risking heavy losses which could decimate their ranks. If the enemy can be destroyed, he must be fought; if not, it is better to clear out: a Red general has no vanity.

The underground forces, for example, do best to gather in ambush against a small enemy unit. Mao Tse-tung: "In every battle, concentrate an absolutely superior force (two, three, four, and sometimes even five or six times the enemy's strength). This way the revolutionaries can divide the enemy's forces, surround them, and annihilate them without letting any escape from the net."

The aim of the guerillas, in fact, is to reduce the enemy's forces, both troops and materiel—not simply to drive them back. In his "Problems of Strategy in China's Revolutionary War," Mao Tse-tung leaves no doubt about this: "Injuring all of a man's ten fingers is not as effective as chopping off one, and routing ten enemy divisions is not as effective as annihilating one of them."

This principle of annihilation has an absolute value. Only the destruction of the enemy can eliminate an immediate danger and procure arms and ammunition. It is the only thing that can lower the morale of the enemy troops and incite them to desert. Only annihilation can make the tactical strike truly effective and serve the overall strategy by changing the larger balance of forces, though it may be by very little. And so one should always attack a weaker force, and not hesitate to divide the units of this weaker force even further in order to assure complete destruction.

If the enemy is to be divided, it must come out from its barracks, leave its camps behind. It must be allowed to penetrate into territory held by the underground forces. It should be lured far inside, the way should be open for it. The revolutionaries abandon the region, leave the towns, or at least blend into the background, giving enemy troops the illusion of easy victory and leading them to make mistakes, to be incautious, to scatter their units. Then the enemy has "its ten fingers occupied and its legs tied." A lightning attack can wipe out one of its units.

This situation shows how strategically superior a defensive position is. Not only can the guerillas move about their terrain freely, mingle with the civilians (for they too are civilians), and strike only if victory is certain; but the more the enemy advances, the weaker it becomes, the more difficult becomes contact with its bases. And so the revolutionaries gain the initiative and freedom of action. People's war is a defensive war against an invader from the cities. It hardly matters whether or not the invader is a foreign one: the Kuomintang troops and high civil servants appointed in the capital were like foreigners—they knew nothing about the small, poor, but unified socialistic world established in the Northwest for the purpose of fighting Japan.

Yet a people's war is not a nomadic war. The underground needs bases of support in order to survive. This was one of the first of Mao's theoretical discoveries when he arrived in the mountains of Kiangsi in 1928. A soldier tells how Mao described this need:

"While speaking of the relationship between armed combat and revolutionary bases, Chairman Mao used an amusing popular comparison. The revolution's need for bases, he said, is like an individual's need for a rear end. If he didn't have one he wouldn't be able to sit down. He would have to go around in circles or remain standing up, and he would not be able to go on for long like that. His tired legs would give way and he would fall down. Only when a revolution has a base can it rest and gather its forces again, recruit soldiers and continue the war on an increasingly large scale until its final victory."

There were more than 100 million men in Communist bases in China at the beginning of the last civil war (1946). The bases had been formed under the protection of revolutionary troops, after successful struggles against the invader and social reforms which had won the poorest people over to the Communist cause. The revolutionary bases in Vietnam were formed under these same conditions, or very nearly. The French *maquisards* during World War II did not have time to form impregnable bases: the tragic end of the Vercors *maquis* has not been forgotten in France.

The principle of concentrating forces in an attack and dividing enemy units can be found in all military textbooks along with the rules about ambush, strike, and search missions. These are the very basics of military art. Mao Tse-tung's originality does not lie in his adoption of these principles but in that he showed how guerilla warfare presupposes a struggle for political and social progress or at least for national dignity: people's war is a just war, and no reactionary army can ever apply its principles.

Only underground forces, supported by large sections of the population, can effectively wage a people's war. They are not well equipped with arms; their leaders have not taken courses in the military academies; they do not have guaranteed pay; and, in the beginning at least, their enemy greatly outnumbers them. On the other hand, the guerillas can depend on part of the population to carry out reconnaissance missions, furnish information, guide troops toward combat zones, and watch enemy movements. When the supply of arms and ammunitions permits, active elements of the population can join the ranks of the Liberation Army or form militias charged with performing acts of sabotage, or slowing down or diverting the enemy.

The population therefore helps to isolate enemy forces, whether actively—by destroying the enemy's means of communication with its rearguard or interfering with its procurement of supplies—or passively—by refusing to give information. As for the troops themselves, they are asked to be more vigorous and energetic than mercenary troops could ever be. The succession of attacks and withdrawals, of strikes and evasions, calls for a level of self-denial and discipline possible only in units fighting for the well-being of the nation.

Discussion a Vital Aspect of the Underground

Relations between fellow fighters, between members of the underground, are different from relations in a barracks. This was evident in the French Resistance. Leaders and fighters share the same hardships and the same convictions. The unity, the active solidarity, produce devotion and heroism. Fatigue and danger do not slow down the fighting as much as they do for the enemy. The leaders have often come up from the ranks; the working class, and—in the case of China—the peasants rise from their subordinate positions to positions of equality with the other classes. The revolutionary war helps to spread popular values.

This type of war is also based on respect for democracy. Within the limits required by discipline, freedom to discuss, to suggest, to criticize, is a sign of efficiency. Blind discipline must give way to group examinations of attack plans—underground fighters know the conditions for success better than anyone else. What is more, the experience of the French shows that when the heads of resistance networks forget these principles and start acting like "leaders," giving orders to their subordinates from a distance, they sometimes make tragic mistakes.

You Can't Put the Chick Back into Its Shell
Mao learned from Algerian friends that during the Algerian war the French had read his works in order to use his methods against the NLF. He explained to the Algerian leader, Ferhat Abbas, that his essays were based on Chinese experience and that their conclusions would not work in reverse. They could only be adapted to wars of people's liberation and were of little use in conducting a war against the people. Reliance on these books had not stopped the French from losing the Algerian war. Chiang Kai-shek had studied the works of the Communists too and that had not saved him either.

On another occasion, Mao remarked that to apply the tactics of revolutionary war to counterrevolution was as difficult as "to put a chick back into its shell."
Interview published by Edgar Snow in *le Nouveau Candide*, December 11, 1965.

The fact that an underground fighter knows about a particular plan of attack and agrees with it contributes to the success of the operation. Guerilla warfare is based on flexibility of execution—both of individual tasks and of larger plans. The intelligence and resoluteness of an isolated fighter is crucial to the outcome of the undertaking. Discussion beforehand also constitutes a personal commitment on the part of the guerilla and reduces the risk of desertion under fire. It would have been quite simple for Red Army soldiers to shed their uniforms and drop their guns and pass into the opposite camp. The fact that this practice did not become widespread was in part because of political education campaigns and in part because of the fighters' awareness of what was at stake.

This need for democracy was all the more urgent because the Party hardly formed a majority in the Red Army or among the population in the liberated zones. During the war against Japan, the "united front" policy led the Party to ally itself with everyone who was determined to fight the invader. This meant the majority of the population; intellectuals and bourgeois businessmen also joined the United Front. To maintain a sense of unity, group discussion was indispensable.

In all the liberated zones, the Party avoided taking overt control of the resistance by assuming positions of command. It preferred to put the "three-thirds" formula into practice: the Party held a third of the seats in the organs of power, another third were held by progressive Leftists, and the remaining third were held by Centrist or Rightist elements. To keep control over the whole apparatus it sufficed to win over the progressive elements patiently, then ultimately to persuade the conservative elements to join in.

To make sure that conservatives would enter the alliance against Japan, the Party suspended its plans for socialization and confined itself to moderate reforms (such as the reduction of farm rents and interest rates and the lowering of taxes), which reassured landowners while improving the lot of the people. This subtle policy made the fight against Kuomintang influence easier: it lessened the bourgeoisie's hostility toward Communism and made the attacks of Chiang's troops against the underground unpopular. This moderation put the Communists in the right: ten years later they reaped the benefit.

The West and People's War

Most military experts in the West are very severe in their judgment of Mao's ideas. They credit him with having formed an army of peasants but deny that his ideas have any significance in today's world. These theories might have been valid for China in the thirties, they say, but they have become completely outmoded with the development of new weapons, as much in China as in the countries who are China's potential enemies. Atomic bombs and nuclear missiles call for another kind of war.

But let me clarify. People's war as Mao Tse-tung defined it is decisive "behind the lines." Even in Korea, Chinese troops were behind the socialist lines and were on somewhat the same terms with the population as was the North Korean army.

Obviously guerilla warfare cannot effectively leave its own territory and attempt to conquer foreign countries. Mao Tse-tung continued to invoke the principles of people's war near the end of his life because he believed that an invasion of China (or more than one invasion) was possible. In spite of the overwhelming superiority of Soviet arms, most experts think that after some initial success, a Russian offensive on the Chinese continent would eventually bog down. This was also Mao's hypothesis. He wanted to form a "national defense" army in the true sense of the term, not euphemistically—and be content with that. As for the nuclear deterrent, its aim was to prevent not an invasion but a nuclear attack.

A Maoist people's war, military authorities say, is valid only in Third World countries. It has no place in the West. This is a debatable opinion. The French Resistance contradicts it in part. Let me cite two widely respected Resistance leaders: "There is a place for guerilla warfare in every period and every country," Colonel Rémy has written, "and an occupying force will never cease to be an enemy to every honorable soul, because of the very fact that occupation brings with it constraint." For Rémy, however, guerilla warfare plays only a supportive role, with "allied" forces providing the main thrust.

This point of view is not shared by the former head of the FTP,[1] Charles Tillon, who does not hesitate to quote Mao Tse-tung. Tillon realizes that the resistance of the French underground fighters could only grow little by little, and that the part they played only became really important during the last year before the liberation. Yet he believes that "the tactical contribution of the Resistance was greater than that of the armies who landed, and the planned insurrection carried out by the Resistance within the country was more important than the strategy of the Allies in France." Whether or not these statements are valid, one thing is certain: at the end of 1943, the Resistance swelled considerably, and if the German occupation had been prolonged, the role of the Resistance would have become more important with each passing year.

People who met Mao Tse-tung during the last period of his life were struck by the importance with which the head of the Chinese Party regarded the French *maquis*. Based in wooded and mountainous regions, it evidently reminded him of the underground forces he had once led. Mao seemed to think that future serious conflicts might put the French people face to face with another invader, and that guerilla warfare, always the last resort after the regular army has been defeated, would be the ultimate guarantee that the country would not bow its head.

As for Third World countries, Mao believed that only people's war could free nations from the yoke of imperialism. In this re-

---

[1]FTP = *Franc-tireurs et partisans*. French underground resistance group during World War II [translators' note].

spect the Third World would follow the same course as China. Mao did not explicitly say this, though his followers have. Guerilla warfare should not, however, exclude other forms of combat. People's war depends on political combat, on the education of the peasant and urban masses. It should never be considered a series of terrorist attacks; it assumes that parallel activities will be pursued intensively in parapolitical organizations—trade unions and associations for the masses.

People's war therefore is not the only form of combat; and if this is true for Third World countries, it is all the more true for industrialized nations. Mao Tse-tung rarely expressed his ideas about the struggle in capitalist democracies. In 1938 however he showed that he had very clear opinions about this: the legal struggle must play a very important part before civil war—the final test—breaks out.

This text deserves to be quoted, because it specifically defines both the general conditions and the limits of guerilla warfare: "In capitalist countries . . . the conditions are these: within the country, feudalism no longer exists, the regime is a bourgeois democracy; in their foreign relations, these countries do not suffer from national oppression—on the contrary, they oppress other nations. This is why the task of the proletarian Party in capitalist countries must be to educate the workers and to gather forces through an extended legal battle, thus preparing itself for the eventual overthrow of capitalism. In these countries it is a matter of sustaining a long legal battle, of making use of the parliamentary courts, of staging economic and political strikes, of organizing the trade unions and educating the workers. There the forms of organization are legal ones, and the forms the struggle takes are not bloody." Civil war, therefore, will only occur as a last resort, and clearly in Mao's opinion it is not imminent in the West.

4/A Nonstatist Economic Strategy

Unlike Marx or Lenin, Mao Tse-tung did not make lengthy economic analyses. He neither defined new concepts nor produced a body of theoretical work. The problems of development as such hardly held his attention at all before he took power. After 1949 he followed the national economic effort closely, but he devoted much less time and far fewer pages to it than to the great political questions.

In fact for Mao, once the ideological questions have been settled, the economic problems resolve themselves in the same spirit. "Political work," he wrote in 1955, "is the essence of all economic work. And this is particularly true when the economic system is going through profound changes."

This statement, like the slogan "put politics in a position of command," has helped spread the idea that Mao Tse-tung is not interested in problems of production. In fact the opposite is true, despite the apparent unambiguity of his formulations. During the entire period of preparation for the Cultural Revolution—from 1962 to 1966—Mao Tse-tung did not miss any opportunities to call attention to the urgent need for production. He wanted revolution because he believed it would free the forces of production blocked by an increasing rigidity in the nation.

Oppression discourages the worker and makes him impotent. In the last century, Hegel expressed man's disenchantment in a society which mutilates him and "drives him back into an inner world": "His unhappiness comes from his awareness of the limits imposed on him, which make him scorn life as he is allowed to live it;" and again: "The man who thirsts for an inner life, the man who seeks a better reality in which to live, is offered only the privileges of a cold and dead existence and is told: this is life." There can be no passion for life, and thus for work, except in a free society.

When Mao Tse-tung talked about economics, he did not use the vocabulary of the experts. He did not discuss production costs or material inducements, or "optimal utilization of production factors." He spoke of men working in China, a poor country threatened by war and natural disasters. At a time when the science of economics in the West was accumulating models, equations, and matrices, Mao was interested only in the worker—his attitude toward the machine, his desire for change. Did the worker feel comfortable in the factory, did he want to work more, did he have confidence in the regime, in the Party, did he have the courage to devise better adapted equipment or to propose a more efficient organization of the workship? This kind of positive attitude, he felt, was the key to successful development.

Capitalist economy is based on personal and private interest. This motivation does not exist in the socialist economy. Since it is collective, it can make progress only if the collective becomes animated and believes actively that progress is possible. Mao Tse-tung applied the "mass line" to economics. "The riches of society are created by the workers, the peasants, and the working intellectuals. If they take their own destiny in hand . . . and apply themselves to resolving problems actively instead of evading them, they will be able to find their way out of any and all difficulties."

Mao's economic strategy was both original and ambitious.

General Economic Concepts

Collective drive will reach its height when all the people participate in economic development. All the actual or potential resources of the workers must be mobilized (and the potential resources are far greater than what is presently available).

The idea of strict profit-earning capacity is abandoned, the notion of an enterprise that balances its books twice a year. A firm exerts its influence, spreads its activities throughout an entire region and on its own workers: this is what economists in the West call "external economies." Mao Tse-tung attached the greatest importance to this idea, placing it at the center of his strategy.

Profitability in the larger sense includes advantages to be gained in the future: an enterprise educates the workers, teaches methods of production, develops the workers' minds. The factory would make the peasant into a worker, agriculture would toughen the intellectual. In "poor and blank" China, as Mao called it, almost everything remained to be done. The people would learn to produce by producing.

In the world of free enterprise, business develops wherever conditions are most favorable—where there is existing manpower, an adequate transportation system, and cheap raw materials. Maoist strategy is prepared to ignore these practices: manpower will be created on the spot, the people's communes will make the necessary roads, mine shafts will be opened. In Mao's system everything looks toward the future—and is interested in more than just putting factories into operation.

Mao Tse-tung wanted to do the job rapidly: "We cannot follow the beaten paths of technical development in other countries and trail far behind them." China was in a hurry, it had to take short cuts toward growth.

Economists have said for some time that in the Third World it is often preferable, solely from an economic point of view, to improve the level of health and education rather than immediately establish new businesses. To raise the productivity of an undernourished labor force by feeding it better has often proved to be more effective than buying more machines. Food and education for the workers are highly "profitable" expenditures. Economists specializing in underdevelopment call these costs "human investments." Mao took this idea much further. What mattered to him was the enthusiasm, energy, and creativity of the millions of Chinese workers in the cities and countrysides, and their skill, acquired in the very act of production itself.

At the moment, less is being produced; in ten years, more will be produced. There is nothing wasteful here—but neglecting to train a people would be to squander resources. In any case, Maoist strategy is based on an extremely tight control over collective goods.

Frugality is also an economic necessity. "The principle of strict economy," said Mao Tse-tung, "is one of the basic principles of socialist economy. China is a large country and still very poor; it will take several decades to become prosperous and even then, we must continue to apply the principle of diligence and economy."

What does this mean in concrete terms? Instead of buying large factories and modern equipment as a matter of course, one will not be too proud to transform old machines at a lower cost, to employ processes that are outmoded elsewhere and improve them. Plans will be calculated down to the last detail, to avoid "over-extensions;" technical innovations will aim at saving raw material and equipment; supplies will be kept at the lowest possible level; potential raw materials will be salvaged from the slag and fumes of industrial waste.

This conception of economic development serves as a model for the agricultural sector as much as for industry.

A Non-Stalinist Form of Agricultural Collectivism

"Agriculture is the basis of the economy and industry the dominant factor within it." This somewhat confusing slogan, formulated by Mao Tse-tung in 1960, sums up the principle governing the overall structure.

Mao Tse-tung's ideas ignore Soviet practice, not only of the post-Stalinist USSR, but even of Stalin's first five-year plans. In 1966, Mao Tse-tung stated without the least ambiguity: "The Soviet Union's agricultural policy has always been wrong, because it drains the pool to catch the fish, and is cut off from the masses."

There is no antagonism, said Mao, between the development of agriculture and the development of industry. "It is necessary to ensure the simultaneous expansion of industry and agriculture." One could not be developed at the expense of the other. Here, instead of quoting Mao Tse-tung himself, I will quote an article in the Central Committee's journal, *Red Flag*, which reflects his thought:

"There are two ways of developing heavy industry: the first is to pay less attention to the development of light industry and agriculture in order to concentrate on heavy industry. This method does not make the people happy, and heavy industry cannot develop normally because it is held back by light industry and agriculture." (This method corresponds to the Soviet five-year plans of Stalin's period; the burden of forced industrialization crushed agriculture.) "The second method," *Red Flag* goes on, "is the one which Chairman Mao advocates: to develop light industry and agriculture in order to accelerate the development of heavy industry." An abundant agricultural production and numerous industrial consumer goods will satisfy the needs of the people and accumulate funds with which to finance heavy industry.

Instead of competing for national resources, the two sectors support one another—which is the basis of the slogan "to walk on two legs."

Mao Tse-tung did not renounce the Marxist thesis of the priority of heavy industry. Industry, he says, is the dominant factor (the adjective is "Zhudao," a term which can also be translated as "controlling" or even "dynamic"). Only industrialization can transform the country and its agriculture. Heavy industry, *Red Flag* specifies, allows the means of production to be augmented and provides the tools for mechanizing agriculture. And in the end, says Mao, "the solution for agriculture is mechanization."

So there is no question of buying grains from the peasants at a low price and charging them exorbitant prices for industrial products, demanding massive deliveries of agricultural produce to the state, or establishing a system of point work disadvantageous to the rural areas as a whole. Agriculture is the basis of the economy, and that basis should be solid.

But the mechanization of agriculture is not the first stage in the transformation of the rural world. The countryside can only make progress through a collective effort: socialization of agriculture must come before mechanization. Here again Mao Tse-tung turned his back on Soviet theses. The collectivization of farms and of the work force is the only way to avoid stagnation.

The 1950 agrarian reform freed the countryside from the oppression of the idle rich and the speculators. But could this collection of poor, isolated peasants fight effectively against natural disasters; could it dig irrigation canals, change the course of rivers, terrace the hillsides, forge tools, thresh the harvest, educate the children, and care for the sick? Certainly not. The small private landholdings had to yield to more efficient group organizations.

Even without machines there was a good deal to do—no need to wait for the arrival of tractors and harvester combines. First the countryside had to be reorganized, then mechanical equipment could be provided. This logic—the formation of cooperatives first, then mechanization—was also discovered by North Korea, two years after China. But it was China who led the way, beginning in 1955–56 with the establishment of a system of cooperatives.

Even at the point of mechanizing agriculture, China would not follow the Soviet model. The tractor stations of the USSR were not suitable, the Chinese leaders decided in 1954: they were too great a burden on the countryside, and too dissociated from it. In 1958, at the conference held in Chengtu in Szechwan province,

Mao asked that the tractors be given to the rural collectives that needed them: the collectives would buy them and use them as they saw fit. Then people's communes came into being: they received 70% of the available tractors. The traditionalists revolted and held up the movement, stressing, and sometimes provoking, excesses within it. For a time they were successful. Again in 1963 Mao tried to give a new impetus to mechanization by creating a specialized ministry to deal with it. His adversaries caused the project to fail. The debate started again at the beginning of 1966 and was temporarily settled by the Cultural Revolution, when Liu Shao-ch'i and P'eng Chen were eliminated.

Heavy equipment is not essential to mechanization nor is it even a principal component. First farm implements had to be improved with respect to local soils and crops. Within the village, small factories or even workshops could produce or repair the peasants' equipment. Small units could provide chemical fertilizers and accelerate the fermentation of vegetable-based composts. Manure would continue to play an important part, and the "small fertilizer factory"—a pig in its pen—would remain essential. Tractors and chemical fertilizers are not always the answers, as agronomists know.

Statist control can result in rigidity. The peasants accept collectivization within the framework of cooperatives and people's communes, but the basic echelon is still the production team, which includes about thirty households—about one hundred people—sometimes more. Except in the vast pioneer regions of the west, there is no thought of establishing state farms. "There exist now and will exist for a long time two sorts of socialist ownership: state ownership and collective ownership."

The latter is made up of three echelons: the production team, the brigade (for the village or the cooperative), and the people's commune (at the level of the district). To transfer the center of decision-making from the production team to the commune would disturb the peasant economy: this "Leftist" mistake would have the same result as abandoning socialization: a black market and speculation would develop alongside such a rigid system, as was clearly shown during the Great Leap Forward.

The rural economy should therefore remain decentralized. The state, which must keep the cities supplied, has certain needs. But the five hundred million Chinese peasants must be satisfied. Concerning the allotment of agicultural production, Mao Tse-tung said it very clearly: "We must take into consideration the interests of the state, the collectivity, and the individual." Pressure exerted by the state must remain tolerable. Accumulation of funds by public powers or rural collectivities must not keep the standard of living from rising: "We must do everything we can to make sure that in years of normal harvest the personal revenues of the peasants increase from year to year as a result of the increase in production."

The nation needs to build up grain reserves. Not only must the state's silos be filled, but the economy as a whole will benefit if reserves are built up in each village and each home as well. In this way all households would participate in the strategy for national defense—and they would undoubtedly be more willing to accept a form of politics which allowed them to keep near them the sacks of rice they had worked so hard to earn.

This great flexibility of organization is even more apparent in the industrial sector.

The Need to Build Autonomous Industrial Regions

"Local administrations," Mao Tse-tung explained, "must do whatever is necessary to establish autonomous industrial systems: this would first consist of cooperative regions, then extend to several provinces. Once the right conditions obtain, the latter should construct relatively independent industrial complexes which would also be adapted to the local situation."

These industrial systems must serve agriculture, begin the production of equipment or develop it further if it already exists, and furnish the essential industrial consumer goods. Regional autonomy fulfills the needs of national defense: it precludes the invasion and occupation of large centers; it makes it impossible for production to be totally paralyzed. But the preoccupations of the leaders alone do not determine industrial policy. What Mao wanted above all was to bind agriculture and industry more closely together, and to do that it was necessary to reject the Soviet system of large combines and regional specialization linked by a system of long-distance heavy transport.

What Mao Tse-tung wanted was a balanced system combining enterprises of all sizes and maintaining—though not slavishly— distribution of the stages of production, especially raw materials, over all the different regions. "We must gradually develop a number of large, modern enterprises as the indispensable basis upon which we will build our country into a modern industrial power within a few decades," he stated in 1957. Priority in public investment must still be given to heavy industry, which provides the essential durable goods for other sectors of the economy. Coal mining in large open mines, the metallurgy of regular and special steels, the extraction and refining of oil, the construction of heavy-duty equipment, and industrial chemistry constitute some of the main elements of this industrial base.

However, Mao added, these large units cannot be enough: "It is necessary to create more small- and medium-sized industries. We must also make the best possible use of the entire industrial base left over from the old society . . . and accomplish a great deal with relatively small sums of money."

The primary advantage of small units is that since there are so many of them, they can use the natural resources which are scattered all over the place, though often in small quantities. Pitcoal, peat, and lignite can be found almost everywhere: each region can acquire some cheaply, without importing it from distant provinces. This is why South China is nearly at the point where it no longer has to purchase fuel from Northeast China.

A second advantage is that exploitation of local resources eases the burden on the system of transport, which is indispensable to large industry and was for many years vitally important to the Vietnamese fighters.

Third, light industry allows the economy of backward regions to be diversified, particularly the districts inhabited by national minorities. It provides a foundation for future heavy industry which is expensive and takes time. Yet modernization cannot wait.

The fourth point is that the simplicity and low cost of the equipment allow local collectivities—provincial municipalities, large villages, small villages, and middle-sized city neighborhoods—to take responsibility for the project. Usually all that is needed is the equivalent of less than $100,000, which local coffers can advance. Projects are chosen for their high profitability and yield a quick return.

Fifth, these industries directly serve local interests. They provide steel for agricultural machinery, build the equipment required by the peasants, and provide them with chemical fertilizer. They give the village the cement and bricks for building homes, electricity for their handicraft workshops and telecommunications networks, and fuel for homes and factories. They employ whatever manpower has been freed by mechanization and thus avoid a rural exodus.

The development of small industries, in the opinion of the Chinese leaders, inevitably results in the acceleration of economic development. Mao Tse-tung wanted to proceed very quickly with industrialization. Chinese production is not in proportion to the country's size or its population: "The rapidity of Chinese industrial development," said *New China* on August 26, 1970, "is strategically important in the fight against time that we are engaged in, in competition with imperialism [the Soviet Union] . . . . The law of development is always to proceed from small things to big . . . . The proliferation of small industries will turn out more products for the state, result in more investments and produce more technicians, which will, in turn, allow for the construction of large enterprises serving as the basis for the national economy."

When this law of "small to big" was formulated in 1970, not all planners went along with it. Two years later, they returned to more complex conceptions. The focus shifted to the *simultaneous* encouragement of central and local initiatives, on the *parallel* development of large, middle-sized, and small centralized and localized industries. These variations, however, do not affect the validity of the strategy as a whole nor diminish its originality.

A Course for Third World Countries

The agricultural and industrial structures proposed by Mao Tse-tung hold no great interest for countries with industrialized economies. On the other hand, they provide the Third World with an example of how to industrialize rapidly and—what is more important—independently. Certain countries in Africa and Asia have experienced a monetary growth as rapid as China's, yet none has been able to prevent an increase in its dependence on the outside world.

China's economic progress started with financial and technical aid from the Soviet Union. But from 1960 on, its growth has been based on domestic resources alone. China has paid back all its debts, foreign and domestic. Its commerce with foreign countries represents only an infinitesimal part of the national product (less than 5%). Its imports are limited first to equipment which it has not yet been able to build or which it builds in insufficient quantity, then to the most technically advanced products (American or European planes for its airlines), and lastly to cheap foodstuffs (Australian, American, or Canadian wheat) which go to form its reserves. Its foreign trade differs radically in this respect from the commerce of countries with colonial economies, where sometimes more than half the currency resources are spent on buying food.

The originality of the Chinese model extends beyond economic independence. Only North Korea and North Vietnam have anything similar to China's interconnection between agriculture and industry, between town and country—and North Vietnam was actually forced into it by the war. The mobilization of all rural forces, the use of whatever is available, the preferential treatment accorded the endeavors of individuals and of village communities, the distrust of large-scale mechanization ordered on credit from abroad—these rigorous principles have stood the test of experience over the past fifteen years.

Finally, China's contribution in the area of technical innovation has been of the first importance. Contrary to the belief in the West that it is impossible to industrialize the Third World other than by the techniques used in industrial nations, China has shown that rural development is possible *only if one abandons* the idea of using mainly Western equipment. Each of China's small factories provides only several thousands of tons of fertilizer or steel; the units proposed in African countries often begin at one hundred thousand tons. In Mali or Nigeria people invoke the imperatives of "profitability," but in poor countries the presence of factories that are too large can block development and paralyze the national effort. In such countries a profitable factory is one that is in full use, one whose product immediately serves to modernize the country. China is the first Third World country to develop modern techniques that effectively equip the countrysides—techniques which are cheap enough for poor countries to adopt but ambitious in that they are trying to augment primary industry quickly. These techniques of the small basic industries are in part, of course, linked to political decisions. But they can be gradually adapted to any country which wants above all to rely on its own resources, to develop a cooperative movement in the rural areas after the necessary agrarian reform, and to avoid the old formulas that can lead to stagnation.

5/Mao Tse-tung
the Feminist

Clearly a man as anxious as Mao Tse-tung to free all the latent forces within the Chinese people would have to be a feminist. And he was a feminist—both intellectually and morally. It is not the purpose of this book to discuss the status of Chinese women, their legal equality with men, and their gradual winning of real equality. In the People's Republic the status of women is the highest in all of Asia, because of certain resolves which Mao Tse-tung made long ago. The great May 1, 1950, law concerning marriage passed on to China as a whole the reforms already carried out in "liberated" areas held by the Communists in South China and then in the Northwest.

Mao said what he thought about the question of women very early. Even before he became a Marxist his ideas were clear. When he was thirteen his father wanted to marry him to an older woman who would help in his family's home until the boy was old enough to form his own household—this was the custom. Mao rebelled, fleeing from his father's house and refusing to return as long as his father persisted in his plan.

After he was twenty, Mao adopted the ideas of other young radicals of that time. The New People's Study Society, which he started at Changsha in 1917, rejected the traditional system of marriage. At first, Mao Tse-tung and his comrades swore never to marry. Not that they advocated free love: they believed the subject was of minor importance and did not deserve to be dwelt upon when there was a revolution to be prepared. They felt it was enough to denounce prostitution, concubinage, and bourgeois debauchery. The young men of Hunan believed that the first concern of women should be to take part in the revolution.

Once in Peking, Mao Tse-tung organized an Association for Work and Study in France. These groups of students migrating to

Europe quite frequently adopted anarchist ideas. But many of the travelers shortly afterward became Communists. Strong feelings about the emancipation of women were widespread in these circles. Mao Tse-tung wrote to one of the leaders of the emigration association founded at Changsha: "I hope you will be able to take a large group of female comrades abroad; because every girl you take you save." Several of these girls were later to assume high positions in the Party, both before and after the foundation of the People's Republic.

The May 4th Movement of 1919 helped draw attention to the question of women. In a series of articles in his *Hsiang River Review,* Mao indignantly protested that women were oppressed by men, though they had the same right as men to belong to the "human species." Why were women locked up at home? "Since we are all human beings, why not give us all the right to vote? And why not permit us to mingle freely with one another?" He denounced the fact that men imposed chastity on women while allowing themselves whatever they wished, from prostitution to concubinage. "What is this chastity," he asked, "which is reserved entirely for women, with temples raised everywhere to female martyrs? Where are the temples honoring chaste men?"

Mao Tse-tung took every opportunity to challenge conventional ideas. In a Hunan daily paper, *Ta Kung Pao,* he wrote nine articles about the suicide of a young lady, forced by her parents to marry a man she hated, who cut her throat the day of her wedding. These commentaries reveal the distinctness and depth of Mao's feelings: he does not criticize the young woman's decision even slightly, throwing the whole responsibility for the suicide onto society.

"A person's suicide is entirely determined by circumstances. Was Miss Chao's original idea to seek death? On the contrary, it was to seek life. If Miss Chao ended up seeking death instead, it was because circumstances drove her to this. The circumstances in which Miss Chao found herself were the following: (1) Chinese society; (2) the Chao family of Nanyang Street in Changsha; (3) the Wu family of Kantzuyuan Street in Changsha, the family of the husband she did not want. These three factors constituted three iron nets, composing a kind of triangular cage. Once caught in these nets, it was in vain that she sought life in every way possible. There was no way for her to go on living: the contrary of life is death, and Miss Chao thus felt compelled to die . . . . If, among these three factors, there had been one that was not an iron net, or if one of these nets had opened, Miss

Chao would certainly not have died."

The suicide of this young girl called the entire society into question, and threw light on its murderous aspects. Mao continued: "Since there are factors in our society that have brought about the death of Miss Chao, this society is an extremely dangerous thing. It was capable of causing the death of Miss Chao; it could also cause the death of Miss Ch'ieh, or Miss Sun, or Miss Li. It is capable of killing men as well as women. All of us potential victims must be on our guard before this dangerous thing that could inflict a fatal blow on us. We should protest loudly, warn other human beings who are not yet dead."

Less than ten years later Mao Tse-tung became one of the leaders of the revolutionary movement. He did not repudiate any of his earlier feminist beliefs. In his investigation of peasant rebels in his native province he observed that "usually the men are subject to three systems of authority (political authority, the authority of the clan, and the authority of religion). The women are also under the authority of men in general or subject to the power of their husbands." Thus women find themselves at the very bottom of the pyramid of exploitation. They need to be freed, they need a new order even more than men do.

After the founding of the People's Republic, Mao Tse-tung quickly did away with the legal inequality between the sexes. But the law cannot always control the actual situation. It was time for women to hold a place in society as well as in the home. "The women of China constitute a vast reserve of labor. We must call on this reserve and use it in the fight to build a powerful socialist country." Discrimination between the sexes would not disappear by magic. "True equality between men and women can only be brought about in the course of a socialist transformation of the whole society."

All the Communist leaders shared this desire for equality of the sexes. Most of the high officials of the Chinese Communist Party chose as female companions prominent militant women who played a very large role both in the period of the underground and in the People's Republic. Among them were T'eng Ying-ch'ao, the wife of Chou En-lai; Ts'ai Ch'ang, the wife of Li Fu-ch'un; Wang Kuang-mei, the wife of Liu Shao-ch'i; Yeh Chun, the wife of Lin Piao; and of course Chiang Ch'ing, Mao Tse-tung's third wife.

In the sixties, particularly during the Cultural Revolution and the period of its preparation, Mao Tse-tung and Chiang Ch'ing worked in very close political cooperation. But the couple's collaboration had begun much earlier. In 1939, Chiang Ch'ing began to awaken Mao Tse-tung's interest in the problem of the arts. They discussed ideological questions together, and this might have contributed to the Yenan interviews published shortly afterwards in which Mao talked about literature and art.

In 1963 Mao Tse-tung decided that Chinese art was not being sincerely inspired by socialist collective values. This was true of film, poetry, popular songs, and especially opera. The following year Chiang Ch'ing took over the reform of the Peking Opera and pointed it definitively in the direction of the exaltation of socialist virtues. In the following years, during the tough battles of the Cultural Revolution, Chiang Ch'ing undeniably served as Mao Tse-tung's spokesman to the youth organizations. She was popular with the Red Guard and therefore took the liberty of scolding them—something out of the question for anyone the young rebels regarded with suspicion.

In the last years of his life, Mao Tse-tung spoke little about women's problems as such. As a result of the great reforms carried out in the first years of the regime and the development of social services (such as day care centers and nursery schools), women have come far along the road of liberation. Yet total equality with men will probably not come about until much later, in the period of true Communism—which the Chinese continue to believe in and even prepare for, but which they do not expect to see in the near future. Total equality of the sexes will not be any easier to bring about than elimination of the opposition between peasants and workers, between towns and countrysides, and between manual labor and intellectual work.

6/Mao Tse-tung and the Soviet Union

The first differences between the leaders of the Soviet and Chinese Communist Parties date back to the twenties. An unimportant territorial dispute, to which the West generally attaches too much importance, serves as a background to certain questions of principle—China's quest for an authentic and independent form of socialism, Soviet Communism's loyalty to the memory of Stalin, the affirmation of national dignity—which are the most important differences between the countries.

A Minor Territorial Dispute

The background of the Sino-Soviet dispute was the active part played by the Czarist Empire in the pillaging of China during the 19th century. Parts of Siberia, Turkestan, and the Himalayas—more than 575,000 square miles in all, which historically fell under the rule of the Peking emperor—came under Russian administration. By having the army apply pressure on the northern frontiers, the Czarist regime was able to join with other powers to take advantage of the weaknesses of the decaying regime in China. The "unequal treaties" sanctioned this pillaging.

Today the problem is that the Soviets do not want to give up what they inherited from the Czar, and they refuse to admit that it was stolen. On September 15, 1964, in an interview with members of the Japanese parliament, Krushchev left no doubt about Moscow's point of view:

"Mao Tse-tung implies that the Soviet Union is too large. Peking is fond of pointing out that the government of the Czar seized extra territory and added it to its frontiers. We do not wish to

defend the Russian Czars. Like other emperors, they were pre-
dators; they started wars for the purpose of pillaging and tried to
seize other people's property in order to add to their own posses-
sions. But our attitude is the same towards all aggressors in the
past, whether Russian Czars or Chinese emperors. The Russian
Czars plunged into wars of conquest. But what did the Chinese
emperors do? They engaged in the same wars of conquest, the
same pillaging as the Russian Czars . . . . Thus, if we look at
history to see how the different states were formed, we see that
in both the large states and the small ones, the emperors waged
wars of conquest. The only difference was that the large pillager
seized more than the small pillager.''

It did not help the Chinese Party to point out that in 1920
Lenin had denounced the unequal treaties—to the great satisfaction of the leaders of the Kuomintang, Sun Yat-sen in particular.
Lenin was prepared to restore all of the Czar's acquisitions without demanding anything in return. However the two countries had
more urgent problems to attend to than the reexamination of
treaties. In 1926, after the death of Sun Yat-sen, discussions
began about jointly redefining the frontiers. But before these discussions could yield any result the Kuomintang, in 1927, broke
with the Communists. Later, Stalin said nothing about the 19th
century treaties. Krushchev and his successors said that there was
no territorial problem between the Soviet Union and China. The
treaties were fair, and the Chinese were only trying to start an
unpleasant quarrel in order to satisfy ''their expansionist aims.''

To preserve the unity of the socialist camp, Mao Tse-tung at
first said nothing about Moscow's attitude. The aging Stalin was
too stubborn to allow his policies to be directly challenged. Mao
may have been waiting, like his friends in the Kremlin, for the
old leader to die. In any case he tried to discuss the matter with
Stalin's successors. In 1955, he succeeded in having the Russian
troops withdrawn from Port Arthur, while the ''mixed'' industrial
companies in Sinkiang were put under completely Chinese control. But he wanted to go further: he wanted to challenge the
whole Yalta policy, as he intimated to Japanese journalists in
1964:

''The Soviet Union is occupying many areas. In accordance
with the Yalta agreements, it has taken control of Mongolia,
claiming that by doing this it is protecting Mongolia's independence . . . . When Krushchev and Bulganin came to China in
1954, we raised the question of Mongolia, but they refused to
talk about it. They annexed part of Rumania in order to integrate

it into the Soviet Union. They took away part of East Germany and drove the West Germans out of it. They took part of Poland's territory, incorporated it into Russia and gave part of East Germany to Poland in exchange. The same thing happened with Finland. They took over everything that could be taken over. Some people have said that Sinkiang and the territory north of Amur should be given back to the USSR.

"The area of the Soviet Union is more than 85,000,000 square miles and its population is reaching 200 million. The time has come for it to stop annexing territories . . . . The area to the east of Lake Baikal became Russian territory only one hundred years ago, and at that time Vladivostok, Khabarovsk, the Kamtchatka Peninsula, and several other places could be considered Russian dependencies. We have not yet settled this matter."

In spite of that statement, China has not demanded the return of territories acquired in the last century. At the time of the 1964 negotiations and during the 1969 open negotiations on frontier questions, China asked only for the return of regions occupied by Soviet troops in violation even of the unequal treaties. These regions included about half of the six hundred islands situated on the Chinese side of the Hei-lung Chiang (Amur) and Ussuri Rivers, comprising nearly 400 square miles, and also nearly 8,000 square miles situated in the Pamir region, seized in violation of an 1884 agreement.

This territorial dispute, which provoked violent incidents first in 1962 and then in 1969, still prevents the two regimes from peacefully coexisting today. But Mao Tse-tung's disagreements with the Soviet leaders go back much further—to the early days of the Communist International. At that time, Mao's writings and actions were based on ideas very different from those prevalent in the Socialist movement as a whole.

The Mistakes Made by the International

"Stalin," Mao Tse-tung told André Malraux, "understood nothing about peasants." Socialists of the twenties were mainly preoccupied by questions concerning the workers; they drew their ideas from Marx and Lenin, who were themselves involved with problems of the industrial proletariat. Lenin was categorical: "The city necessarily leads the way for the countryside. The countryside necessarily follows the city." The International tended to apply these conclusions without modification to a very poor, nonurbanized Third World. In 1931 even Ho Chi Minh believed that the revolution would have to begin in the large urban centers, though he emphasized the importance of the role to be played by the peasants.

Yet what Mao Tse-tung held against Stalin was not so much perhaps the fact that he had underestimated the peasants. In fact, Stalin and the Comintern were in favor of absorbing peasant revolts into the anti-imperialist movement led by workers. The Communists were to ally themselves with the antifeudal movement in the countrysides. Stalin's polemic against Trotsky concerned precisely this point. Trotsky felt that the alliance of the proletariat with the peasant movement would give bourgeois overtones to the revolution. Stalin and the International, on the other hand, believed that agitation in the cities should be combined with the development of the agrarian movement in the countrysides.

However Stalin and the International made an unpardonable mistake in Mao Tse-tung's eyes: they issued directives on a subject with which they were not acquainted—they did not take the trouble to make serious investigations. Revolution cannot be organized from a distance. The political situation in every country is complex; sometimes it changes very quickly and requires an immediate, appropriate, and flexible response. In 1943 Mao explained the dissolution of the Comintern: "There is no way a unified international organization can adapt to complex and rapidly changing circumstances . . . . An international center of control is no longer necessary."[1] The International, he went on, was "at a great distance from the concrete struggles of each country." Besides, he said, "the leading cadres of the Communist Parties are politically mature now." The revolutionary movement in China was complex, "even more complex than the Russian revolution." In short, the Chinese Communist Party could very well accomplish what it had to accomplish by itself.

Mao Tse-tung went on to say that from 1935 on the Comintern had no longer intervened in the internal affairs of the Chinese Communist Party—in some sense an acknowledgment that the Party had submitted to its authority during the first fifteen years of its existence. Not without some feeling of relief, he hailed the dissolution of the International as "a great event which marks the end of one period of history and the beginning of another." Not

[1]See Stuart Gelder, *The Chinese Communists,* London, 1946.

without irony—unless for some reason the translation is inadequate—he reduces to almost nothing the list of the Comintern's actions in China: "Comrade Mao noted two historical facts: that Chiang Kai-shek was sent to Moscow by Sun Yat-sen, and that a representative of the Kuomintang participated in one of the meetings of the Comintern. He said that this was enough to show how much the Comintern had helped the revolution in China and how great its influence on the Chinese people was."

The mistakes made by the International, starting in 1927, would not be repeated. In the midst of the war the Chinese Communist Party and Mao Tse-tung definitively won the right to make their own decisions.

Mao's Disagreements with Stalin

Mao Tse-tung was always discreet about his differences with Stalin. He remained silent about the help Moscow gave the Kuomintang while it was fighting the Communists. He remained silent about the Kremlin's lack of interest in the Chinese revolution (former Belgian ambassador Rotschild reports in *La Chute de Tchiang Kaichek* that there was a United States military mission in Yenan in 1944 as well as British agents, but there were only two Soviets—journalists from the Tass agency). He did not reproach the Soviets for the freedom they allowed Japanese troops in the border regions of Manchuria or for the glory they claimed for their late campaign against Japan when the latter had already been mortally wounded by America's atomic bomb. There was also no mention, at least not officially, of the Soviet army's pillaging of factories in Northeast China, as compensation for its lightning war against Japan.

Only much after the fact did Chinese leaders express reservations about the Yalta agreements and about the attitude of the Soviets at the time of the negotiations, when they made decisions about the Chinese either without consulting them or by putting pressure on them. What was more, Moscow chose to side with the Nationalists up to the very end; in 1945 the USSR agreed to the joint American and British request that the Japanese surrender only to Kuomintang troops. Stalin urged the Communists to come to an agreement with the Kuomintang; but, as he later complained to Djilas, "They agreed with us on paper, but in practice, once they had returned home they did whatever they liked." "In

1945," said Mao Tse-tung in a speech before the Central Committee in 1962, "Stalin refused to let us organize a revolution and told us: 'No civil war. Collaborate with Chiang Kai-shek. Otherwise, the Republic of China will collapse.' But we did not follow his orders, and the revolution won out.'' (The text of this speech was published in March 1967 by the journal *Mainichi* of Tokyo.) It is also known that one year before the 1949 victory over the Kuomintang Stalin had said that any attempt at revolution would be premature. What was more, the Soviet embassy maintained diplomatic ties with the Kuomintang until the end of the civil war. Also, the Soviet Union demanded from the Chinese fighting in Korea a high price for some of their equipment.

Actually, the friction between Mao Tse-tung and Stalin only increased after the founding of the People's Republic. When he arrived in Moscow on his first trip abroad, Mao Tse-tung did not receive the warm welcome he was expecting. Negotiations for the conclusion of a peace and friendship treaty were difficult. The economic and technical aid was more expensive than China had anticipated. Even worse, there were damaging conditions attached to it. According to an article published in *The New York Times* on June 4, 1956, Krushchev had stated a few months before in Warsaw that the main object of his trip to Peking in 1954 was to remove the causes of tension, because Stalin "had demanded too much in return for aid" and Mao Tse-tung had been very embittered by Stalin's insistence on mining concessions and jointly owned companies. Krushchev also said that "the tension in our relations continued until the death of Stalin in 1953."

Sinkiang, that great borderland of Western China, in effect passed under the economic control of the USSR in 1950 because of these jointly owned mining companies. The Russians easily dominated the companies through their capital and their technicians. Mao and other Chinese leaders could hardly help pondering the similarities between the foreign economic presence which they had driven from their eastern coast and this interference by the USSR in the deserts of the west, which China was forced to accept because of its poverty.

In the last years of his life, Stalin made blunder after blunder on China—with, it must be said, the agreement or tacit acceptance of most of the Kremlin leaders. If Krushchev's memoirs are to be believed, Stalin was dreaming of legendary mines full of gold and diamonds which would contribute much to his country. He wanted to turn China's tropical agriculture to the USSR's advantage; he contemplated starting plantations of rubber trees on

Hainan Island and setting up Russian canneries in China for canning tropical produce such as pineapples—in short, Stalin talked as if new worlds were opening up for Soviet workers to colonize. Mao Tse-tung was deeply hurt.

Why did he remain silent? First, because Stalin was fairly skillful at mingling the favorable with the not so favorable. In 1945 for example, after accepting the capitulation of the Japanese army in the northeast of China, the Soviets turned over to Communist troops the war booty taken from the enemy: 1,200 machine guns, 600 tanks, 800 airplanes, 3,700 pieces of artillery, mortars, and grenade launchers—all of which were to prove very useful in the civil war. And in any case Stalin was much too stubborn a man to pay attention to what he called "margarine Communists." Mao Tse-tung might enrage him, but he probably could not make him change his mind on a major point. What was more, China, involved in dangerous operations in Korea and contained on its eastern coasts by the U.S. 7th Fleet since June 1950, urgently needed its powerful ally. From a military point of view, all the armament factories were in the USSR. And from a diplomatic point of view, the Soviets had a seat in the Security Council of the United Nations, where they were using their veto freely. In the area of economics, China was no less dependent. Its first five-year plan began in 1953; Soviet credits assured the financing of a number of industrial projects. A last point in favor of the Russians: in 1955 the Kremlin wiped out a vestige of the colonial era by giving up its bases at Port Arthur and Dairen and by bringing the garrison home.

On a more general level, Mao had no desire to follow the example of Tito, who was rejected by Stalin and resorted to compromises in order to survive, by flirting with the West. It was better to put up with its share of the Kremlin's mistakes and to assert the Chinese way actively, reorganizing the rural economy without eliminating the kulaks, and fighting against bureaucracy with mass campaigns. For Mao Tse-tung and for those close to him, this was the most essential thing. Autonomy was well worth the sacrifice.

Furthermore, the Chinese felt profound respect for Stalin. And they believed that it was really the Soviet Party as a whole that had taken the wrong course. Stalin's death did not change their feelings in the least, as Russian leaders realized. On his return from China in 1954 Krushchev, after remarking how deep the gulf was that separated the two Parties, told his comrades that "conflict with China is inevitable."

In addition, there could be no doubt about Stalin's desire to build socialism in his country and to eliminate reaction. As a consequence Stalin was "relatively good" according to the Chinese formula, and his faults were not serious enough for him to be subjected to international invective. So that Krushchev's speech to the 20th Party Congress and his denunciations of Stalin did not help bring closer ties between the Soviets and the Chinese based on suffering shared in the past; on the contrary, these remarks opened a gap between the two Parties that grew deeper and deeper with each passing year.

"Then what was it that Comrade Stalin did? He developed this principle, he developed Marxism-Leninism and on behalf of oppressed people throughout the world defined a series of theses which are completely specific, vivid, and clear— namely, an entire theory about the establishment of a revolutionary front, the overthrow of imperialism and capitalism, and the formation of a socialist society."
Speech celebrating Stalin's birthday, Yenan,
December 21, 1939

The two regimes still disagree about the question of Stalin. And the question has not been satisfactorily settled in either Moscow or Peking. Mao Tse-tung's position is expressed in two texts published in 1956 entitled "On the Historical Experience of the Dictatorship of the Proletariat." Mao Tse-tung told Edgar Snow that they reflected his point of view on the question.

These two articles clearly show that the Chinese leaders, with Mao at their head, had long known where to stop in their criticism of the Secretary-General of the Soviet Party. These are the essential points:

"During the last period of his life [Stalin] made certain serious mistakes in his work as principal leader of the Party and the state. He became infatuated with himself, and lacked perspective . . . . He accepted and encouraged the personality cult and made arbitrary personal decisions." He made "serious mistakes which affected the whole nation for a long time . . . . He placed too much emphasis on the problem of repressing counter-revolutionaries. Although he punished a number of counter-revolutionaries who had to be punished, and essentially did what he had to do in this area, he also gratuitously accused many loyal Communists and good citizens, which gave rise to serious miscarriages of justice . . . . At times, he interfered unduly in the domestic affairs of certain fellow countries and certain fellow Parties, and this had many serious consequences.'' Mao Tse-tung was more explicit on this last point in the interview given to Japanese journalists which I quoted earlier.

"Late in his life the series of victories and panegyrics about him turned his head . . . . He began to have a blind faith in his own wisdom and his own authority. He refused to devote himself to investigation and to the serious study of complex situations, or to listen attentively to his comrades' opinions or to the voice of the masses.''

This, then, is the essence of Mao's (and China's) criticism of Stalin. This official text is very moderate; nevertheless, it calls a spade a spade. It is enough to show that for a long time Peking felt little esteem for Lenin's successor.

Clearly, China's criticisms were inspired by Krushchev's speech to the 20th Party Congress. Mao Tse-tung said that the efforts of the new leader of the Soviet Party to wipe out the mistakes of the past were "courageous." But at that time he hardly approved of the way in which Stalin was being exposed to public indignation. Stalin had faults, but the Soviet Party and its leaders had also made mistakes. What was open to question was the whole "working method" of the Russian Communists—their weak ties with the popular masses, the fact that the ruling class was more and more cut off from the people, and because of this was losing its revolutionary impetus. In short, Stalin had sinned not through an excess of socialist zeal but through insufficient confidence in the masses and thus through a lack of belief in socialism and a failure to practice socialism: "As soon as he places himself above the Party and the masses instead of remaining among them, as soon as he separates himself from the masses, any leader of the Party or the state necessarily ceases to have a complete, penetrating view of the affairs of state.''

But, said Mao and his comrades, "Stalin's mistakes are in no way a result of the socialist system" and so one should not "throw out the baby with the bath water." And because of this the discussions within the Communist movement in 1956 marked a turning point. Up to then the socialist bloc had somehow or other maintained its unity. After the 20th Congress this unity was shattered. Mao Tse-tung and Krushchev came to diametrically opposite conclusions about Stalin's record.

Let me sum up the Chinese point of view: Stalin led the life of a great revolutionary; he fought Czarism, helped organize the taking of power by the Bolsheviks, and struggled to defend the revolution; he was an intransigent enemy of imperialism. "The tragedy of Stalin was that even while he was making mistakes he believed that what he was doing was necessary to defend the interests of the workers against the attacks of the enemy . . . . We believe that if one compared Stalin's mistakes to what he accomplished, the mistakes would seem of secondary importance."

The problem, Mao and his friends went on to say, was that not only Stalin had to be judged, but "all the comrades who made similar mistakes under his influence." Mao Tse-tung was well aware that most of those comrades were still in power in 1956, and so he urged the Kremlin to practice collective self-criticism, and not be content with abusing Stalin as a scapegoat. Besides, wasn't Moscow continuing to make the same mistakes the dead dictator had made, by almost interfering in Poland, by sending troops into Hungary—which Mao Tse-tung opposed? The Chinese leaders pointed out that their own Communist Party had always earnestly endeavored to apply the principles of democratic centralism and collective control, and had included among its 1956 Congress resolutions to fight against "large-power chauvinism."

Eagles and Hens

Seven years later the break became definitive. Mao Tse-tung was completely against the direction in which Krushchev was taking the Soviet regime, both in domestic and in foreign affairs. The Soviet criticism of Stalin seemed to him to constitute the starting point of "Soviet revisionism." Mao Tse-tung therefore became Stalin's defender. In the 1963 pamphlet entitled "On the Question of Stalin," he insisted upon the need to make a fair appraisal of the Soviet leader's mistakes and was ironical about "revisionist poultry," quoting Lenin:

"It sometimes happens that eagles fly lower than hens, but hens never manage to rise to the height of eagles!" August Bebel and Rosa Luxemburg (and Mao implicitly included Stalin too) were "great Communists," even though they made mistakes. They remained "eagles," while the revisionists (here the reference is to the Soviet leaders of 1963) were nothing but "poultry" on the "dung heap" in "the backyard of the workers' movement."

The Two Swords

"I believe there are two 'swords': one is Lenin and the other Stalin. The Russians have now rejected the sword which is Stalin. Haven't certain Soviet leaders rejected the sword which is Lenin as well? I think they largely have. Is the October Revolution still valid? Can it still serve as an example to other countries? In his report to the 20th Congress of the Communist Party of the Soviet Union, Krushchev says that it is possible to come to power in a parliamentary way. Put another way, other countries need no longer follow the example of the October Revolution. Once this door is opened, Leninism has virtually been rejected."

Speech before the Central
Committee of the Chinese Communist Party
delivered on November 15, 1956

At the time the discussion about Stalin was only part of the larger controversy over the line of the international Communist movement. Starting in 1956, this controversy evolved rather quickly from purely theoretical debates into a cold war punctuated by exchanges of gunfire at the border.

Earlier, I described Mao Tse-tung's theoretical ideas and showed how different from the Soviet point of view they were. Mao saw the Soviet Union as a class state, with an exploitative ruling class and an oppressed majority. This dictatorship of the bourgeoisie wore a socialist disguise. Worst of all it was pushing other workers' parties in the same direction—toward betrayal of revolution, and the revision of Marxism until it had no more revolutionary content.

Behind the ideological controversy between the Parties developed a dispute between the states. The alliance of the two countries, conceived in 1950 as everlasting, underwent some rude shocks. Krushchev's bluntness, his extemporaneous speeches, and his aggressiveness only made matters worse.

By 1956, Mao Tse-tung knew that the Soviet Union could no longer be set before the Chinese people as a model. His own Party was actually richer in experience, and it had not made mistakes like Stalin's massive purges of 1937–38. The Chinese press opened its columns to popular criticism and did not close them until 1957, when the fault-finders passed from denouncing faults to questioning the regime itself. Mao Tse-tung systematized his doctrine, asserting that the dictatorship of the proletariat was not directed against the people, but only the former ruling classes. He thus suggested what the Soviet Union should have done in the past, what it should be doing at the moment—what it was not doing, he insinuated.

The Break

In 1957 the productive forces in cities and rural areas were working in collective organizations; the economy was at least as socialist as in the USSR. Why not go further? Starting the following year, China continued on the path toward socialism on its own, all energies gathered behind the Party Chairman.

In the meantime two disputes had arisen, pushing Mao Tse-tung to choose an independent way. Both were related to military problems. In 1958 Krushchev reported, "We needed to have a radio station in Chinese territory in order to remain in contact" with submarines situated at a distance from Soviet territory. The Chinese refused. The following year the Soviets, finding Vladivostok an inadequate base for their Asian strategies, asked for a base where they could provision crews, repair ships, and rest men on leave. Mao Tse-tung personally refused. His later interpretation of the request was extremely dry. In September 1962 he stated before the Central Committee: "During the second half of 1958, Krushchev conceived the plan of having a combined Chinese and Soviet fleet and in this way attempted to place the coasts of China under the control of the USSR and to organize a blockade of China" (see *Mainichi,* March 9, 1967). The following year, the *People's Daily* gave an official tone to this accusation: in 1958 the leaders of the Communist Party of the Soviet Union "had wanted to put China under Soviet military control."

Then in August 1958 the second crisis over the Straits of Taiwan erupted. It seemed Chinese strategy was based on support supposedly forthcoming from the Soviet Union should the United States decide to save the Nationalist regime by bombing the mainland. Krushchev refused to involve his country, promising only that the USSR would provide China with all the material and moral support it needed to defend itself. In preparing for the reconquest of Taiwan, Mao Tse-tung and Chou En-lai had undoubtedly misunderstood Krushchev's attitude. Once again they were forced to realize that China could rely only upon its own forces. When in the following year Krushchev broke his commitments of 1957 and decided not to provide the technical assistance that would have allowed China to build atomic weapons, it was the last straw.

In the preceding few months the country had become a seething cauldron for the experimental application of revolutionary formulas to the economy, technology, administration, universities, and so on. Caught in the fever of the Great Leap Forward, China searched for its own path without the help of the Soviets. Mao Tse-tung ran the risk of tense relations with Moscow. A number of Soviet experts, whose duties were to work out plans and install equipment, no longer found themselves usefully employed, although this was not true in heavy industry which still needed them.

By 1960 Chinese agriculture had come to a sorry pass. Too much technical improvisation had worn out the soils; lower echelon cadres often had trouble following "the movement," moving too fast or hanging back, and sometimes even openly hostile to the experiment; and lastly, catastrophic droughts hit a number of provinces for the second year in succession. Grain production fell dramatically. Without its agricultural base, China's entire economy tottered. This was the moment Krushchev chose to recall all Soviet experts without warning.

In retrospect, the silence maintained by the two parties immediately afterward, especially the silence of the Chinese, is astonishing. In 1960 Chou En-lai said piously and untruthfully that "the departure of a large number of Soviet experts was quite natural. They came to work in China for a temporary period, so they were bound to leave eventually." Four years later the Central Committee—on Mao's initiative, no doubt—denounced this violation of the friendship treaty and emphasized its gravity: "A large number of our scientific research projects had to be cut off in the middle; other construction projects had to be suspended and certain factories and mines which had reached the stage of trial production could not be put into operation according to plan."

The silence between 1960 and 1963 did not stop the conflict from becoming gradually more and more bitter. China challenged the frontiers and in 1960 asked to open negotiations. Gunfire broke out in the disputed regions. In 1962 the Sinkiang frontier was closed after 60,000 Chinese nationals, mostly Uigurs, crossed into Kazakhstan. Peking asserted that they had been "incited" and "coerced" by the Soviet government. The 1964 talks came to nothing.

By 1963 Mao Tse-tung was no longer content with "insulting the mulberry tree by pointing to the acacia"—in other words abusing Yugoslavia as a way of denouncing the Soviet Union. He decided to name his target, and he concentrated his attacks on Krushchev. The departure of Krushchev began a brief period of hope. But the polemic began again all the more vigorously in 1965. Mao was followed, though at a certain distance, by the Cubans, the North Koreans, and the Japanese Communist Party; the Albanians were right beside him. The Vietnam war intensified. In socialist circles everywhere leaders wondered: shouldn't we accept a United Front with the Russians in order to help Hanoi and the National Liberation Front more effectively? The question was asked by the Vietnamese, the Koreans, the Japanese, and also by Moscow, which because of its financial and military strength could be sure of being in command. No, said Chairman Mao Tse-tung and Minister of Defense Lin Piao: The most important thing was not foreign military aid but what was going on inside Vietnam—the people's war itself. Help for Vietnam was indispensable, but it did not require an alliance with Moscow.

The Cultural Revolution swept out most of those members of the army, the state and the Party who were in favor of reestablishing some contact with the Soviets. Mao Tse-tung urged the people of China to say what they knew about their bourgeois leaders. Chief of State Liu Shao-ch'i and Chief of Staff Lo Juiching joined former Defense Minister P'eng Teh-huai, ousted in 1959, in the ranks of Soviet supporters. The ghost of Kao Kang was evoked—a former Vice-Prime Minister and Party leader in the northeast, who had been seduced by the Kremlin and who died in 1955. Much later still—but not without good reason, given the circumstances under which he disappeared—the last great man ousted by the Cultural Revolution, Lin Piao, would be accused of having had the support of the USSR in his conspiracies.

Of all Chinese leaders, Mao Tse-tung was undoubtedly the one who felt the most profound scorn for the Krushchev and post-Krushchev Soviet regimes. During an interview given on May 11, 1964, he did not mince words: "In the Soviet Union at present there is a dictatorship of the bourgeoisie, of the upper bourgeoisie, a dictatorship like the German fascist dictatorship, like Hitler's dictatorship.'' No compromise was possible where principles were concerned, because, as he said in August of the same year, ''revisionism in power means the bourgeoisie in power.''

Yet the harshness of this judgment had no direct connection with what happened in 1967. Moscow's embassy in Peking was ransacked by Leftist elements, and Soviet diplomats subsequently left China.

Volleys of Gunfire

In 1968 there was a new development: the Soviet Union invaded Czechoslovakia. China denounced this ''social imperialism''—defined by Mao Tse-tung as socialism in words, imperialism in action. And comparing it to the U.S. invasion of Vietnam, the Chinese said that the Kremlin was ''a little brother of the White House,'' its nature was the same, they were two badgers from the same hill.

The following year tensions reached their height: hundreds of dead lay on the frozen banks of the Ussuri River and on the sandy islands tucked away in the bends of the Amur River. There were numerous incidents on the Sinkiang border, the weakest point in China's defenses. China feared a raid on its atomic installations in the northwest, a move which obviously tempted some of the Soviet general staff. Mao Tse-tung composed a slogan which was adopted by all of China: ''If no one attacks us, we will not attack; if we are attacked, we will counterattack.''

At last, Kosygin made a quick stopover in Peking in September, and negotiations were opened on October 20. There were fewer incidents, but even so the two countries strengthened their border garrisons. The countries could not agree on how to approach the border problem. Even negotiations about navigation in the Ussuri, Songhua, and Amur Rivers, used by the fishermen and bargemen of both countries, came to nothing. Yet in 1970 the ambassadors returned to their posts and commercial exchanges tentatively started up again. Mao Tse-tung did not concentrate on these specific problems. Anyway, the era of large-scale controversy was over, and Mao no longer felt there was any use in arguing with adversaries who were ideologically ''incurable.''

A Small Compromise

At the end of May 1971, the Lebanese newspaper *An Nahar* published an interview with Chou En-lai by Arab journalists. This passage is taken from it:

"Prime Minister Kosygin stopped off in Peking in 1965 and met with Mao. The latter sarcastically suggested to him that he send Krushchev—'now that you have defeated him'—to study Marxism in the Chinese universities. 'No,' said Kosygin, 'we should concentrate on the fundamental controversy between the two parties.' Chairman Mao answered: 'That controversy could go on for ten thousand years.' Kosygin: 'That would be longer than necessary.' Mao: 'We will accept a small compromise. We will reduce that period by one thousand years, so that it will last nine thousand years. But the fundamental controversy will not affect relations between our two states.' Kosygin, Chou En-lai added, 'was completely satisfied with this statement.'"

However, Mao Tse-tung urged his fellow citizens not to lose hope for the USSR. In its Leftist phase, the Cultural Revolution supported and publicized certain clandestine Russian organizations, for example the "Stalin Group." Such support soon became out of the question however.

Still, some of Mao's quotations have always urged the Chinese to expect a revolutionary upsurge from its large neighbor—the Soviet Party as a whole could be put back on the right path if only its present leaders were thrown out:

"Even though control of the Soviet Party and state have at present been usurped by revisionists, I advise my comrades to maintain the firm conviction that the Soviet people—the great mass of Party members and cadres—are good or relatively good and want revolution, and that this domination by revisionism will not go on for long" (January 1962).

"The popular masses, including those in the Soviet Union, want revolution. In the international Communist movement, the overwhelming majority of Communists and cadres, including those of the Communist Party of the Soviet Union, want revolution . . . . It is possible that for a while certain people will not see the situation clearly and will allow themselves to be deceived or will even make mistakes, but since they want revolution, in the end they will sooner or later break with revisionism and go over to the side of Marxism-Leninism.'' (Commentary on the Moscow meeting of March 23, 1965.)

It might seem as though these statements contradict the ones reported by Chou En-lai in the box above. In fact, after the 1971 crisis these quotations were hardly read any more. One can easily imagine how useful they could be to people in favor of compromise with Moscow. It is equally possible that in the last few years of his life Mao changed his analysis of the Soviet regime, becoming more aware of the importance of revisionism and its influence on very large sectors of the Soviet population. Whatever the case, Mao remained convinced that all countries would one day come to socialism. For Chinese history—which thinks of itself in terms of millenia—''one day'' could mean in several years, or in a century, or perhaps even longer.

7/Mao Tse-tung the Poet: Classicist and Revolutionary

What place should we give Mao Tse-tung the poet in a work entirely devoted to Mao Tse-tung the political man? A leader who retires from the world in order to compose a poetic image of it is not a ruthless, power-hungry politician, nor is he one of those militants who inevitably become impoverished by a constant involvement with immediate concerns. The beauty of Mao Tse-tung's poetry adds a human dimension to the political figure, a depth and tenderness lacking in most professional revolutionaries.

He was never a prolific poet. Since 1957, thirty-eight small texts have been published—belatedly and after some hesitation. While Mao Tse-tung wrote in the old style, his desire was that younger generations free literature from the conventions of the past, that they write free verse, or at least verse free of the strict demands of assonance and the alternation of tones. This was why he was reluctant to publish his poems, afraid of serving as a model and slowing down creativity.

Mao's art is classical in form and in the shaping of a thought, but its content has a revolutionary tension. Its attitude is detached. Mao's verses are heavy with the past, laden with reveries, rising above the moment to express the nature of things, a little as Lucretius once did.

> So long desiring to be near the clouds,
> I returned to climb the peaks of Chingkang . . .
> Everywhere the oriole sang and the swallow danced
> And the murmuring water flowed.
>
> *Return to Chingkangshan*

But there is no resemblance to Western romantic poetry in this return to the mountain stronghold of the underground.

In 1965 the poet looks at how far they have come; man has liberated himself:

> A snap of the fingers, and thirty-eight years pass
> Through the ninth heaven, we embrace the moon
> At the bottom of the sea and catch turtles—
> Joy and triumphal songs return.

He concludes:

> Nothing in this world is difficult,
> We need only have the will to climb.

The process is typical. There can be no love of life without love of the world, no love of the world without contemplation, and all contemplation arouses the will. One look at the world unleashes in Mao Tse-tung the reveries of the will.

Even in his dreams he is still the man of action, the man of courage, in pursuit of a present a thousand times more beautiful than the past, at least for the people; he rejects the idea of the Golden Age.

On a February day in 1936, he contemplates the snow on the plains of the North, "A thousand li* sealed with ice, and snow flies over ten thousand li . . ." then sees the river with its frozen waters, as though it had not moved for centuries. But countless heroes, he muses, were needed to defend this beautiful country. Suddenly he cuts short his patriotic outburst: the men of today are just as worthy as those of yesterday:

> Alas, the Tsin emperor and the Han warrior
> neglected culture,
> Tsung of the T'ang and Tsu of the Sung
> wrote no verse,
> Genghis Khan, the pearl of heaven,
> Could only string his bow against the eagles.
> They are all gone.

---

*Chinese unit of measurement.

And Mao Tse-tung concludes:

> To find men of talent,
> Let us look to our own time.

What is expressed in these two verses—the desire to act and to sense the grandeur of the present—was later transposed into the symbolic slogan "Yesterday's heroes are dead, today's heroes are working."

Mao writes in an epic tone when he celebrates the exploits of the Red Army. "High are the mountains and shadowy the valleys," went the *Song of Roland*—of which Mao's verses are reminiscent:

> The clatter of horses' hooves rings sharp,
> And the bugle's note is muted.
> Do not say the strong pass is guarded with iron.
> This very day with long steps we shall pass its summit.

And later, with the nostalgia of an Asian Homer:

> Happiness to see the rice flow in a thousand waves
> And the hero return in the evening mist.

And with the pride of a fighter whose resoluteness and boldness have made him victorious, in the Chingkang mountains again, birthplace of the People's Army:

> At the foot of the mountain wave banners and flags,
> At the peak of the mountain our horns and drums resound,
> The enemy has encircled us a thousand, ten thousand times
>> around.
> Unyielding, we are like the highest peak . . .

The strength of man is as apparent in his work as on the battlefield. In earlier days the Red Army fought to conquer China; now the People's Republic is fighting to master the elements. One day in June 1959, when the Great Leap Forward still seemed full of promise, Mao Tse-tung returned to Shaoshan, his birthplace, and meditated:

Ready for sacrifice, firm and resolute,
They dare demand the sun and moon
To shine in a new sky.

Mao dreamed of a bridge that men would build over the great river that divides China in two, the majestic Yangtze:

The wind stirs the masts,
The tortoise and the snake are still.
A grandiose plan appears to me:
From south to north a bridge will be built
Connecting the two sides of the mighty abyss.

All of Mao Tse-tung's poems are constructed this way: written according to a strict form, they draw on two thousand years of culture to exalt the beauties of China, which has been liberated from its troubles—from foreigners, from sickness, from apathy. As he says one autumn morning in Changsha:

Every being, under this frosty sky, struggles to be free.

The past and the present are also combined this way in the new Chinese opera: "Let us make new verses with the old rhythms." Songs about the fight against Japan are written in the pentatonic scale, and Mao evokes the same theme within the formal pattern of the ch'ing p'ing lu ("pure and calm air") poem:

When will we bind the green dragon?

Mao showed that formal purity is perfectly compatible with revolutionary themes, that far from diminishing the effect, it increases and accentuates it. Of course, he did not renovate poetic form; others have devoted themselves to that, and have been successful. Nonetheless, he made a major contribution. By using classical versification and entirely ignoring free verse, he showed that revolutionary emotion could adapt to the most implacable formal rigor.

He explained himself straightforwardly in his famous Yenan interviews: "What we need is the unity of politics and art, the unity of content and form, the unity of a revolutionary political content and an artistic form of the highest possible level."

three/
Mao Tse-tung: Extracts from His Speeches and writings

Marxism—a Guide, Not a Dogma[1]

The great complexity of Marxism can be summed up in one phrase: "We are right to revolt." For centuries, people said it was right to oppress and exploit the people, but that it was wrong to rebel. Marxism says just the opposite. It is a great contribution, this thesis which Marx formulated on the basis of the proletarian struggle. Taking this thesis as their fundamental principle, people resist, fight, and work for socialism.

On the occasion of Stalin's sixtieth birthday, 1939

We are Marxists, and Marxism teaches that in our approach to a problem we should start from objective facts, not from abstract definitions, and that we should derive our guiding principles, policies, and measures from an analysis of these facts.

"Talks at the Yenan Forum on
Literature and Art." 1942 (P.E.)

The most fundamental method of work which all Communists must firmly bear in mind is to determine our working policies according to actual conditions. When we study the causes of the mistakes we have made, we find that they all arose because we departed from the actual situation at a given time and place and were subjective in our working policies.

"Speech at a Conference of Cadres in
the Shansi-Suiyan Liberated Area,"
1948 (P.E.)

---

[1]Texts marked "P.E." are taken directly from the "Peking Editions": *Selected Works of Mao Tse-tung* (Peking: Foreign Language Press, 1961, 1965). The remaining texts, except where otherwise indicated, are the author's and translators' renderings.

If we are so used to China's problems that we no longer see them; if we put on glasses and still do not see them; if we see only the works of Marx, Engels, Lenin, and Stalin on our bookshelves, then our theoretical work will undoubtedly be very bad.

"Reform our Study," 1942, from the original
edition as quoted by Stuart Schram

The theory of Marx, Engels, Lenin, and Stalin is universally applicable. We should regard it not as a dogma, but as a guide to action. Studying it is not merely a matter of learning terms and phrases but of learning Marxism-Leninism as the science of revolution.

"The Role of the Chinese Communist Party
in the National War," 1938 (P.E.)

Some people have read a few Marxist books and think themselves quite learned, but what they have read has not penetrated, has not struck root in their minds . . . . In order to have a real grasp of Marxism, one must learn it not only from books, but mainly through class struggle, through practical work and close contact with the masses of workers and peasants.

"Speech at the Chinese Communist
Party's National Conference on
Propaganda Work," 1957 (P.E.)

Marxism must certainly advance; it must develop along with the development of practice and cannot stand still.

Ibid.

While we recognize that in the general development of history the material determines the mental, and social being determines social consciousness, we also—and indeed must—recognize the reaction of mental on material things, of social consciousness on social being and of the superstructure on the economic base.

"On Contradiction," 1937 (P.E.)

If we have a correct theory but merely prate about it, pigeonhole it and do not put it into practice, then that theory, however good, is of no significance.

"On Practice," 1937 (P.E.)

When applying Marxism to China, Communists should join the general truth of Marxism to the specific practice of China's revolution fully and appropriately; in other words, Marxism will not be useful unless it is combined with the characteristics of the nation and assumes a particular national form; there is no way it can be applied in a subjective or rigid manner. Rigid Marxists are only making a mockery of Marxism and the Chinese revolution; there is no place for them among the ranks of our revolution.

"On New Democracy," 1940

Movement and Contradiction Are Universal

Mankind will never cease to move forward and nature will never cease to develop; neither will ever stop at a certain level. Man, too, should constantly appraise his experience and discover, invent, create, and move forward. Points of view which are inspired by opposition to progress, pessimism, a feeling of impotence, pride, or presumption are erroneous. And the reason they are erroneous is that they do not correspond to the historical facts of the development of human society over the past million years or so, nor to the historical facts of nature as far as we are able to know them (nature as it is reflected, for example, in the history of the celestial bodies, Earth, life, and other natural sciences).

Quoted by Chou En-lai in his report
to the National Assembly, 1964

There is no construction without destruction, no flowing without damming and no moving without halting.

"On New Democracy," 1940 (P.E.)

Nature and society are full of contradictions. As soon as one is resolved, another appears. There is no such thing as a world or a society without contradictions. Sometimes we are not able to point to a specific contradiction and yet it still exists. Contradictions are the moving force behind the development of all things. This was true in the past, it is true today, and it will continue to be true tomorrow.

1966

In a society in which there are classes, the class struggle will never end, and in a classless society the struggle between what is old and what is new, between what is true and what is false, will continue indefinitely.

Quoted by Chou En-lai before
the National Assembly, 1964

The fundamental cause of the development of a thing is not external but internal; it lies in the contradictoriness within the thing . . . . External causes are the condition of change and internal causes are the basis of change, and external causes become operative through internal causes. In a suitable temperature an egg changes into a chicken, but no temperature can change a stone into a chicken.

"On Contradiction," 1937 (P.E.)

The existence of contradictions is universal, but their nature is different according to the nature of things. In each specific thing, the unity of opposites is conditional, temporary, transitional, and therefore relative; while the struggle of opposites is absolute.

Ibid.

If in any process there are a number of contradictions, one of them must be the principal contradiction playing the leading and decisive role, while the rest occupy a secondary and subordinate position. Therefore, in studying any complex process in which there are two or more contradictions, we must devote every effort to finding its principal contradiction. Once this principal contradiction is grasped, all problems can be readily solved.

Ibid.

Of the two contradictory aspects, one must be principal and the other secondary. The principal aspect is the one playing the leading role in the contradiction . . . . But this situation is not static; the principal and the nonprincipal aspects of a contradiction transform themselves into each other and the nature of the thing changes accordingly.

Ibid.

Class Conflicts Are Permanent

If it is true that even today there are still royalist deputies in that bourgeois institution, the French National Assembly, then it is highly likely that long after all exploitative classes have finally disappeared from the surface of the earth, representatives of Chiang Kai-shek's dynasty will still be active here and there. The most recalcitrant of them will never admit their defeat. They feel the need not only to deceive others but to deceive themselves as well. Otherwise they could no longer live.

> "Commentaries to Materials for a
> Critique of Hu Feng's Counter-
> revolutionary group," *People's
> Daily,* June 10,1955

Classes and the class struggle continue to exist in a socialist society, as does the struggle between the socialist way and the capitalist way. A socialist revolution on the economic front alone—taking over ownership of the means of production—is not enough and does not guarantee that it can keep what it has won. There must be a parallel socialist revolution on the political and ideological fronts.

Socialist society lasts for quite a long period of history, during which classes and class contradictions continue to exist . . . as well as the danger that capitalism will be restored. We must realize that this struggle will be a long and complex one, we must increase our vigilance and continue socialist education [otherwise] it will not be long—a few years, perhaps, or a decade, several decades at most—before a nationwide counterrevolutionary restoration will take place, the Marxist-Leninist Party will become a revisionist party, a fascist party, and all of China will change color . . . .

Starting now, we should discuss this question—day after day, month after month, year after year—in order to understand it clearly enough and be able to follow a Marxist-Leninist line.

> Central Committee conference of
> August 1962, and Central Committee
> 10-point decision of May 1973

When circumstances are against them, members of the exploitative classes usually resort to attack in order to defend themselves, to protect their present existence and arrange possibilities for their future development. Either they fabricate stories and spread rumors among the people, or they take advantage of certain superficial incidents to attack essential things, or they sing the praises of some people while attacking others, or else they take the slightest excuse to divide us and make trouble for us. In short, they are constantly seeking ways to oppose us and are always on the lookout for a chance to carry through their schemes successfully. Sometimes they lie low and wait for a chance to return to the attack. They are experienced in the class struggle and know how to fight in every way—legal and illegal. As members of a revolutionary Party, we ought to become familiar with their tricks and study their tactics in order to overcome them; in any case we certainly should not be as naive as the scholars buried in their books, who view the class struggle simplistically when it is actually so complex.

People's Daily, June 10, 1955

Opposition and struggle between ideas of different kinds constantly occur within the Party; this is a reflection within the Party of contradictions between classes and between the new and the old in society. If there were no contradictions in the Party and no ideological struggles to resolve them, the Party's life would come to an end.

"On Contradiction," 1937 (P.E.)

Beyond one party, there exist other parties, and even within a party there are different groups; it has always been this way.

People's Daily, April 27, 1968

We have already won great victories. But the defeated class will continue to struggle against us. Those people are still there, and that class still exists. This is why we cannot speak of a final victory, even over the next few decades. We must not relax our vigilance. According to Leninist thinking, the final victory of a socialist country depends not only upon the efforts of the proletariat and the great popular masses of that country, but also on the victory of a worldwide revolution, on the elimination of the system of exploitation of man by man in the world, resulting in the emancipation of all of humanity. As a consequence, it is an anti-Leninist mistake to speak lightly of the final victory of our revolution; and what is more, it does not correspond to the real situation.

Quoted in Lin Piao's report to the 9th Congress of the Chinese Communist Party, 1969

The transition period is full of contradictions and struggles. The revolutionary struggle we are engaged in now goes even deeper than the earlier armed revolutionary struggle. It is a revolution which will bury the capitalist regime and all other systems of exploitation forever.

Quoted in "The Struggle between the Two Tendencies in the Chinese Countrysides," *Red Flag,* November 1967

Later, the proletarian parties and the dictatorship of the proletariat will no longer exist, but today they are absolutely indispensable: without them we would not be able to suppress the counterrevolution, resist imperialism, and build socialism. In order to attain these objectives, the dictatorship of the proletariat must remain to a large extent coercive. This makes it necessary to fight bureaucracy and the proliferation of organizations. I propose that we get rid of two-thirds of the Party and government organizations.

"Ten Major Relations," April 1956

"A Communist Party Is Necessary"

In order to bring about the revolution, there must be a nucleus at its center.

Quoted by Chou En-lai, September 1966

Without a revolutionary Party, without a Party based on the Marxist-Leninist theory of revolution and the Marxist-Leninist style of revolution, it is impossible to lead the working class and the great popular masses to victory . . . . Revolutionary forces throughout the world, unite and fight against imperialist aggression.

1948

In order to conduct a large-scale revolution, one must have a large Party and many first-rate cadres . . . . These cadres and these leaders must assimilate Marxism-Leninism, be politically perceptive, competent in work, filled with the spirit of self-sacrifice, capable of resolving problems by themselves, unshakable in the face of difficulties and completely devoted to the nation, their class, and the Party . . . . Let us fight to draw the masses by the millions into the anti-Japanese national united front.

1937

In order to unite the Party and the people, we must put democracy fully into practice. This holds true both inside the Party as well as outside it . . . . As long as the minority accepts the decisions of the majority, it can hold to its different opinions. It is a good thing to apply this principle as much within the Party as outside of it. If you allow the others to keep their erroneous opinions for a time, it will be easier for them to abandon them later. Besides, it often happens that the minority is in the right.

> Speech to the enlarged session of the January
> 1962 Central Committee, printed in *Théorie et
> Politique*, No. 2, April 1974

Man has arteries and veins; through the heart they circulate his blood, and he breathes with his lungs, breathing out carbon dioxide and breathing in fresh oxygen—that is he rejects what has been spoiled and absorbs what is new. In the same way the proletarian Party must reject what has been spoiled and absorb what is new, in order to be fully dynamic. Without rejecting waste and absorbing new blood, the Party could not be dynamic.

> *Red Flag,* No. 4, 1968

[In the Party] a political atmosphere must be created in which there are both centralism and democracy, discipline and freedom, unity of will and—in each individual—a spirit of satisfaction and liveliness.

> "Chengtu Speech," 1958. Printed in
> the Party statutes in 1969 and 1973

We must affirm anew the discipline of the Party, namely: (1) the individual is subordinate to the organization; (2) the minority is subordinate to the majority; (3) the lower level is subordinate to the higher level; (4) the entire membership is subordinate to the Central Committee.

> "The Role of the Chinese Communist Party
> in the National War," 1938 (P.E.)

Of these seven sectors—industry, agriculture, commerce, culture and teaching, the army, the government, and the Party—it is the Party which controls them all.

> Quoted in the reports of Chou En-lai
> and Wang Hong-wen before the 10th
> Congress, 1973

[We must] unify the various points of view, the political measures, the plans, the leadership, and the actions.

> Meeting of the Central Committee of January
> 1962, quoted in Wang Hong-wen's report
> to the 10th Congress, 1973

Who gave us this power? The working class, the poor and middle peasants, the working masses who form more than 90 percent of the population. We represent the proletariat and the popular masses, we have overthrown the enemies of the people, and the people support us. A fundamental principle of the Communist Party is to rely directly on the great popular masses.

Red Flag, No. 4, 1968

Repressing the Counterrevolution

A counterrevolutionary is a negative, destructive element; he is the opposite of a positive element . . . . There are inevitably some diehards, some stubborn counterrevolutionaries, but in the social conditions that exist today, most of those counter-revolutionaries will change sooner or later. Of course, some won't have time to change before the God of Hell invites them down to join him. As for the others, who knows when they will change?

[Because of our policy of reeducation through work] some of them are doing useful work and doing it enthusiastically for the benefit of everyone.

[Who was executed during the 1951–52 campaign?] Those whom the people hated the most, those who had contracted a series of blood debts. In a revolution which has affected six hundred million people, if we did not kill a few villains, if we put up with their presence, the masses would certainly object. It is important to state that the execution of these people in the past was justified. That is the first point.

The second is that the number of counterrevolutionaries is much lower . . . . But there are still a few who continue their work of sabotage. For example, they have killed animals, burned grain, destroyed factories, stolen information, and pasted up reactionary posters. From now on, we should go by this principle where they are involved: fewer arrests and fewer executions. Most of them should go into agricultural cooperatives for forced labor and reeducation. But we cannot yet stop executions altogether: if a counterrevolutionary kills someone or blows up a factory, should he be executed? Without any question.

The third point concerns the elimination of counterrevolution in administrations, schools, and army units. According to the principle adopted at Yenan, "do not kill a solitary wolf; do not arrest a crowd." Some are not executed, not because their crime was slight, but because there would have been no point in executing them. It would be better to let them live. Where is the harm in not killing a solitary wolf? If he can change through working, let him do it, and what was useless will become useful. Besides, a head is not like a leek: it will not grow again once it has been cut off. If one cuts it off by mistake, there is no way to put right this mistake . . . .

We must allow counterrevolutionaries to live, and leave them a way out. This will have a good effect on the people and will improve our image abroad.

"Ten Major Relations," April 1956

The Attitude toward Non-Communist Parties

Our policy towards these people is to encourage unity rather than conflict, since we want to mobilize them in the cause of socialism.

There is no official opposition in China, because all the democratic parties have accepted the leadership of the Chinese Communist Party. But in actual fact, certain members of the democratic parties constitute a form of opposition. On the question of "carrying the revolution to the very end," of the direction of our foreign policy [in favor of socialist countries—Author's note], of opposing America by helping Korea, and also on agrarian reform, these people equivocate. They have their own ideas about eliminating counterrevolutionaries. They support the Common Program but show no interest in a Constitution. Yet when the project of forming a Constitution was announced, they raised their hands in approval . . . . They are the opposition and at the same time they are not. Their patriotism often induces them to switch from a position of opposition to one of acceptance.

Relations between the Communist Party and the democratic parties must be improved. We must allow them to express their own views. As long as these people are reasonable, we will accept their ideas, no matter what they are. That is the rational thing to do—for the Party, for the state, for the people and for socialism.

"Ten Major Relations," April 1956

Encourage Debates and Accept Criticism

We must not be afraid of opening wide, nor should we be afraid of criticism and poisonous weeds. Marxism is scientific truth; it fears no criticism and cannot be defeated by criticism. The same holds for the Communist Party and the People's Government; they fear no criticism and cannot be defeated by it. There will always be some things that are wrong, and that is nothing to be afraid of.

"Speech at the Chinese Communist
Party's National Conference on
Propaganda Work," 1957 (P.E.)

If Marxism feared criticism, and if it could be overthrown by criticism, it would be worthless . . . . Fighting against wrong ideas is like being vaccinated—a man develops greater immunity from disease as a result of vaccination. Plants raised in hothouses are unlikely to be sturdy.

"On the Correct Handling of Contradictions among the People,"

Just because you let the people speak the sky is not going to collapse, and you won't fall down either. On the other hand, if you deprive other people of the chance to speak, then sooner or later you will inevitably fall.

Speech to an enlarged conference
of the Central Committee, 1966

What are you afraid of? Those who are bad will show it. But why be afraid of good elements? Replace your fear by daring. You must show that in the end you are capable of passing the test of socialism.

Speech to various Party leaders, 1966

Communists must listen attentively to the opinions of non-Communists and give them a chance to express themselves. If what they say is right, we will commend them and we will profit by their strong points; if what they say is false, we should still allow them to say all they have to say, and then patiently explain whatever has to be explained.

Speech to the Assembly of the border region
of Shensi-Kansu-Ningsia, 1941

To educate the people, we must begin by learning from them.
People's Daily, July 15, 1967

The only way to get rid of these evil-minded people is to let them first appear. The only way to root out poisonous plants is to let them come up out of the earth. Don't peasants weed several times a year? Once these plants have been pulled up, they can still be used as fertilizer. "The capitalist line of *Wen-hui Pao* must be criticized."
People's Daily, July 1, 1957

One cannot build without destroying. To destroy is to criticize, to wage a revolution. In order to destroy we must reason, and to reason is to build. So it is that destruction comes first, bearing construction within it.
Circular of the Central Committee, May 16, 1966

Truth is not afraid of being refuted; whatever is afraid of being refuted is not the truth. Anyone who fears criticism is a coward, and anyone who dreads countercriticism is also a coward. Not to permit criticism is to behave like a despot; but isn't it another kind of tyranny to prohibit countercriticism? One must renounce despotism, and reject neither criticism nor countercriticism. To overcome our inadequacies in accomplishing socialism and in our Party work, we must completely open the debate, firmly initiate a constructive revolutionary critique, and continue to remove all obstacles to useful criticism. At the same time, in order to defend socialism, to oppose those "critiques" which destroy socialism, we must resolutely initiate a correct countercriticism. This is the only way our rectification movement will be able to develop in a wholesome way.
People's Daily, June 9, 1957 (attributed to Mao Tse-tung)

The Danger of Revisionism

If it happened that revisionists seized control in China, Marxist-Leninists from all countries would have to denounce them and fight them firmly and help the working class and popular masses of China to oppose revisionism.
People's Daily, November 11, 1965

What would you do if revisionism appeared in the heart of the Central Committee? It is quite possible that this might happen, and that is the greatest danger.

Directive of December 1967

The revisionists, the Right opportunists, pay lip-service to Marxism; they too attack "dogmatism." But what they are really attacking is the quintessence of Marxism. They oppose or distort materialism and dialectics, oppose or try to weaken the people's democratic dictatorship and the leading role of the Communist Party, and oppose or try to weaken socialist transformation and socialist construction.

"On the Correct Handling of Contradictions among the People,"

It is revisionism to negate the basic principles of Marxism and to negate its universal truth. Revisionism is one form of bourgeois ideology. The revisionists deny the differences between socialism and capitalism, between the dictatorship of the proletariat and the dictatorship of the bourgeoisie. What they advocate is in fact not the socialist line but the capitalist line. In present circumstances, revisionism is more pernicious than dogmatism.

"Speech at the Chinese Communist Party's National Conference on Propaganda Work," 1957 (P.E.)

Left to itself, mankind would not necessarily reestablish capitalism . . . . But it would reestablish inequality. The forces which bring new classes into being again are powerful . . . . Krushchev seemed to believe that once a Communist Party took power, the revolution had been completed—as if this were simply a national liberation!

Interview with André Malraux reported in *les Antimémoires*

[Rightist and revisionist elements] appreciate bourgeois liberalism and are opposed to the Party leadership. They are opposed to the idea that culture and education (including the press) be subject to control, planning, and supervision, which are necessary but should not be overly centralized, and are indispensable to the realization of a planned economy. They echo the rightist

intellectuals in society, associate with them, and treat them as
brothers.

"Things are Changing," May 1957

For the People—Democracy

In trying to resolve contradictions among the people one cannot
resort to insults, fistfights, or worst of all, the use of arms. Such
contradictions can only be resolved through discussion, reasoning, criticism, and self-criticism—in short, through democratic
methods which give the masses a chance to express themselves.

Directive of May 1967

In advocating freedom with leadership and democracy under
centralized guidance, we in no way mean that coercive measures
should be taken to settle ideological questions or questions involving the distinction between right and wrong among the
people. All attempts to use administrative orders or coercive measures to settle ideological questions or questions of right and
wrong are not only ineffective but harmful. We cannot abolish
religion by administrative decree or force people not to believe in
it. We cannot compel people to give up idealism, any more than
we can force them to believe in Marxism. The only way to settle
questions of an ideological nature or controversial issues among
the people is by the democratic method, the method of discussion, of criticism, of persuasion and education, and not by the
method of coercion or repression.

"On the Correct Handling of Contradictions among the People,"

Within the Party as outside the Party, democracy must be put
fully into practice . . . . We must really get the problems out in
the open and let the masses speak, even those who insult us.

Directive of March 1966 (P.E.)

Without large-scale democracy for the people, the dictatorship
of the proletariat could not establish itself firmly and political
power would lack stability. Without democracy, without the
mobilization of the masses and their supervision, it would be impossible to exercise an effective dictatorship of the proletariat
over the reactionaries and bad elements, and impossible to go
ahead effectively with their reeducation. They would continue to

provoke disturbances and might even bring on a restoration. This matter calls for your vigilance.

Directive of May 1968

Among the people the advanced and backward elements can compete with one another, making free use of our newspapers, periodicals, forums, etc., so that the former can educate the latter using democratic methods and persuasion, and so that old-fashioned ideas and systems can be eliminated.

May 1955

Sympathy for those who have made mistakes can help us win them over. One way to judge whether a man's nature is good or bad is by seeing whether he is hostile to those who have made mistakes or is willing to help them.

It is necessary to distinguish clearly between what is true and what is false. Then one can begin to educate the others and build Party unity. Debate, criticism, and fights within the Party are necessary. In certain circumstances, allowing some specific criticisms and even a few fights helps people to correct their own faults and other people's faults.

"Ten Major Relations," April 1956

People's War

The Kuomintang controlled a vast region containing many people and large cities. It had the support of the imperialists, and its army was large and well-equipped. But the basic point was that it was not with the masses, the peasants, and the soldiers. It had its own internal contradictions. Our army was smaller and poorly equipped (with only millet and guns). We controlled very few areas and no large cities. We received no foreign aid. But we were with the masses . . . we represented the people's will, and that is the essential point.

"Hangchow Interviews," December 1965

Reading is learning, but applying is also learning, and the more important kind at that. Our chief method is to learn warfare through warfare. A person who has had no opportunity to go to school can also learn warfare—he can learn through fighting in war.

"Problems of Strategy in China's Revolutionary War," 1936 (P.E.)

Of the officers in the Kuomintang, those who had graduated from the War College did not know how to fight, while those who had spent several months in training at the Whampoa Military Academy could fight. [The Academy, which was set up by the Kuomintang in 1924 with Soviet aid, trained cadres for the first revolutionary war under the direction of Chiang Kai-shek, at the time of the alliance between the Chinese Communist Party and the Kuomintang—Author's note.] Very few of our marshals or generals were university graduates. Even I never read any treatises on strategy . . . . When we fight, we do not take any books with us. All we do is analyze our situation in relation to the enemy's situation—the concrete situation.

"Hangchow Interviews," 1965

The phenomenon that within a country one or several small areas under Red political power should exist for a long time amid the encirclement of White [i.e., reactionary—Author's note] political power is one that has never been found elsewhere in the world. There are peculiar reasons for this unusual phenomenon. It can exist and develop only under certain conditions.

First, it cannot occur in any imperialist country or in any colony under direct imperialist rule . . . . For this unusual phenomenon can occur only in conjunction with another unusual phenomenon, namely, in warfare within the White regime . . . .

Secondly, the places where China's Red political power first emerges and can last long are not those unaffected by the democratic revolution . . . but those . . . where, in the course of the bourgeois-democratic revolution of 1926 and 1927, the masses of workers, peasants and soldiers rose in great numbers . . . .

Thirdly, whether the people's political power in small areas can last long depends on whether the nation-wide revolutionary situation continues to develop . . . .

Fourthly, the existence of a regular Red Army of adequate strength is a necessary condition for the existence of the Red political power . . . .

Fifthly, another important condition besides those mentioned above is required for the prolonged existence and development of the Red political power, namely, that the Communist Party is strongly organized and commits no mistakes in policy.

"Why Is It That Red Political Power
Exists in China?" 1928 (P.E.)

Our principles of operation are:

1. Attack dispersed, isolated enemy forces first; attack concentrated, strong enemy forces later.
2. Take small and medium cities and extensive rural areas first; take big cities later.
3. Make wiping out the enemy's effective strength our main objective; do not make holding or seizing a city or place our main objective. Holding or seizing a city or place is the outcome of wiping out the enemy's effective strength, and often a city or place can be held or seized for good only after it has changed hands a number of times.
4. In every battle, concentrate on absolutely superior force (two, three, four and sometimes even five or six times the enemy's strength), encircle the enemy forces completely, strive to wipe them out thoroughly and do not let any escape from the net. In special circumstances, use the method of dealing crushing blows to the enemy, that is, concentrate all our strength to make a frontal attack and also to attack one or both of his flanks, with the aim of wiping out one part and routing another so that our army can swiftly move its troops to smash other enemy forces. Strive to avoid battles of attrition in which we lose more than we gain or only break even. In this way, although we are inferior as a whole (in terms of numbers), we are absolutely superior in every part and every specific campaign, and this ensures victory in the campaign. As time goes on, we shall become superior as a whole and eventually wipe out all the enemy.
5. Fight no battle unprepared, fight no battle you are not sure of winning; make every effort to be well prepared for each battle, make every every effort to ensure victory in the given set of conditions between the enemy and ourselves.
6. Give full play to our style of fighting—courage in battle, no fear of sacrifice, no fear of fatigue, and continuous fighting (that is, fighting successive battles in a short time without rest).
7. Strive to wipe out the enemy through mobile warfare. At the same time, pay attention to the tactics of positional attack and capture enemy fortified points and cities.
8. With regard to attacking cities, resolutely seize all enemy fortified points and cities which are weakly defended. Seize at opportune moments all enemy fortified points and cities defended with moderate strength, provided circumstances permit.

As for strongly defended enemy fortified points and cities, wait till conditions are ripe and then take them.

9. Replenish our strength with all the arms and most of the personnel captured from the enemy. Our army's main sources of manpower and materiel are at the front.

10. Make good use of the intervals between campaigns to rest, train and consolidate our troops. Periods of rest, training and consolidation should in general not be very long, and the enemy should so far as possible be permitted no breathing space.

"The Present Situation and Our Tasks," 1947 (P.E.)

A Different Way for the West?

[In capitalist countries] this insurrection and war should not be launched until the bourgeoisie becomes really helpless, until the majority of the proletariat are determined to rise in arms and fight, and until the rural masses are giving willing help to the proletariat. And when the time comes to launch such an insurrection and war, the first step will be to seize the cities and then advance into the countryside, and not the other way about. All this has been done by Communist Parties in capitalist countries, and it has been proved correct by the October Revolution in Russia.

China is different however.

"Problems of War and Strategy," 1938 (P.E.)

Therefore the proletariat, the peasantry, the intelligentsia and the other sections of the petty bourgeoisie undoubtedly constitute the basic forces determining China's fate. These classes, some already awakened and others in the process of awakening, will necessarily become the basic components of the state and governmental structure in the democratic republic of China, with the proletariat as the leading force . . . .

This new-democratic republic will be different from the old European-American form of capitalist republic under bourgeois dictatorship, which is the old democratic form and already out of date. On the other hand, it will also be different from the socialist republic of the Soviet type under the dictatorship of the proletariat which is already flourishing in the USSR, and which, moreover, will be established in all the capitalist countries and will undoubtedly become the dominant form of state and governmental structure in all the industrially advanced countries. However, for a certain historical period, this form is not suitable for the revolutions in the colonial and semi-colonial countries. During this period, therefore, a third form of state must be adopted in the revolutions of all colonial and semi-colonial countries, namely, the new-democratic republic. This form suits a certain historical period and is therefore transitional; nevertheless, it is a form which is necessary and cannot be dispensed with.

"On New Democracy," 1940 (P.E.)

Neither the old social democracy, which has been in existence for several decades, nor modern revisionism, which appeared more than ten years ago, have ever allowed the proletariat the least equality with the bourgeoisie. They categorically deny that the history of mankind, which is several thousand years old, is the history of a class struggle; they categorically deny the need for the proletariat to fight the bourgeoisie, for a revolution to be staged by the proletariat against the bourgeoisie, or for a dictatorship to be exercised upon the bourgeoisie by the proletariat. What is more, they are the faithful lackeys of the bourgeoisie and of imperialism.

Circular of May 16, 1966

Economic Development Based on Frugality and Diversity

Diligence and economy should be practiced everywhere, in the management of factories, stores, state or cooperative enterprises, and all other forms of work. This is the principle of strict economy, one of the fundamental principles of the socialist economy. China is a large country, but it is still very poor and will need several decades to become prosperous. And even then, the principle of diligence and economy will still have to be applied. It will be particularly necessary during these decades, and during the next few five-year periods, to encourage diligence and economy and especially to practice a strict economy.

"The Socialist Upsurge in China's Countryside," 1955

It must be affirmed that heavy industry is the core of China's economic construction. At the same time, full attention must be paid to the development of agriculture and light industry . . . .

Industry must develop together with agriculture, for only thus can industry secure raw materials and a market, and only thus is it possible to accumulate fairly large funds for building a powerful heavy industry . . . . But it is not yet so clearly understood that agriculture provides heavy industry with an important market. This fact, however, will be more readily appreciated as gradual progress in the technical improvement and modernization of agriculture calls for more and more machinery, fertilizer, water conservancy and electric power projects and transport facilities for the farms, as well as fuel and building materials.

> "On the Correct Handling of Contradictions among the People," 1957 (P.E.)

We must build up a number of large-scale modern enterprises step by step to form the mainstay of our industry, without which we shall not be able to turn our country into a strong modern industrial power within the coming decades. But the majority of our enterprises should not be built on such a scale; we should set up more small and medium enterprises and make full use of the industrial base left over from the old society, so as to effect the greatest economy and do more with less money.

> *Ibid.*

With these two things, grain and steel, everything becomes easier.

> *People's Daily,* August 16, 1958

In the end, the most important thing for agriculture is mechanization.

> *People's Daily,* May 8, 1969

The workers will mainly devote themselves to industrial production while at the same time acquiring knowledge in military, political, and cultural matters. They must also participate in the movement for socialist education and should criticize the bourgeoisie. Where conditions permit, they will also work in agricultural and subsidiary production, following the example of the workers in the Taching oil industry.

Peasants in the people's communes will devote themselves mainly to agricultural production, including forestry, animal husbandry, subsidiary production, and fish breeding, but they will also have to have some training in military, political, and cultural matters. If conditions permit, they will set up small collective factories. They must also criticize the bourgeoisie.

Letter to Lin Piao quoted in circular of May 7, 1966

We cannot trail behind other countries, following the beaten path, as we develop our techniques.

People's Daily, December 29, 1968

We must break with routine and use advanced techniques as much as possible, in order to transform our country into a powerful, modern socialist state in a fairly short time.

Directive of October 1966

The aim of socialist revolution is to liberate the forces of production. The transformation of private property into socialist collective property in the domain of agriculture and handicrafts, and the transformation of capitalist property into socialist property in private industry and commerce will necessarily result in a considerable liberation of the forces of production. And in this way the social conditions will be created for an enormous development of industrial and agricultural production.

Address to the Supreme State Conference, 1956

In industrializing the country, is it a good idea to allow some rewards to individual producers and to give production teams a certain degree of initiative? Undoubtedly. Otherwise, we would have to stop it. It would be bad to centralize everything, to deduct what the factories owe, or to deprive production units of all initiative. We are still inexperienced in this area . . . .

A peasant economic collectivity, like a factory, is a unit of production. Relations between the collectivity and its members should be correct. Every error, every case of neglect of the peasants welfare will result in the failure of the collective economy. It is possible that certain socialist countries have made mistakes in the area. Some of the collective units in these countries are running smoothly and others less smoothly. If they are badly managed, agriculture will not be able to prosper. The collectivity must accumulate its own capital. In this respect, we must be careful not to ask too much of the peasants, not to make things too difficult for them.

"Ten Major Relations," April 1956

We need both uniformity and individuality. In order to develop regional enthusiasm, each region must assert its personality according to local conditions; this also satisfies the interests of the whole and strengthens the unity of the country.

Ibid.

Revolution Is the Main Trend in the World Today

A new upsurge in the struggle against U.S. imperialism is now emerging throughout the world. Ever since World War II, U.S. imperialism and its followers have been continuously launching wars of aggression and the people in various countries have been continuously waging revolutionary wars to defeat the aggressors. The danger of a new world war still exists, and the people of all countries must get prepared. But revolution is the main trend in the world today . . . .

While massacring the people in other countries, U.S. imperialism is slaughtering the white and black people in its own country. Nixon's fascist atrocities have kindled the raging flames of the revolutionary mass movement in the United States. The Chinese people firmly support the revolutionary struggle of the American people. I am convinced that the American people who are fighting valiantly will ultimately win victory and that the fascist rule in the United States will inevitably be defeated . . . .

U.S. imperialism, which looks like a huge monster, is in essence a paper tiger, now in the throes of its death-bed struggle. In the world of today, who actually fears whom? It is not the Vietnamese people, the Laotian people, the Cambodian people, the Palestinian people, the Arab people or the people of other countries who fear U.S. imperialism; it is U.S. imperialism which fears the people of the world . . . . Innumerable facts prove that a just cause enjoys abundant support while an unjust cause finds little support. A weak nation can defeat a strong, a small nation can defeat a big. The people of a small country can certainly defeat aggression by a big country, if only they dare to rise in struggle, dare to take up arms and grasp in their own hands the destiny of their country. This is a law of history.

"People of the World, Unite and Defeat
the U.S. Aggressors and All Their
Running Dogs!" May 20, 1970 (P.E.)

As far as world war goes, there are really only two possibilities: either war provokes revolution, or revolution averts war.

April 1969

In order to bring about complete emancipation, oppressed peoples must first put their faith in their own struggle, and only then rely on international help. Peoples whose own revolution has been successful should help those who are fighting for their freedom. That is our internationalist duty.

"Interview with African Friends," 1963

The popular masses, including those of the Soviet Union . . . want revolution. And as regards the international Communist movement, an overwhelming majority of Communists and cadres, including those in the Communist Party of the Soviet Union, want revolution. The ones like Krushchev, with his mulishness, who obstinately follow a revisionist course, make up only an infinitesimal minority, hardly a handful.

March 1964 (P.E.)

In short, more than 90 percent of the population, in China as well as in other countries in the world, will eventually support Marxism-Leninism. At present many people in the world are still deceived by social democracy, revisionism, imperialism, and the whole reaction, and have not yet awakened. But in the end they will awaken and will support Marxism-Leninism. The truth of Marxism-Leninism is irresistible. The popular masses will sooner or later bring about a revolution. Worldwide revolution will triumph in the end.

Speech at the enlarged work
meeting of January 1962

The Communist's Morale

All men must die, but death can vary in its significance. The ancient Chinese writer Szuma Chien said, "Though death befalls all men alike, it may be weightier than Mount Tai or lighter than a feather." To die for the people is weightier than Mount Tai, but to work for the fascists and die for the exploiters and oppressors is lighter than a feather . . . .

Wherever there is struggle there is sacrifice, and death is a common occurrence. But we have the interests of the people and the sufferings of the great majority at heart, and when we die for the people it is a worthy death.

"Serve the People," 1944 (P.E.)

There is an ancient Chinese fable called "The Foolish Old Man Who Removed the Mountains." It tells of an old man who lived in northern China long, long ago and was known as the Foolish Old Man of North Mountain. His house faced south and beyond his doorway stood the two great peaks, Taihang and Wangwu, obstructing the way. With great determination he led his sons in digging up these mountains, hoe in hand. Another greybeard, known as the Wise Old Man, saw them and said derisively, "How silly of you to do this! It is quite impossible for you few to dig up these two huge mountains." The Foolish Old Man replied, "When I die, my sons will carry on; when they die, there will be my grandsons, and then their sons and grandsons, and so on to infinity. High as they are, the mountains cannot grow any higher and with every bit we dig, they will be that much lower. Why can't we clear them away?" Having refuted the Wise Old Man's wrong view, he went on digging every day, unshaken in his conviction. God was moved by this, and he sent down two angels, who carried the mountains away on their backs. Today, two big mountains lie like a dead weight on the Chinese people. One is imperialism, the other is feudalism. The Chinese Communist Party has long made up its mind to dig them up. We must persevere and work unceasingly, and we, too, will touch God's heart. Our God is none other than the masses of the Chinese people. If they stand up and dig together with us, why can't these two mountains be cleared away?

"The Foolish Old Man Who Removed
The Mountains," June 1945 (P.E.)

Every Communist working in the mass movements should be a friend of the masses and not a boss over them, an indefatigable teacher and not a bureaucratic politician.

"The Role of the Chinese Communist Party
in the National War," October 1938 (P.E.)

It has to be understood that the masses are the real heroes, while we ourselves are often childish and ignorant, and without this understanding it is impossible to acquire even the most rudimentary knowledge.

"Preface to *Rural Surveys,"* 1941 (P.E.)

[Communists] must be modest and prudent, restrain themselves from any presumption and any precipitation, be capable of practicing self-criticism and have the courage to correct inadequacies and errors in their work. In any case, they should not hide their errors, take all the credit for themselves and lay all the blame on others.

Quoted in "Krushchev's Pseudo-
Communism," 1964

There are many people who are loaded down with ideological burdens: self-satisfaction, hunger for fame, and even age can become burdens; for example, old people think they are very experienced and extraordinary; young people contemplate their youth and also think they are extraordinary; some people seem very fine but are really primarily concerned about themselves, marked by feudal and totally bad thinking . . . . All these attitudes are ideological burdens, they are enemies, we must reject them, uproot them.

1944 speech reported in *Ta Kung Pao,*
November 13, 1951

Connect Teaching to Practical Activity and to Politics

Less time should be spent in school. The program of studies should be cut down and improved. The subjects taught should be radically reformed, and to begin with, some should be simplified. While devoting themselves mainly to their regular studies, pupils and students should learn other things as well. In other words they should not only acquire cultural knowledge but also knowledge about industrial and agricultural production and the military arts; and every time there are campaigns to criticize the bourgeoisie, within the Cultural Revolution, they should participate in them.

16-point decision of August 8, 1966

The universities must be maintained: by that I mean principally the technical and scientific universities. In any case, the length of study should be reduced, teaching should be revolutionized, proletarian policy should be put in command, and we should follow the example of the machine tool factory at Shanghai, which draws its technical personnel from among the workers. Students should be taken from among the skilled workers and peasants, and should return to production after several years of study.

People's Daily, July 22, 1968

If we are to revolutionize teaching in a proletarian manner, the working class must take command of it . . . . Propaganda teams of workers should be in charge of the schools from now on. In rural areas, the schools will have to be run by the former poor and middle peasants, who are the most solid allies of the working class.

People's Daily, July 26, 1968

It is truly necessary for the educated young to go into the country to be reeducated by the poor and middle peasants. We must convince city people to send their children to the country after the first or second stage of secondary school and university . . . . Comrades in the rural areas should warmly welcome these young people.

People's Daily, December 22, 1968

In the future, the schools should have factories, and vice versa. Professors should do manual work. This cannot work if they move only their lips and not their hands.

Interviews at the University of
Tientsin, July 1958 (P.E.)

In short, these materials [documents on past and present inventors, both Chinese and foreign—Author's note] prove that humble people are the most intelligent, and high ranking figures the most stupid. We must strip them of their capital—these great intellectuals with all their affectations. Let us see less servility and instead, the pride of a man who is master in his own home. We should encourage the workers, the peasants, the old cadres, and the small intellectuals to have confidence in themselves, to stand up straight and be creative.

Interviews with delegation heads, Second
Session of the 8th Congress,
May 18, 1958

Ever since ancient times, people who made discoveries, who founded schools, started out as young, relatively uncultivated people, scorned and oppressed . . . . One cannot say this is a rule—more research would have to be done—but one can say that on the whole it is true.

Celebrities are the most backward people, the most fearful, the ones with the least creativity. Why? Because they already have a name. Of course one cannot dismiss all celebrities; there are exceptions. But it often happens that the young overcome the older people, that the less cultivated people get the better of the more cultivated.

"Speech at the Second Session of the 8th Congress," May 8, 1958

Methods of teaching: (1) Stimulate people's minds (abolish the system of stuffing heads); (2) Start with what is close and proceed to what is far away; (3) Start with the superficial and go on to the profound; (4) Use ordinary speech; (5) Talk about what can be understood; (6) Talk in an interesting manner; (7) Support words with gestures; (8) Review the ideas presented in the last class; (9) A plan is necessary; (10) Classes for cadres should include discussions.

Resolution of the 9th Congress of the 4th Red Army, December 1929

On Art and Culture

In the world today all culture, all literature and art belong to definite classes and are geared to definite political lines. There is in fact no such thing as art for art's sake, art that stands above classes, art that is detached from or independent of politics. Proletarian literature and art are part of the whole proletarian revolutionary cause . . . . Works of art which lack artistic quality have no force, however progressive they are politically. Therefore, we oppose both works of art with a wrong political viewpoint and the tendency towards the "poster and slogan style" which is correct in political viewpoint but lacking in artistic power. On questions of literature and art we must carry on a struggle on two fronts.

"Talks at the Yenan Forum on Literature and Art," 1942(P.E.)

It is not good for students to acquire knowledge without practice, from books alone. Tsinghua University has its own workshops and it trains scientists and engineers. However, it is not possible to set up workshops for fine arts departments or for literature, history, economics, or novel writing. Schools of the fine arts must take society as a whole as their workshop.

Interview with a Nepalese delegation
on the problems of education, 1964

A given culture is the ideological reflection of the politics and economics of a given society. There is in China an imperialist culture . . . . Into this category falls all culture embodying a slave ideology. China also has a semi-feudal culture . . . . Its exponents include all those who advocate the worship of Confucius, the study of the Confucian canon, the old ethical code and the old ideas in opposition to the new culture and new ideas. Imperialist culture and semi-feudal culture are devoted brothers and have formed a reactionary cultural alliance against China's new culture . . . . Unless it is swept away, no new culture of any kind can be built up. There is no construction without destruction, no flowing without damming and no motion without rest; the two are locked in a life-and-death struggle.

"On New Democracy," 1940 (P.E.)

China needs to assimilate a good deal of foreign progressive culture, not enough of which was done in the past . . . . However, we should not gulp any of this foreign material down uncritically, but must treat it as we do our food—first chewing it, then submitting it to the working of the stomach and intestines with their juices and secretions, and separating it into nutriment to be absorbed and waste matter to be discarded—before it can nourish us.

Ibid.

We must make all the opera singers, poets, playwrights, and men of letters leave the cities and go one by one to the base of the country—to the villages and factories; they should not stay in organization offices for very long. If they did that, there would be no way for them to leave. If you do not go out to the base, you will not have anything to give us to chew on; if you do go, you will have something to give us.

Directive of 1967 (P.E.)

To study foreign productions does not mean to import them in huge quantities; if we bring something in from outside, we must absorb it in a critical manner. The past is studied for the sake of the present, and what is foreign is studied for the sake of China . . . . It is not easy to combine what is Chinese and what is foreign . . . . We can also make something that is neither Chinese nor foreign; neither donkey, nor horse, a mule isn't so bad . . . . In art, one must show originality and a creative spirit, one must reflect the vivid characteristics of the period and the nation. It should not be the case that the more Chinese art is made, the older it gets and the more foreign it gets. It must contain the characteristics of its time and the nation, and here one should not be afraid to be innovative.

"Chairman Mao's Directives on
Artistic Work," 1967 (P.E.)

The Future Belongs to Socialism

We have witnessed the successive downfalls of many counter-revolutionaries: the government of the Tsin dynasty, the Peiyang "warlords," the Japanese militarists, Mussolini, Hitler, and Chiang Kai-shek; they made mistakes both in their thinking and in their actions, and it could not have been any other way. In our time, the imperialists inevitably fall into the same errors too.

"Commentary on the Critique of Hu Feng's
Counterrevolutionary Group," *People's
Daily*, June 10, 1955

Like us, our enemies are constantly trying to form an idea of the balance of forces in the class struggle, in this country and a-broad. But because they are reactionaries, and are backward and corrupt, they are in for a disappointment; they do not understand the laws of the objective world; since their way of thinking is subjective and abstract, their estimates are always wrong. Their class instincts always lead them to think they are all-powerful and that the revolutionary forces are in a weak position. They overes-timate their own forces and underestimate ours every time.

Ibid.

In the end, the socialist regime will replace the capitalist re-gime; this is an objective law, independent of human will. Whatever efforts the reactionaries make to slow down the wheel of history as it moves ahead, the revolution will break out sooner or later and will necessarily be victorious.

> Speech at the meeting of the Supreme
> Soviet of the USSR to celebrate the
> 40th Anniversary of the October
> Revolution, November 1957

Things develop ceaselessly. It is only 45 years since the revolution of 1911, but the face of China today is completely changed. In another 45 years, that is, in the year 2001, the start of the 21st century, China will have undergone even greater changes. She will have become a powerful, socialist, industrial country . . . . China . . . ought to have made a greater contribution to humanity. Her contribution over a long period has been far too small. We are rather ashamed of that.

> "In Commemoration of Dr. Sun Yat-sen," 1956 (P.E.)

The period we are entering, which will last fifty or even a hundred years, will be a great period. It will see a radical change in the social system on an international scale; it will be a period of great upheaval, a period unique in history. In such a period, we should be prepared to engage in awe-inspiring struggles which will in many ways be different from the kinds of struggles which went on in the past.

> Speech at a Mass Meeting, 1962

four/
Appendices

1/The Leaders

Mao Tse-tung's Titles and the Positions He Held in the Party and the Government

1921. Member of the founding Congress of the Chinese Communist Party. Secretary of the Communist Party of Hunan and secretary of the province's trade union.

1923. Member of the Politburo of the Chinese Communist Party.

1927. Loses his membership in the Politburo for a few months when he takes control of the Chingkangshan Army.

Spring 1928. Political commissar of the army. July: reelected a member of the Central Committee.

1931. Chairman of the Chinese Soviet Republic.

1935. Chairman of the Party's Politburo (effectively leader of the Party).

1945. Chairman of the Party's Central Committee (a post held until his death), and of the People's Revolutionary Military Council.

1954. Deputy from Peking, reelected in 1958 and 1964. Chairman of the Republic until 1959. Chairman of the National Council of Defence until 1959. Honorary Chairman of the People's National Congress.

Party Comrades

In 1921, Mao Tse-tung took part in the founding of the Chinese Communist Party held in a girls' school in Shanghai. With him were: Ho Shu-heng, Li Han-chun, Chang Kuo-t'ao, Lin Jen-ching, Chen Kung-po, Chou Fu-hai. Ch'en Tu-hsiu, who was absent, was nevertheless appointed Party Secretary. Only Tung Pi-wu managed to remain with Mao Tse-tung up to the end, through half a century, surviving the many conflicts which arose within the Party and escaping the massacres of the civil war. Li Ta was ousted a short time before his death at the beginning of the Cultural Revolution.

In the fall of 1922, Mao Tse-tung worked closely with Liu Shao-ch'i in organizing the large-scale strike of the Anyuan miners. In 1923, he met Li Li-san, who became Party leader in 1930 and who left the Central Committee only in 1969. For many years, Mao Tse-tung was supported by the small group of military leaders who had come to join him at the base in the Chingkang mountains: Chu Teh, P'eng Teh-huai, Lin Piao, Ho Lung, Yeh T'ing, and Hsiao K'e.

Chou En-lai joined the underground fighters later. In 1931, he arrived at the base in Kiangsi and the following year became the Red Army's political commissar. From the time of the Tsunyi Conference (1935) he maintained very close relations with Mao Tse-tung.

When Mao Tse-tung became Chairman of the Party in 1935 at Tsunyi, he was supported in his opposition to the former leadership by Chu Teh, Lin Piao, Nieh Jung-chen, P'eng Teh-huai, Liu Po-ch'eng, and Teng Hsiao-p'ing.

The Long March itself helped to bind the group of leaders together, in spite of the dissidence of Chang Kuo-t'ao. The list of members of the Politburo appointed by the Central Committee in 1966 is enough to show the importance of the ties formed during that epic journey. Taking part in the Long March were Chou En-lai, Chu Teh, Li Fu-ch'un, Ch'en Yun, Tung Pi-wu, Liu Po-ch'eng, Li Hsien-nien, T'an Chen-lin, Hsiuo Hua, Hsu Hsiang-ch'ien, Yeh Chien-ying, and Nieh Jung-chen, all of whom were still active in the Party in the last days of Mao; Hsieh Fu-chih, who died in 1972 at his post of Vice-Prime Minister; Lin Piao, Ho Lung, Li Hsueh-feng, and T'eng Hsiao-p'ing, victims of the upheaval during and after the Cultural Revolution.

The membership of the Politburo over the past fourteen years is as follows.

1962. Mao Tse-tung, Liu Shao-ch'i, Chou En-lai, Chu Teh, Ch'en Yun, T'eng Hsiao-p'ing, all members of the standing committee, and Tung Pi-wu, P'eng Chen, Ch'en Yi, Li Fu-ch'un, P'eng Teh-huai, Liu Po-ch'eng, Ho Lung, Li Hsien-nien, Li Ching-ch'uan, T'an Chen-lin, Ulanfu, Chang Wen-t'ien, Lu Ting-yi, Ch'en Po-ta, K'ang Sheng, Po I-po, K'o Ching-shih,

Luo Jong-huan, and Lin Po-ch'u.

1966. Mao Tse-tung, Lin Piao, Chou En-lai, T'ao Chu, Ch'en Po-ta, T'eng Hsiao-p'ing, and K'ang Sheng, all members of the standing committee, and Liu Shao-ch'i, Chu Teh, Li Fu-ch'un, Ch'en Yun, Tung Pi-wu, Ch'en Yi, Liu Po-ch'eng, Ho Lung, Li Hsien-nien, Li Ching-ch'uan, T'an Chen-lin, Hsu Hsiang-ch'ien, Yeh Chien-ying, Nieh Jung-chen, Po I-po, Li Hsueh-feng, Hsieh Fu-chih, Liu Ning-yi, and Hsiao Hua.

1969. Mao Tse-tung, Lin Piao, Chou En-lai, Ch'en Po-ta, and K'ang Sheng, all members of the standing committee, and Yeh Chun, Yeh Chien-ying, Liu Po-ch'eng, Chiang Ch'ing, Chu Teh, Hsu Cheyu, Chen Hsi-lien, Li Hsien-nien, Li Tso-peng, Wu Fa-hsien, Chang Chun-chiao, Chiu Hui-tso, Yao Wen-yuan, Huang Yung-sheng, Tung Pi-wu, and Hsieh Fu-chih. In addition, there were four deputy members; Chi Teng-kui, Li Hsueh-feng, Li Te-sheng, and Wang Tong-hsing.

1973. The Politburo elected at the 10th Congress did not include any of Lin Piao's partisans. On Mao Tse-tung's side, five Vice-Chairmen of the Central Committee were elected: Chou En-lai, Wang Hong-wen, K'ang Sheng, Yeh Chien-ying, and Li Te-sheng (in order of precedence). Chang Chun-chiao, Secretary-General of the Presidium of the Congress, entered the standing committee alongside the members listed, as well as Chu Teh and Tung Pi-wu. The other members of the Politburo were Wei Kuo-ching, Liu Po-ch'eng, Chiang Ch'ing, Hsu Che-yu, Hua Kuo-feng, Chi Teng-kui, Wu Teh, Wang Tung-hsing, Chen Yong-gui, Chen Hsi-lien, Li Hsien-nien. Deputy members were: Wu Gui-hsien, Su Chen-hua, Ni Chi-fu, and Saifudin.

September 1976 (at the death of Mao Tse-tung). Vice-Chairmen of the Central Committee were: Hua Kuo-feng, Wang Hong-wen, Yeh Chien-ying. Other members of the politburo were: Chang Chun-ch'iao, Wei Kuo-ching, Liu Po-ch'eng, Chiang Ch'ing, Hsu Che-yu, Chi Teng-kui, Wu Teh, Wang Tung-hsing, Chen Yong-gui, Chen Hsi-lien, Li Te-sheng, and Li Hsien-nien, Yao Wen-yuan. Deputy members were: Wu Gui-hsien, Su Chen-hua, Ni Chi-fu, and Saifudin.

October 1976: Hua Kuo-feng becomes Party Chairman. Wang Hong-wen, Chang Chun-chiao, Chiang Ch'ing, Yao Wen-yuan are ousted (without formal decision) from the Politburo.

Chairmen and Vice-Chairmen of the National People's Congress

1949. Standing committee of the People's National Congress. Chairman: Mao Tse-tung. Vice-Chairmen: Chou En-lai, Li Chi-shen, Shen Chun-ju, Kuo Mo-jo, Chen Shu-tong. Secretary-General: Li Wei-han.

1954. Standing committee of the People's National Congress. Chairman: Liu Shao-ch'i. Vice-Chairmen: Soong Ch'ing-ling, Lin Po-ch'u, Li Chi-shen, Chang Lan, Luo Jong-huan, Shen Chun-ju, Kuo Mo-jo, Huang Yen-pei, P'eng Chen, Li Wei-han, Chen Shu-tong, Dalai Lama Tansengchiatso, Saifudin. Secretary-General: P'eng Chen.

1959. Chairman: Chu Teh. Vice-Chairmen: Lin Po-ch'u, Li Chi-shen, Luo Jung-huan, Shen Chun-ju, Kuo Mo-jo, Huang Yen-pei, P'eng Chen, Li Wei-han, Chen Shu-tong, Dalai Lama Tansengchiatso, Saifudin, Ch'eng Ch'ien, Panchen Erdeni, Chuji Deltseng, He Hsiang-ning, Liu Po-ch'eng, and Lin Feng. Secretary-General: P'eng Chen.

1965. Chairman: Chu Teh. Vice-Chairmen: P'eng Chen, Liu Po-ch'eng, Li Ching-ch'uan, K'ang Sheng, Kuo Mo-jo, He Hsiang-ning, Huang Yen-pei, Chen Shu-tong, Li Hsueh-feng, Hsu Hsiang-ch'ien, Yang Min-hsuan, Ch'eng Ch'ien, Saifudin, Lin Feng, Liu Ning-yi, Chang Chih-chong, Ngapo Ngawang Jigme, Chou Chien-jen. Secretary-General: Liu Ning-yi.

January 1975. Chairman: Chu Teh. Vice-Chairmen: Tung Pi-wu, Soong Ch'ing-ling, K'ang Sheng, Liu Po-ch'eng, Wu Teh, Wei Kuo-ching, Saifudin, Kuo Mo-jo, Hsu Hsiang-ch'ien, Nie Rong-chen, Ch'en Yun, T'an Chen-lin, Li Ching-ch'uan, Chang Ting-cheng, Tsai Chang, Ulanfu, Ngapo Ngawang Jigme, Chou Chien-jen, Hsu Teh-heng, Hou Jue-wen, Li Su-wen, Yao Lien-wei.

Leadership of the Socialist State

1931–34. Chinese Soviet Republic (proclaimed at Juichin). Chairman: Mao Tse-tung. Vice-Chairmen: Chang Kuo-t'ao and Hsiang Ying.

1949. Central Council of the People's Government. Chairman: Mao Tse-tung. Vice-Chairmen: Chu Teh, Liu Shao-ch'i, Soong Ch'ing-ling, Li Chi-shen, Chang Lan, and Kao Kang.

1954. Chairman of the Republic: Mao Tse-tung. Vice-Chairman: Chu Teh.

1959. Chairman of the Republic: Liu Shao-ch'i. Vice-Chairmen: Soong Ch'ing-ling, Tung Pi-wu.

1965. Chairman of the Republic: Liu Shao-ch'i. Vice-Chairmen: Soong Ch'ing-ling, Tung Pi-wu.

1974. Before convening of the National People's Congress: Interim Chairman: Tung Pi-wu. Vice-Chairman: Soong Ch'ing-ling.

The constitution of 1975 eliminated the post of Chairman of the Republic, whose functions were divided between the Party Chairman and the Chairman of the National People's Congress.

Mao Tse-tung's Co-workers in the Government since 1949

(Prime Minister, Vice–Prime Minister, Secretaries-General of the government, and principal ministers)

1949. Prime Minister: Chou En-lai. Vice–Prime Ministers: Tung Pi-wu, Ch'en Yun, Kuo Mo-jo, Huang Yen-pei. Secretary-General: Li Wei-han. Economic and financial affairs: Ch'en Yun. Foreign affairs: Chou En-lai. Finance: Po I-po. Agriculture: Li Chu-cheng. Commerce: Yeh Chi-chuang.

1954. Prime Minister: Chou En-lai. Vice–Prime Ministers: Ch'en Yun, Lin Piao, P'eng Teh-huai, Teng Hsiao-p'ing, Teng Tzu-hui, Ho Lung, Ulanfu, Li Fu-ch'un, Li Hsien-nien. Secretary-General: Hsi Chung-hsun. National Defense: P'eng Teh-huai. Planning Commission: Li Fu-ch'un. Finances: Li Hsien-nien. Foreign Affairs: Chou En-lai. Agriculture: Liao Lu-yen. Foreign Commerce: Yeh Chi-chuang.

1959. Prime Minister: Chou En-lai. Vice–Prime Ministers: Ch'en Yun, Lin Piao, P'eng Teh-Huai, Teng Hsiao-p'ing, Teng Tzu-hui, Ho Lung, Ch'en Yi, Ulanfu, Li Fu-ch'un, Li Hsien-nien, Nieh Jung-chen, Po I-po, T'an Chen-lin, Lu Ting-yi, Lo Jui-ching, Hsi Chung-hsun. Secretary-General: Hsi Chung-hsun. National Defense: P'eng Teh-huai, replaced by Lin Piao. Planning Commission: Li Fu-ch'un. Finances: Li Hsien-nien. Foreign Affairs: Ch'en Yi. Agriculture: Liao Lu-yen. Foreign Commerce: Yeh Chi-chuang.

1965. Prime Minister: Chou En-lai. Vice–Prime Ministers: Lin Piao, Ch'en Yun, Teng Hsiao-p'ing, Ho Lung, Ch'en Yi, K'o

Ch'ing-shih, Ulanfu, Li Fu-ch'un, Li Hsien-nien, T'an Chen-lin, Nieh Jung-chen, Po I-po, Lu Ting-yi, Lo Jui-ch'ing, T'ao Chu, Hsieh Fu-chih. Secretary-general: Chou Jong-hsin. National Defense: Lin Piao. Planning Commission: Li Fu-ch'un. Foreign Affairs: Ch'en Yi. Agriculture: Liao Lu-yen. Foreign Commerce: Yeh Chi-chuang.

1975. Prime Minister: Chou En-lai (successor in 1976: Hua Kuo-feng). Vice–Prime Ministers: Teng Hsiao-p'ing, Chang Chun-chiao, Li Hsien-nien, Chen Hsi-lien, Chi Teng-kui, Hua Kuo-feng, Chen Yong-gui, Wu Gui-hsien, Wang Chen, Yu Chiu-li, Ku Mu, Sun Chian. National Defense: Yeh Chien-ying. Agriculture: Sha Feng. Foreign affairs: Chiao Kuan-hua. Planning Commission: Yu Chiu-li. Foreign Commerce: Li Chiang.

2/Maoism outside China

Maoism[1] is a new phenomenon in the West. The originality of China's positions and of Mao Tse-tung's ideas only became apparent in the West in the early sixties, at the time of the great ideological controversy between China and Russia (1960–64). In the beginning this controversy did not clearly involve an opposition between Mao's doctrines and Krushchev's theses; Krushchev was attacking the Albanian Workers' Party and Mao was attacking the Yugoslav leaders.

At the time European Communists were finding it hard to accept the line followed by Krushchev in Moscow since 1956. In most organizations, a nonliberal segment on the Left challenged the positions of the leaders in the name of loyalty to the revolutionary tradition and to Marxism-Leninism, identifying with the ideas of both Stalin and Mao Tse-tung.

Later, mainly from 1965 to 1968, the development of the student movement started a second wave of Maoism. This time it was less a matter of carrying on a tradition; the emphasis was on the originality of the Chinese experiment, particularly as embodied in the Cultural Revolution. According to these Maoists, Mao was breaking with the past, particularly with the Stalinist period. Maoism was expressed at that time in certain movements and in a style of political work, rather than in Parties with well-structured organizations.

It was the first time in the history of the world that ideas originating in Asia had had such a great influence on the political

---

[1]By Maoism I mean the fact that a fraction of the Left in the West identifies with Mao Tse-tung's ideas. The problem, however, is to find out if these Leftists really apply Mao's ideas. Maoism and Marxism are different kinds of concepts: the first refers to an influence; the second is an official doctrine.

life of the West—in the streets, in universities, in the factories. It
has been said that Chinese analyses derive from a society that is
very different from the society of the industrialized West and
cannot be suitable for the latter. But this is not really the issue.
After all the ideas of Lenin—a Russian—and Marx—a
German—gave the Chinese a way of analyzing their society; from
the very beginning, the Chinese revolution has relied on Western
theses. A reading of the works of Mao shows that he felt he was
following directly in the path of Marx and Lenin. The developments of Mao's doctrine do not contradict socialist thinking in the
West. Also, though Maoism adheres to Mao Tse-tung's doctrinal
concepts, it does not adopt Mao's specific directives—except in
caricature form. These after all are intended for Chinese society.

Historically Maoism is primarily a political and ideological
challenging of the line followed by the Soviet Union and by the
Parties strictly or in principle faithful to the fundamental theses of
the Communist Party of the Soviet Union. As Mao would say,
Maoism considers the Moscow leaders to be "instructive examples of the wrong direction." Most often, this challenging takes
the form of separate organizations, unconnected with the Communist Parties. Sometimes, however—and this was notably the
case in the Italian Communist Party—"pro-Chinese" positions
are expressed within the organization itself.

Maoism and the Ideological Debate in the West

The Cultural Revolution allowed Western socialists to define
their own positions. The Maoists contested Moscow's theses
more vigorously than before. On the whole they accepted the
most intransigent analyses of the Chinese revolutionaries. However, certain groups or parties kept their distance. Several organizations in various places—though in fact they were few—
endorsed the moderate ideas officially defended by Liu Shao-ch'i.
Outside Europe, the Japanese Communist Party drew away from
Peking, the Workers' Party of North Korea expressed reservations, and the North Vietnamese did not commit themselves.
Cuba made more than one move towards Moscow.

But, confining ourselves primarily to the West, here are the
main points on which Maoists were opposed to the classical
Communist and socialist positions:
1. The Maoists believe that struggles against the authorities

should be carried out from class positions. When there is a united front of several social classes against the bourgeoisie, the proletariat should be the moving force in it and should control it.

The Parties they criticize are usually in favor of a "large group of democratic and popular forces," without being specific.

2. The Maoists believe that divergences within the workers' movement and the socialist movement reflect class oppositions in the rest of society, particularly the differences between the ideologies of the proletariat and the bourgeoisie.

The criticized Parties and their leaders, who are often old militants, believe their work has stood the test. They do not think the proletariat can be contaminated by adverse ideas, and they would certainly never think it necessary to carry out systematic campaigns to combat "revisionism."

3. The Maoists believe that one must try to take power and then try to ensure a dictatorship of the proletariat. The need for this dictatorship should not be concealed, and one should be prepared to explain what it involves, if this is necessary.

The Parties criticized by the Maoists may fight in the name of "advanced democracy," for example. They refuse to speak of a dictatorship of the proletariat because that idea is unpopular.

4. The Maoists believe that the taking of power is inevitably a violent episode in the class struggle, because the ruling classes "do not retreat of their own accord." Control of the parliament does not give real power in the country: it does not ensure either control of production or control of the armed forces. Resistance by the enemy necessarily entails a phase of violent fighting.

The Parties criticized believe that parliamentary power can become a springboard for progressive reforms leading to socialism.

5. The Maoists believe that an authentic Communist militant should work with the popular masses. The cadres, members of the Party, are not the "functionaries of the revolution," nor do they run it. They must remain in contact with the world of production.

Militants in the criticized trade unions and political organizations believe they need a certain apparatus for information and organization; difficult living conditions could only be harmful to the efficiency of their action.

Having posed these principles however, I must say that Maoists in the West are profoundly divided. They do not agree about the practical conclusions to be drawn from their basic positions. They are very alert as to the faults of rival movements but extremely indulgent about their own. Each usually believes it is the only one capable of defining the true revolutionary line, or of interpreting Mao's thought correctly.

If we take the broadest meaning of the word, we could consider certain new and persistent trends in the far Left movement to be Maoist. In particular:

1. This trend is manifested in the most intense forms of trade union struggle. Since 1968 in France a section of the workers often rejects agreements negotiated between their union and management. Strikes take place against the wishes of the unions, who are accused of confining themselves to legislative, contractual, nonviolent struggles. Lock-ins of heads of enterprises have increased. In some factories, machinery has been sabotaged. The idea is to give the class struggle a violent overtone, and for certain "theoreticians," to formulate principles for a people's revolutionary war in industrialized countries, to "lay the base" for an "urban guerilla force."

2. Militants, often from nonworker backgrounds, seek to involve themselves in the working class world, to become workers. Taking as their example the Chinese Red Guards who left the city to bring about a revolution in the country and to reeducate themselves through manual labor, young intellectuals have infiltrated the factories. This phenomenon exists not only in Europe and America, but also in Japan, for example, and in India. It is impossible to estimate how many are involved. For one thing the militants applying for factory jobs hide their social origins, for fear of not being hired. Also, during school vacations, movements of the far Left arrange for training sessions in the country, where militant members work in the fields.

Non-Maoist movements also organize this sort of activity, particularly the so-called Trotskyite organizations. But insofar as these Maoist groups question the traditional role of the revolutionary organization—conceived as a guide and vanguard—they reflect the influence of Chinese ideas more than the ideas of Trotsky, which were very classical on this point.

Maoist Organizations

It is impossible to draw up a complete list. Every month new groups come into being and old ones break up. The Chinese newspapers cite come of these organizations during visits from their delegations, in special articles, or in speeches made by them on various occasions—such as a Party Congress, a nuclear explosion, the launching of a satellite, or the October 1st national holiday. Peking generally refuses to choose among rival groups, even when they insist—which often happens—on being recognized as the only revolutionary organization; the Chinese Party is obviously reluctant to award certificates of Marxist-Leninist authenticity which they feel can be granted only by the people—the Chinese Communist Party does not want to play the role of "father Party."

Evidence of this refusal is seen in the windows of post offices in China where *Servire Il Popolo,* the newspaper of the "Marxist-Leninist Communist Party," of Italy is displayed along with *Nuova Unità*, the bi-weekly of the "Communist Party of Italy (Marxist-Leninist)." Various different Japanese publications are also displayed together.

The People's Republic cannot establish ties with all the organizations seeking its patronage or calling themselves Maoist. Besides, many of the latter do not make contact with Peking and are unknown to the Chinese press. This silence is not in the least significant. If China expressed any preference, it would no doubt be for organizations that form Parties or claim to be Parties (because "in order to make a revolution, there must be a revolutionary party"), and for the largest mass organizations.

Maoist groups have multiplied in Europe. Several of them are illegal, some are content with being semiclandestine. In Portugal these organizations came to the surface again after the fall of the Caetano dictatorship. There is a small Marxist-Leninist core in Greece. In Spain the Communist Party, which has some fellow feeling for China (its publication is *Nuestra Bandera*), coexists with the Marxist-Leninist Communist Party (whose publication is *Vanguardia Obrera*).

The Communist Party of Holland publishes *De Kommunist*; in the same country, the Movement for Marxist-Leninist Communist Unity distributes *Rode Tribune*. The KPD (Marxist-Leninist) of West Germany puts out *Roter Morgen*. The Belgian Party publishes a biweekly called *Clarté*. There are organizations in all the Scandinavian countries. In Norway, the Communist Workers'

Party publishes *Klassekampen*. Little is known about the small Austrian group and the Maoist faction within the Irish revolutionary movement.

I have already mentioned the two Italian organizations. In 1968 the MLCPI claimed that its membership numbered 150,000, certainly greater than it actually was at the time and even greater than it was to be in following years. I should also mention the place occupied, at least for a time, by the group that brought out *Manifesto,* whose circulation went as high as 50,000. Mrs. Macciocchi, former Communist deputy from Naples, and A. Jocaviello, former head of the foreign policy service of *Unità*, were for a long time able to make statements in favor of China within the Italian Communist Party (which its enemies called "revisionist").

In Eastern Europe, of course, Albania must be mentioned: it was the first country openly to denounce the leadership of the Soviet Party (in Enver Hodja's speech at the 1960 Moscow Conference) and, both in words and in actions, has consistently adhered to a line very close to that of the Chinese Party; what is more, it has done this quite independently of China. Some time ago, Peking listed the Marxist-Leninist organizations in Eastern Europe—in Hungary, Poland, Yugoslavia, and East Germany. It seems that only the Polish Marxist-Leninist Communist Party has been able to continue its activity. It publishes a newspaper whose articles are sometimes reprinted in the Albanian press.

In France—to schematize a fluid and confused situation—there are two currents among the Maoists. One has formed around *l'Humanité rouge,* the newspaper of the Marxist-Leninist Communist Party of France, which was dissolved at the time of the May 1968 popular movement and keeps itself mostly underground. The other gravitates around *Quotidien du peuple,* the official organ of the Revolutionary Communist Party (Marxist-Leninist). Each of these two organizations includes a few thousand militants.

I should also mention the existence of a number of French groups which are either ephemeral or have minimal support. Like the preceding ones, they call themselves Marxist-Leninist, and they often spring from splits in the organizations I have already cited.

In Great Britain one finds a strong current of sympathy for the People's Republic, shared by such eminent academic personalities as Joseph Needham and Joan Robinson. But the political organizations inspired by Mao's ideas are of little importance. I can only mention the Communist Federation of Great Britain (Marxist-Leninist), the Association of Communist Unity (Marxist-Leninist), and the Communist Party of Great Britain (Marxist-Leninist), which publishes a newspaper called *The Worker*.

In the United States the Maoist current was long dormant. The American Communist Party was vigorously attacked at the beginning of the sixties by the Chinese leadership for sharing the revisionist ideas of the Soviets and adopting an ambiguous attitude toward John Kennedy and American imperialism.

Mao himself was most interested in the problem of the American blacks; in his two declarations of 1963 and 1968 he affirmed that what the whole racial problem boiled down to was the question of class struggle. From this he gained a few sympathizers in the most politicized black American circles. In Peking during the sixties, he maintained relations with Robert Williams. In 1970 a delegation of Black Panthers led by Eldridge Cleaver stopped over in Peking.

With the development of Sino-American relations, the current of goodwill extended beyond the black minority. Nevertheless it did not give rise to any powerful political organizations which openly identified with Mao Tse-tung. At any rate I should cite the Revolutionary Communist Party of the United States with its newspaper *Revolution* (once the organ of the Revolutionary Union, based in Chicago), the October League (Marxist-Leninist) with its newspaper *The Call,* and a little group which calls itself the Organizing Committee for a Marxist-Leninist Party.

In Canada there is nothing to mention other than the Communist League of Canada (Marxist-Leninist), which publishes a bimonthly newspaper, *The Forge*.

It is very difficult to determine the exact influence of Mao Tse-tung's ideas in the West. But it would not be too much to say that all the organizations which claim kinship with Marxism-Leninism and which challenge the line followed by the Soviet Party without identifying themselves with the Trotskyite trend are, willy-nilly, more or less influenced by the Maoist doctrine.

It would be underestimating the importance of Maoism to overlook the fact that Mao's influence is primarily on Asia. The military aspects of Mao's thought receive more attention there, and the leaders of Asia's numerous guerilla bands draw the fundamental principles for their own struggle from strategic ideas developed by Mao. The ideas behind North Vietnamese strategies obviously owed a great deal to Chinese theories about people's war, though they differed on several points; Cambodian guerillas, before they took over, openly acknowledged their reliance on the Vietnamese and Chinese experience, and the same was true of the Laotians.

But Mao's influence travels beyond the Indochinese peninsula. The People's Republic maintains contact with the Communists of Ceylon, with the Marxist-Leninist Communist Parties of Bangladesh and India (the Naxalite movement), and with the guerilla war developing at the southern border of Burma. The people's resistances in Thailand and Malaysia claim kinship with Mao Tse-tung's thought, and so does a faction of the Philippine guerilla movement, which depends on the Philippine Communist Party—reestablished in 1969 "on the theoretical basis of Mao Tse-tung's thought." Also, the People's Republic approves of the general line of the Indonesian Communist Party, which was reestablished with difficulty after the massacres of 1965. Peking newspapers published the self-criticism of the leaders of the destroyed organization.

In Japan the influence of Mao's ideas appears in far Left student organizations, and sometimes in a spectacular way during certain peasant struggles. Pro-Chinese organizations play a very important part within the coalition of the far Left fighting for the departure of American troops and the closing down of American bases. They have many publications: in particular I can mention *Xianfeng,* the newspaper of the Communist Youth League, *The People's Star,* a publication of the Marxist-Leninist Communist Party, the Toho press agency (Orient), and the review *Mao Tse-tung's Thought.*

The affinity of North Korean leader Kim il Sung's doctrines with those of Mao Tse-tung is striking and would justify an entire study.

Even farther East, mention should be made of the Australian Marxist-Leninist Communist Party and its newspaper, *Vanguard,* and the New Zealand Communist Party and its publication, *People's Voice.*

Finally, in the Middle East, Mao Tse-tung's thought is familiar to Palestinian fighters, at least in a schematic way, and to the underground fighters of Dhofar, in the southern part of the Arabian peninsula.

3/The Judgment of Contemporaries

With the exception of Victor Serge—one of the first non-Chinese Communists to discover the originality of Maoist conceptions—the people I quote have all met the Party leader. Some, like Liu Shao-ch'i, Chang Kuo-t'ao, founder of the Party, and Wang Ming—former member of the Politburo, head of the "Bolshevik" faction, party representative to the Komintern who moved to Moscow in the 1950's and adopted the Soviet line towards China—were his co-workers and enemies within the Chinese Communist Party.

There are three groups: observers, Mao's friends and admirers, and Mao's enemies. It should not be too surprising to find Liu Shao-ch'i and Lin Piao in both of the last two categories. Often, the opinion quoted reflects less the personality of Mao Tse-tung than it does the personality of its author. This is notably the case with Nikita Krushchev. In any case the reflections below, contradictory and often passionate, show the hatred, love, and profound interest aroused by Mao Tse-tung in those who met him.

Observers

Edgar Snow: "He restored China's self-respect," 1968

"In China's 3,000 years of written history the combination of Mao's achievements was perhaps unique. Others had ridden to power on the backs of the peasants and left them in the mud; Mao sought to keep them permanently erect. Dreamer, warrior, politician, ideologist, poet, egoist, revolutionary destroyer-creator, Mao had led a movement to uproot one fourth of humanity and turn a wretched peasantry into a powerful modern army which united a long-divided empire; provided a system of thought shaped by valid Chinese needs and aspirations; brought scientific and technical training to millions and literacy to the masses; laid the foundations of a modernized economy, able to place world-shaking nuclear power in Chinese hands; restored China's self-respect and world respect for or fear of China; and set up examples of self-reliance for such of the earth's poor and oppressed as dared to rebel . . . .

"Maoism had become larger than Mao, and if the Cultural Revolution failed to suppress revisionism, neither could revisionism permanently erase the impact, for better or worse, of the life of Mao Tse-tung."

André Malraux: "Monolithic," 1965

"He has the same kind of round, smooth, young face as the Marshal [Ch'en Yi, at that time Vice–Prime Minister—Author's note]. The famous wart is there on his chin like the sign of a Buddha. There is an air of calm about him, which is all the more unexpected because he is supposed to be violent . . . . 'When poor people are resolved to fight,' he says, 'they always conquer the rich: look at our revolution . . . .'

"He gestures wearily and rises, leaning with his two hands on the arms of his easy-chair. He stands up straighter than any of us, he is monolithic . . . . He walks one step at a time, as stiffly as though he were not bending his legs, more than ever the bronze emperor . . . . No one since Lenin has had such a powerful effect on history . . . . He wanted to make China over and he has; but with the same resoluteness he wants uninterrupted revolution, and it is vital to him that youth should want it too."

Edgar Faure: "The head of a religious community"

"Mao is characterized by his serene bearing and speech; he pronounces his short and dense sentences slowly, pausing each time to reflect.

"Mao—and Krushchev too—are not men in ivory towers, as were Stalin and even Molotov. Mao likes to make unexpected visits to collectives. One day he will suddenly appear in a barracks. When he is planning to swim across the Yangtze, a team of young working-class athletes is brought together and told that an important figure is going to come exercise with them, and only at the last minute do they find out that this figure will be none other than Mao Tse-tung himself.

"Chairman Mao speaks of China with restrained passion, expressing mingled despondency and confidence . . . . He bows his head slightly as though under the overwhelming weight of destiny. He joins his hands. It has been said that Mao Tse-tung combines the qualities of a military man and a peasant, but I find that his bearing makes him more like a man of the church; he reminds me of the head of a religious community, especially from the period of the orders of knighthood.

"The fact that Mao writes poetry is not simply one anecdote in his life. I think it is one of the keys to understanding his character. Unlike many Marxists, Mao is not the author of only one book. In his short pieces, his thought is free of Party jargon and the clutter of dialectics. Here, the themes of the revolution are presented in a simple, picturesque and profound manner; they are accessible to all the people in this country—and will remain accessible to all the people in the future.

"There is something of the humanist in this revolutionary, which also helps to explain certain original aspects of Chinese Communism.

"The Chairman went out to our cars with us. He took me by the arm to point out a step in the shadows. The impression which my last glimpse of him through the car windows gave me—that famous face above the closed collar of the beige jacket, his hand lifted in a friendly wave—was an impression of strength, of an open nature and of 'presence.' "

François Mitterrand: "Severe and Conciliatory"

"Unlike Stalin Mao, who is so severe as far as doctrine goes, actively tries to win people over . . . . This continuity, this unity of viewpoint which is a very important asset for the new China, is obviously a result of the moral and intellectual authority of Mao Tse-tung, who does not need to hold the key position in the Party apparatus, or command the army or the police from within the government, or compel the enthusiasm of the public with postures or rhetoric, to remain in control . . . . He takes trips, keeps himself informed, thinks, receives visitors, and from time to time, on ritual occasions or when a solemn warning is necessary, he intervenes . . . . There are some people who feel that a more active type of leadership is useful and important, but evidently Mao's method is imitated even in the West . . . .

"The care he takes to distinguish between what is essential and what is secondary, to harmonize the Party's interests and the country's interests, not to separate Communism from the specifically Chinese historical contingencies, not to reject any citizen *a priori,* whatever his race, social standing, or politics—this care, so typical of his method, is primarily a result of a judicious appraisal of the capacities, needs, and customs of his people."

L'Express, April 6, 1961

Friends

Victor Serge: "He reminds one of Lenin"

"I am looking at an extremely interesting document on the peasant movement in Hunan. It is a detailed letter written from Changsha on February 18th [1927] by the Communist student [sic] Mao Tse-tung . . . . I have read many things on the Chinese revolution. I have never found Communist thought of higher quality anywhere than the thought of this unknown young militant, Mao Tse-tung. He has coined phrases that are inevitably reminiscent of the phrases Lenin created in 1918–1919. These are his conclusions (and mine):

" 'Leadership by the poor peasants is absolutely necessary. Without the poor peasants, there would be no revolution. To deny their role is to deny the revolution. To attack them is to attack the revolution. They have never been wrong on the general direction of the revolution . . . . If those in charge of the Chinese revolution had been inspired by an equally clear conception of the class struggle, all victories would have been possible. Alas!' "

Liu Shao-ch'i: "This most faithful servant of the people," 1945

"Comrade Mao Tse-tung is an eminent representative of the heroic proletariat of our country and of all that is best in our great country's tradition. He is a Marxist full of creativity and talent, combining the universal truth of Marxism—mankind's highest ideology—with the concrete practice of the Chinese revolution . . . . Comrade Mao Tse-tung is the head of our Party. He is also an ordinary member of our Party, and puts himself entirely at the service of the Party. He scrupulously observes Party discipline in every respect. He is the leader of the masses, but everything he does is based on the will of the people. He stands before the people as its most faithful servant and its most humble pupil.

". . . He is not only the greatest revolutionary and statesman in the history of China, but also the best theoretician and the greatest scholar."

Lin Piao's "Boundless Praiwe": "Better than Marx, Engels, or Lenin," May 18, 1966

"For several decades, Chairman Mao has constantly shown the dialectical relations between mind and matter. The core of Marxism is the dialectic. Chairman Mao applies the dialectic with facility. Dialectical materialism, which is the ideological basis of the proletariat, is expressed in everything he does. Chairman Mao has developed the Marxist dialectic in an exhaustive and creative manner.

"The life which Chairman Mao has led goes far beyond what Marx, Engels, or Lenin did. Of course, Marx, Engels, and Lenin were all great men . . . . But unlike the Chairman, they [Marx and Engels] did not have the experience of personally leading a proletarian revolution, of commanding so many important political campaigns, and particularly military campaigns, in person. Lenin died six years after the victory of the October Revolution, at the age of only fifty-four. He, too, did not experience so many prolonged, complex, violent, and varied struggles, the way Mao did . . . . The Chairman's remarks, his writings and his revolutionary practice prove his great proletarian genius . . . .

"Chairman Mao is a genius . . . . We read books too, but either we do not understand anything in them or we understand only part of what is in them. Chairman Mao reads books and understands them. Several decades ago, Chairman Mao already understood the crux of the dialectic, but we did not . . . . Chairman Mao has applied the theory of Marxism in a broad and amplified way and he is second to no one in the world today. Marx and Engels were the geniuses of the 19th century; Lenin and Mao Tse-tung are the geniuses of the 20th century . . . .

"Mao Tse-tung's thought can change the ideological expression of a man, change the face of the nation, and cause the Chinese people to rise up forever before the whole world . . . . If Mao Tse-tung's thought is used to unite the army and the Party, all problems will be solved. Every sentence the Chairman writes is the truth; one sentence of his is worth more than ten thousand of ours.''

Anna Louise Strong: "Happy and sociable," 1946

"Seldom have I seen a man so happily and sociably set in his environment. What privacy he needed was given by the respect his neighbors held for him. The children above peeped down but made no noise. Even Mao's little daughter had a disciplined sense of what she might do during his interviews.

"Mao Tse-tung is a large man, loose-limbed, with the slow, massive but easy movements of a middle-western farmer. His round, rather flattish face has a placid reserve that lights into vivid humor when he smiles. Under his shock of thick black hair, a powerful head and searching eyes indicate an active, penetrating mind that little escapes. He has an elemental vitality directed by a deep but mobile intellectuality. He wore the usual suit of dark blue cotton. There was no haste or restlessness in his manner but a very poised friendliness.

"It was a delicious meal that Mrs. Mao set before us, much of it from ripe tomatoes, onions, beans and peppers that grew in the hillside garden. For desert there was 'eight treasures rice,' rice sweetened with 'eight delicacies.' In this case there were four: peanuts, walnuts, plums from Mao's garden, and dates from 'Date Garden' upriver.''

Enemies

Liu Shao-ch'i: "A Leftist adventurist," 1937

According to Chang Kuo-t'ao, Liu Shao-ch'i arrived in Yenan in June 1937, to have a talk with the Central Committee. "According to Liu, the Chinese Communist Party had always had a tendency towards Leftist adventurism, and not towards Rightist opportunist errors . . . . The peasant uprisings were thoughtless Leftist moves; the establishment of a soviet government in Kiangsi, and the practical measures which accompanied it, arose even more clearly from Leftist adventurism . . . . Even though the letter did not attack Mao Tse-tung directly, it criticized the policy and the line followed by Mao. Chang Wen-t'ien and others suspected Liu Shao-ch'i of collaborating with me in launching new attacks against the central authorities of the Party.

"Liu was not an admirer of Mao. He once told me that in his opinion, Mao was not very logical in his approach to problems, was stubborn, was not concerned with the choice of options, and lacked personal culture."

Preface to Liu Shao-ch'i's *Selected Works,* URI, Hong Kong, 1968

Chang Kuo-t'ao: "He lacks moral sense."

"Mao Tse-tung attaches little importance to reasoning, he is very interested in hidden maneuvers, and he lacks any moral sense. He is apparently a disciple of Ts'ao Ts'ao, who said: 'I would rather deceive all the people in the world than be deceived myself.' "

Wang Ming: "Unparalleled bestiality," 1969

"The counterrevolutionary crimes of Mao Tse-tung and his group are causing the Chinese Communist Party and the Chinese people to experience an unprecedented tragedy. The conquests of the Chinese revolution are threatened with total destruction. The socialist creation in China is threatened with complete collapse . . . . Mao Tse-tung is an anti-Communist through and through. [He wants to] found his own Communist international, like his predecessor and master, the Judas Trotsky.

"He is afraid of intellectuals and their knowledge. That is why he does not confine himself to persecuting and destroying the best elements among the intellectuals of China, but also tries to intoxicate the people so that China's younger generation will not be able to acquire knowledge and will become a crowd of imbeciles, knowing nothing but Mao Tse-tung and his ideas, unable to be anything but the blind instrument of Mao Tse-tung and his group, doing everything they wish, and sacrificing everything for them.

". . . He has atomic and hydrogen bombs tested in regions populated by national minorities, without worrying about their health or their life.

"This reckless conspirator, this man of unparalleled bestiality, has the body of a tiger and the soul of a serpent . . . . In fact, he sides with the white racists. The proof is that he denigrated Martin Luther King, the leader of the black civil rights movement, who was loved by all American blacks . . . . He welcomes the aggression of the United States in Vietnam and would like it to last as long as possible and become as extensive as possible . . . . Why is Mao Tse-tung so anxious to provoke a war between America and the Soviet Union, and also a world war? Because in this way he could fulfill his extremely selfish and greedy objectives.''

Published by *Novosti,* Moscow, 1969

Chiang Kai-shek: "This offshoot of Marx," March 29, 1974

''By openly identifying himself with the tyrant Tsin [founder of the Tsin dynasty in the 3rd century B.C.—Author's note], by making Confucius into an enemy, shamelessly going 'against the current,' Mao Tse-tung is making a criminal attempt to destroy our history and our culture . . . . Mao Tse-tung, the descendant of Marx, Engels, Lenin, and Stalin, is behaving in a despotic and tyrannical way, deliberately turning his back on the benevolence and decorum of Confucian philosophy . . . Of course he can burn books on the continent and deceive 700 million people with his ''little red book'' of quotations, but how will he be able to burn all the books in the world? . . . How will he be able to prevent the successive rise of his former close comrades, like Liu Shao-ch'i, Lin, and Ch'en Po-ta?

''Mao thinks that he has a perfect right to take away the life, goods and freedom of the 700 million people who live on the continent of China. The targets of his rebellion are the history, culture, philosophy, and art of humanity. But can Mao and his handful of followers really rebel against five thousand years of Chinese history?''

Lin Piao: "A feudal tyrant," (Project 571 from March 1971)

''He is abusing the confidence and the position the people have given him, he is going against history, he has become the Tsinshi Huang [founder of the Tsin dynasty, in the 3rd century B.C.—Author's note] of modern times . . . . He is not a true Marxist, but a disciple of Confucius and of Mencius. Under cover of Marxism, and in the manner of Tsinshi Huang, he is imposing the greatest feudal tyranny in China's history . . . .

''The masses are still very devoted to B52 [Document 571 code name for Mao Tse-tung—Author's note]. The system of rule by division practiced by B52 makes the contradictions within the army quite complex . . . . He goes out very little, his activities remain hidden, and his security system is impressive . . . .

''Down with the Tsinshi Huang of modern times—B52! Overthrow the dynasty which is brandishing the socialist flag!''

Krushchev: "An Asian petty bourgeois," 1970

"If you close your eyes, if you listen to what the Chinese are saying about Mao and if you replace 'Comrade Mao' by 'Comrade Stalin,' you will have some idea of the way things were in our time . . . . Men like Stalin and Mao have at least one thing in common: in order to remain in power, they believe it is absolutely necessary for their authority to appear to come from above, not only so that the people will obey them, but also so that they will fear them . . . .

"Mao is a true owl; he works all night . . . . Politics is a game and Mao Tse-tung has played it with all the cunning of the Asians, making his own use of flattery, treason, pitiless vengeance and deception . . . . Stalin was always rather critical in his judgments of Mao Tse-tung. He found a name for him which describes him very accurately in Marxist terms. He called him 'the margarine Marxist.' . . .

"The fact is that Mao, relying on the peasants and ignoring the proletariat, was victorious. This victory . . . was a new distortion of Marxist philosophy, since it had been won without the proletariat. In short, Mao Tse-tung is a petty bourgeois whose interests are foreign—and have always been foreign—to those of the workers . . . .

"I was never sure I understood what he meant. At the time, I said to myself that this was because of certain aspects of the Chinese mentality and the way the Chinese thought . . . . Certain statements Mao made were shocking to me because of their simplicity, and others because of their complexity . . . . I was never sure what Mao's position was. It is impossible to know which way to turn with these Chinese . . . .

"This cult of Mao's personality reverberated even as far as our country . . . . When the Chinese launched their so-called egalitarian reforms, a whole literature appeared which spread extensively across the frontier into Soviet Siberia. When I saw what was happening, I said to my comrades: 'This must stop at once. The slogans praising Chinese reforms are very alluring. You are mistaken if you do not realize that ideas like these will drop on fertile soil here . . .'

"The Soviet army crushed the forces of the German army, whereas Mao Tse-tung's men spent twenty-five years playing the fool with knives and bayonets.''

4/Short Bibliography

The books that have been written about Mao Tse-tung would fill a library. Few of them really contribute to our knowledge of the man and his work. It will be enough here to point out the essential works and the ones most easily obtainable. I will not name works which are available in the People's Republic and in Hong Kong, of which I have made extensive use but which have not been translated from the Chinese.

Two books by Edgar Snow should be mentioned first: *The Other Side of the River* and, especially, *Red Star over China* (1938), which gave Kuomintang China a picture of life in the liberated zones of the northeast and the personality of the Communist leaders. In *Red Star*, Mao Tse-tung tells about his childhood. In 1968 Edgar Snow brought out an expanded edition (Grove Press) of *Red Star over China*, which greatly enriched the first version of the book.

A reading of Mao Tse-tung's works is indispensable. The most essential of them appear in four volumes published in Peking under the title *Selected Works of Mao Tse-tung* (Foreign Languages Press; vols. 1-3, 1965; vol. 4, 1961).[1] These collections contain only writings of the years prior to the founding of the People's Republic. His later writings have been published in individual pamphlets, of which, in my opinion, the following are particularly important:

"Report on an Investigation of the Peasant Movement in Human," 1927
"On Contradiction," 1937

---

[1] The *Selected Works* in the original Chinese were published in four volumes in 1960.

"Combat Liberalism," 1937
"Oppose Stereotyped Party Writing," 1942
"Some Questions Concerning Methods of Leadership," 1943 as
   well as "Methods of Work of Party Committees," 1949 which
   cover in a few pages the Communists' rules for work and organization.
"On the Correct Handling of Contradictions among the People,"
   1957

Even though the collection of Mao Tse-tung's quotations put
together by the army under the direction of the former Minister of
Defense, Lin Piao, is now much less widely used in the People's
Republic, it seems to me that the *Little Red Book* is still the
simplest and most complete introduction to Mao's work. To understand the intensive use the Chinese made of it between 1964
and 1971, one must read Lin Piao's preface, where he explains
exactly how it should be used and emphasizes the need to combine a reading of the texts with the analysis of concrete problems.

Stuart Schram has put together a fairly complete collection of
translations of Mao's speeches and writings published by Pan-
theon in the U.S. and Penguin in Great Britain: *The Political
Thought of Mao Tse-tung,* which has the advantage of sometimes
referring to the original versions. The Peking Editions struck out
unclear analyses and overly personal remarks from Mao's original
versions, as well as opinions which deviated too openly from
Marxist tradition. The official texts are therefore more exact for
someone interested in Mao Tse-tung's thought as the Party leader
himself propounds it. On the other hand the original editions,
sometimes hastily drafted in the thick of the battle by a leader
who had not yet perfectly formed his system of thought, have the
advantage of showing a more vivid person who often comes close
to heresy—a more spontaneous and less infallible figure than the
official image.

Two books edited by Jerome Ch'en should be mentioned, *Mao*
(Prentice-Hall, 1969) and *Mao's Papers* (Oxford University Press,
1970), which contain many little-known texts. Some of them
were translated from Red Guard newspapers by the American
Consulate in Hong Kong. Others are more recent quotations from
Mao Tse-tung, published in China in small editions.

As for biographies of Mao Tse-tung, one which should be
mentioned is Jerome Ch'en's *Mao and the Chinese Revolution*
(Oxford University Press, 1967). Another is the large, well-
documented *The Morning Deluge* (Little, Brown, 1972) by Han

Suyin. Also see Han Suyin's *Wind in the Tower* (Little, Brown, 1976).

Two short texts, republished in Peking in 1972, give a glimpse of Mao Tse-tung's daily life and supplement Snow's book *Red Star over China*. They are Chen Chang-feng's *On the Long March with Chairman Mao* (China Books, 1972) and Yen Chang-lin's *In His Mind a Million Bold Warriors* (China Books, 1972).

The *Novosti* agency has published a series of violently anti-Maoist pamphlets which tell us as much about the Russian leaders as they do about Mao Tse-tung himself. They are easily available in Soviet hotels and airports, but it is rather difficult to find them in Western countries.